Catholics and the law in Restoration Ireland

Manchester University Press

STUDIES IN EARLY MODERN IRISH HISTORY

SERIES EDITORS
David Edwards
Micheál Ó Siochrú

The study of Early Modern Irish History has experienced something of a renaissance in the last decade. However, studies tend to group around traditional topics in political or military history and significant gaps remain. The idea behind this series is to identify key themes and set the agenda for future research.

Each volume in this series comes from leading scholars from Ireland, Britain, North America and elsewhere, addressing a particular subject. We aim to bring the best of Irish historical research to a wider audience, by engaging with international themes of empire, colonisation, religious change and social transformation.

To buy or to find out more about the books currently available in this series, please go to: https://manchesteruniversitypress.co.uk/series/studies-in-early-modern-irish-history/

Catholics and the law in Restoration Ireland

Paul Smith

Manchester University Press

Published by Manchester University Press
Oxford Road, Manchester, M13 9PL

www.manchesteruniversitypress.co.uk

British Library Cataloguing-in-Publication Data
A catalogue record for this book is available from the British Library

ISBN 978 1 5261 7635 6 hardback

First published 2025

Typeset
by New Best-set Typesetters Ltd

Contents

Series editors' preface

The study of Early Modern Ireland has experienced a renaissance since the late 1990s, with the publication of a number of major monographs examining developments in the country during the sixteenth and seventeenth centuries from a variety of different perspectives. Nonetheless, these works still tend to group around traditional topics in political, military or religious history and significant gaps remain. The idea behind this new series is to identify key themes for exploration and thereby set the agenda for future research. Manchester University Press, a leading academic press with a strong record of publishing Irish related material, is the ideal home for this venture.

This volume explores a long-neglected topic, namely the Catholic experience of Restoration Ireland. Indeed, the study of Restoration Ireland more generally is often overlooked, bookended by the tumultuous upheavals of the mid-seventeenth century and the iconic Jacobite Wars of the 1690s. Paul Smith exploits a wide range of material beyond the legal records, including Gaelic Irish poetry, to counter the bias of colonial governmental sources and reconstruct the efforts of the majority population to survive the new political dispensation, following the return of King Charles II. His analysis challenges the orthodoxy of a reluctant but widespread accommodation with the Protestant newcomers, to present instead a more nuanced, fascinating picture of a vibrant, resourceful community, determined to retain its identity and culture in the face of military and political defeat.

David Edwards
Micheál Ó Siochrú

Acknowledgements

It gives me great pleasure to acknowledge the many types of assistance that I received in writing this book. I am grateful to the many librarians and archivists who helped my research. In particular I would like to thank Mary Higgins and Iris Bedford of Trinity College Dublin, Brigid Clesham and Wesley Geddis who carried out the immense task of preparing the Collection List of the Westport papers in the National Library of Ireland, and the staff of the Bodleian Library Oxford.

In TCD I have had the benefit of the experience and support of Robert Armstrong, Ciaran Brady, David Brown, Brian Cliff, Jessica Cunningham, David Dickson, Susan Flavin, David Hamill, Eoin Mac Cárthaigh, Bríd McGrath, Damian McManus, Deirdre Nic Chárthaigh and Liam O'Rourke. Andrew Carpenter, Jane Fenlon, the late Raymond Gillespie, the late Rolf Loeber and Magda Stouthamer-Loeber, Conleth Manning and Vincent Morley generously shared their time and experience.

I owe a particular debt of gratitude to Hazel Maynard and Eoin Kinsella who generously shared their research with me and gave me every encouragement. I have to thank Catherine Marshall for saving me from innumerable solecisms. I am particularly grateful to Profs. Micheál Ó Siochrú and Mark Hennessy in TCD for their expertise, guidance and unending patience. My research would not have been possible without their scholarship, support and encouragement.

At MUP, Meredith Carroll, Laura Swift, Siobhán Poole, Lianne Slavin and Kate Hawkins steered me cheerfully through the publication process. I am grateful to the readers of my manuscript for their encouragement and suggestions. Jane Robson assiduously refined my text. Once again I have to thank Micheál Ó Siochrú who encouraged me to publish this book and acted as imperturbable sounding board.

This book is dedicated to my husband Brendan Ruddy and the memory of my parents Angela and Patrick Smith.

List of abbreviations

BL	British Library
Bodl	Bodleian Library, Oxford
CSPD	*Calendar of the State Papers, domestic series*
CSPI	*Calendar of the State Papers relating to Ireland*
PROI	*Public Records Office of Ireland*
DIB	*Dictionary of Irish Biography*
EEBO	Early English Books Online
ECCO	Eighteenth Century Collections Online
HMC	Historic Manuscripts Commission
IHS	*Irish Historical Studies*
NAI	National Archives of Ireland
NHI	New History of Ireland
NLI	National Library of Ireland
ODNB	*Oxford Dictionary of National Biography*
TCD	Trinity College Dublin

Introduction: the centrality of law

> *By the Lord Deputy's direction he published the last proclamation throughout the county of Antrim, and in several places caused most part of the county to assemble, and had it interpreted into Irish. This has bred such an impression in them, that they will not endure any more wrongs of their chieftains, but they immediately seek for redress, which formerly they durst never do, but were as bondsmen. They now begin to have the feeling of His Majesty's laws.*[1]

The aim of this book is to explore and illustrate some of the many different ways in which Irish Catholics engaged with and experienced the English common law system during the Restoration. By 1660, English common law was widely, if not universally, applied in Ireland. For the English and Protestant interest in Ireland the law was the principal means for enforcing the mandate of the administration, apart from military intervention. For Catholics in Restoration Ireland the law had several distinct meanings.[2] From a constitutional perspective, Patrick Darcy described the elements of legal authority in Ireland as English common law and the lawful customs and parliamentary statutes of Ireland. This structural analysis was widely accepted and highly influential. Another understanding of the meaning of the law derived from an evolving and dynamic process, as new laws unfavourable to Catholics were enacted and applied in practice, according to the policy of the administration in Dublin, closely overseen by London. To be fully effective, law making and enforcement had to be internalised – accepted and obeyed – but submission to and observance of the law was problematic for Catholics when the legal system was administered by Protestants to protect Protestant interests, and therefore it was contested as immoral or unfair. Finally, although the Catholic majority may have been forced to submit to the law, Catholics understood that the law could be exploited for their own purposes. The law might be experienced as alien and oppressive, but it could also provide opportunities for the restoration of lost estates, protection from arbitrary or unjust administration and the regulation of economic and family relationships. For some Catholics the law provided a career and opportunities for social advancement, and eminent lawyers were prominent in advocating Catholic causes, as well as influencing the nature and effect of new legislation.

While the seventeenth century was a profoundly unsettled period in many parts of Europe, the changes in Ireland were exceptional. The population collapsed by a quarter between 1650 and 1652, Catholic landowners lost perhaps three-quarters of their estates, the trading privileges of Catholic merchants were removed and tens of thousands of Protestant settlers immigrated. For Catholics the 1640s and 1650s were periods of great upheaval and hardship, but the 1660s heralded new possibilities. The Restoration was framed by events in Ireland: after Dublin Castle was seized in late 1659, the Irish Convention of February 1660 called for the restoration of the Stuart monarchy. Charles II was proclaimed king of England by Parliament on 8 May 1660. In Ireland, the initiative was seized by the Protestant interest and Charles II was proclaimed king of Ireland on 14 May. Shortly afterwards a Protestant delegation to London requested that the king call a parliament in Dublin, re-establish the Church of Ireland and restore the royal courts. Despite holding the upper hand politically and militarily, this was an uneasy period for Protestants, fearful that the religious toleration promised by Charles II in the Declaration of Breda in April would encourage a Catholic revanche and a reordering of the Cromwellian land settlement. Notwithstanding the Protestant domination of political developments, this was a period of great optimism for Catholics, hopeful that the new king would be favourably disposed towards Catholics and permit religious freedom. The period covered by this book ends with the Treaty of Limerick in October 1691; the last act of the Stuart Restoration in Ireland. The Catholic interest had been defeated at the Boyne, Aughrim, Galway and finally at Limerick. James II had fled and a Protestant king and a Protestant parliament in London had complete control over Ireland. The Protestant interest was secure, and minded to ensure that the Catholic supremacy they had endured during James's short reign would never recur. In the intervening thirty-one years, the contest between Protestant and Catholic had been fought on many fronts. Frequently acrimonious, occasionally violent, conflict had been joined in parliament and the courts, but generally within the confines of the constitutional and legal system that was restored on Charles's accession.

It is important to note that, while Catholics were optimistic in 1660 that Charles II would improve their religious liberties and social and economic status, their experience of and response to the common law during the Restoration was not uniform. There was no one Catholic experience. Notwithstanding that the Cromwellian persecutions and confiscations had fostered unity in adversity, Catholic society was far from coherent and divisions and distinct points of view emerged quite quickly. The ethnic divisions in the 1640s resurfaced, particularly in regard to the land settlement.

Figures as diverse as Ormond and Tyrconnell made little secret of their bias towards Old English families. The New Catholic Interest, Catholics who had prospered and bought land after the Restoration, feared any upset to the settlement. The Catholic church itself was riven with dissension. Ethnic divisions played a part here too, but could not held liable for dissension within the hierarchy or between secular priests and religious orders. There were marked differences in religious practice and discipline between the elite clergy educated in Europe who had fully adopted Tridentine reforms, and unreconstructed clerics whose formation was principally in Ireland. But while there was considerable diversity in Catholic opinion, the accession of the Catholic James II in 1685 created a commonality of purpose that had not been experienced among Irish Catholics since 1660.

Legal history and history of the law

Legal history and the history of the law are not the same thing. David Ibbetson distinguishes between internal legal history, the history of the elements of the law as they evolved, for example the evolution of the law of contract, from external legal history, the history of law embedded in its social and economic context.[3] He clarified that the concern of external legal history 'is the way that law operates in society, which seems to have law as the given and its operation as the thing that needs to be examined'. In that sense, this book is concerned with external legal history.

Michael Lobban summarised the distinction between legal historians, '[who] remain in danger of being regarded as erudite court jesters in the law faculty, full of curious information, but marginal to the practical and current needs of the law student', and historians using legal sources, '[who] tend to be concerned *not with the law itself*, but other issues, ranging from the nature of violence and its control, to the functioning of the economy, and the nature of political and social relations'.[4] This study falls into a third category – it uses a wide range of legal sources and is fundamentally concerned with the law itself: how it influenced and was influenced by Ireland's Catholics during the Restoration.

The issue is essentially methodological. Lawrence Friedman articulated the divergent approaches of lawyers and historians:

> The dominant ideology of the law schools was such that these were not centers of legal research. They taught legal method, legal reasoning, analytical skills, how to take cases apart, and how to put them back together again. Legal scholars and lawyers were interested in precedents, but not in history; they twisted and used the past, but rarely treated it with the rigor that history demands. Historians, for their part, were not aware of the richness and

> importance of legal history; the lawyers, jealous of their area, showed them only a dreary landscape of concepts; historians were unwelcome there: the landscape was technical and strewn with corpses and mines.[5]

For Friedman, the greatest challenge was to generate an interdisciplinary endeavour in the fields of law and history, not writing the history of the law, but rather writing about the role of law in history. This book recognises the fundamental importance of law in society, and the critical role which the law played in forming the experience of Catholics in late seventeenth-century Ireland.

In Ireland, legal history is a comparatively undeveloped subject. In 1947 Francis Newark remarked that Ireland lacked an elementary monograph on Irish legal history.[6] Writing in 2001, the librarian Janet Sinder noted that Newark's comment still held true.[7] The foundation, however, of the Irish Legal History Society in 1988 was a landmark event.[8] Its founder, Nial Osborough, spelled out the difficulties that a researcher might face, including the loss or destruction of records, the challenge of working in a field where the paucity of records obscures productive lines of enquiry and the judgments required in drawing conclusions from limited evidence.[9] But he also recognised the opportunities and how even modest discoveries can shed light on dark corners of the law and history. The most recent contribution in this field is by Kevin Costello and Niamh Howlin.[10] Theirs is not a general history of the experience of religion or a study of the history of religion in Ireland. It is a legal history of religion in Ireland, narrower and technical, and treats of some of the principal episodes in the legal history of religion in Ireland after the Restoration.

If some lawyers can be accused of shying away from history, how do historians treat the law? In 1970 John McEldowney and Paul O'Higgins wrote that the practice of Irish history undervalued the law: 'Consistently, the word "legal" appears to have less importance attached to it than the social, economic and political emphasis currently in vogue in the study of Irish history. Even where historians become interested in legal history, so often the historians' views of law are markedly different from that of lawyers that the result can be counterproductive.'[11] Twenty-five years later, writing from an historian's perspective, Patrick Walsh noted that the picture had not changed markedly, and that the focus of historians on the law was narrowly defined: 'The law has not always been well served in the historiography of eighteenth-century Ireland. Much of the existing scholarship has either focused on particular pieces or types of legislation or else has concentrated on narrow, and sometimes abstract, constitutional issues.'[12] These observations demonstrate that when historians do engage with the law, outside the boundary of writing the history of the law itself, the scope has been narrow and the results of limited application.

Ted McCormick has reminded us of the all-pervasiveness of the law, and how 'legal issues marked, masked or contributed to (but rarely assuaged) political, economic and cultural fissures' in Ireland.[13] The law was a primary tool of conquest, and making law was the clearest expression of the will of the monarch and parliament. The major land settlements of this period were articulated in and implemented by the law. Between 1685 and 1689 the Catholic counter-revolution found its clearest expression in a multitude of proclamations and the statutes of the 1689 parliament. It is paradoxical that in most histories the law is perceived as incidental, in a very few its importance is acknowledged and rarely is it the central focus of investigation.

The imposition of the common law – the theoretical framework

How and why did it come to pass that English common law was imposed in Ireland? Sir John Davies, the early Stuart legal giant, had a keen sense of the history of the English in Ireland and the critical role played by the law in the conquest. He was one of the major actors in early seventeenth-century Ireland and his career coincided with the extension of the common law throughout the kingdom, a project in which he was intimately involved. Thus he was uniquely positioned to comment on the process. Not only was he experienced in the practical realities, but he could articulate the philosophical basis that underpinned the programme. For Davies, the 'law provided the framework for social interaction which regulated behaviour'.[14] Davies's thought and writings are critical to understanding the commitment of the administration to impose English law on early modern Ireland.

English common law evolved over centuries from the traditional customs of the people of England which had gradually attained the force of law. It was introduced into Ireland with the Anglo-Norman conquest, and for over four hundred years the Brehon and common law systems ran in parallel; the former in those parts of Ireland which had not been conquered, the latter where English power prevailed. Mountjoy's victory over O'Neill at Kinsale in 1601 and the Treaty at Mellifont in 1603 completed the Tudor conquest. For the first time the entire country was, to varying degrees, under the control of an English administration. Mountjoy appointed his protégé Davies as Solicitor General of Ireland in 1603, and in 1606 he became Attorney General, an office he held until 1619. Davies's Irish experience prompted him to publish *A Discoverie of the True Causes Why Ireland was*

Never Entirely Subdued, nor Brought under Obedience of the Crowne of England untill the Beginning of His Majesties Happie Raigne in 1612.[15]

The first part of the book is a short, taut exploration of the military history of the English presence in Ireland up to 1600.[16] Davies's premise was that military hegemony must be first established before civil society can flourish.[17] Conquest of a barbarous country was legally justified and a precedent had been established by the Irish themselves who had won their land by conquest.[18] For Davies, conquest was the first stage in the assimilation of the Irish to English rule: the only alternative was a policy of expulsion and extermination, which he eschewed.[19] But military victory was only a step towards the goal of an enduring conquest. The second part of the book explores the 'defects in the Civil Policy and Government' before 1600.[20] Significant parts of the narrative focus on the over-liberal grants of land to the first Anglo-Normans, the emergence of powerful magnates such as the earls of Kildare and Ormond and the infighting that ensued.[21] But the main thrust of Davies's argument relates to the failure to extend the common law as a powerful agent of social change to all the inhabitants of Ireland. He argued there could be no completed conquest without healthy legal institutions. While Henry II and his son John had introduced English law to Ireland, 'only the English colonies and some few septs of the Irishry ... were admitted to the benefit and protection of the laws of England'.[22] The Irish were considered 'aliens, or rather enemies' and in consequence 'were not only disabled to bring any actions, but they were so far out of the protection of the law as it was often adjudged no felony to kill a mere Irishman in the time of peace'.[23]

When Henry VIII was declared king of Ireland in 1541, the theoretical extension of the law to all subjects failed to ensue because it was not supported by the necessary administrative conditions throughout the whole country.[24] Davies argued that this was 'a great defect in the civil policy'. If the English could not defeat the Irish militarily, and govern them according to the common law, then they would find them 'pricks in their eyes and thorns in their sides till the world's end – and so the conquest never be brought to perfection'.[25] Poynings's parliament in 1494–95 passed laws 'for the making of a commonwealth in Ireland', including the enactment of all prior English legislation for Ireland, 'but these laws did not spread their virtue beyond the English Pale, though they were made generally for the whole kingdom'.[26] Davies admired the work of St. Leger, Sussex, Sidney and Perrot as 'good governors' during the sixteenth century, but even 'they did not abolish the Irish customs nor execute the law in the Irish countries'.[27] It was only under James I that the necessary conditions prevailed for the common law to be applied universally. Specifically English law was to be extended to the Gaelic Irish. Davies proposed that a successful conquest required a system of non-discriminatory laws for the whole population: 'for the conquest is never perfect till the war be at an end; and the war is not at an end till there be peace and unity; and there can never be concord and unity in any one kingdom but where there is but one king, one allegiance and one law'.[28]

The logical outcome was the extension of common law to everyone living in Ireland by a proclamation in March 1605 declaring all persons in the realm to be free natural and immediate subjects of the king, and not subjects of any lords or chiefs.[29] Arthur Chichester, the lord deputy and Davies's patron, ordered the widespread dissemination of the proclamation. There was no doubt that the proclamation was to extend to the Gaelic Catholic population when in May of 1605 Thomas Phillips, the English soldier and planter, and another of Chichester's protégés, had it translated into Irish and read out at Chichester's direction. The effect seems to have been instantaneous: 'They now begin to have the feeling of His Majesty's laws.'[30] Davies hoped that in due course the spread of the law would make the need for translation redundant, as the Irish would have their children learn English to better navigate the law. The effect would be to reform and educate, and eliminate difference: 'we may conceive an hope that the next generation will in tongue and heart, and every way else, become English ... For heretofore, the neglect of the law made the English degenerate and become Irish; and now, on the other side, the execution of the law doth make the Irish grow civil and become English.'[31] Establishing the common law throughout the kingdom was the cornerstone of the civil conquest of Ireland.

Behind the almost abstract legal and constitutional reasoning lay a complex of political imperatives for Davies and the English administration, which Hans Pawlisch has identified.[32] The primary objective was to centralise and redistribute power by assimilating the Gaelic leadership to the sovereignty of the crown, and reducing the influence of the Old English who could no longer be relied upon to rule according to the king's wishes. A second was to undermine the legitimacy of any alternative claims to sovereignty. Phillips was happy to report that the reading of the proclamation in Irish 'has bred such an impression in them, that they will not endure any more wrongs of their chieftains, but they immediately seek for redress, which formerly they durst never do, but were as bondsmen. ... This abates the superiority of their lords, to their great grief, for now they fall from them and follow His Majesty's officers, to crave justice against their lords.'[33] Eliminating Brehon law would mean that the Gaelic leaders could no longer rely on the authority derived from their local sept. There was also a Protestant dividend: it was now clear that all power derived from the monarch and the Old English could no longer trace their legitimacy to the donation of Ireland to Henry II by Pope Adrian IV. Similarly, title to land ultimately derived from the king through surrender and regrant, or the repair of defective titles. Thus, establishment of the common law had consequences far beyond the mere replacement of the Brehon system, and had the potential to permeate social, military and political life. Pawlisch summarised: 'Thus the military victory of 1603 enabled English jurists and administrators to accomplish a variety of reforms that encompassed the defeat and break-up not only of native forms of political organisation and landholding, but also of the *Catholic* [emphasis added] religion and those elements of the social polity that adhered to it.'[34]

It is not clear why Pawlisch could argue that the common law would eliminate the Catholic religion. The subject of religion is a remarkable omission in *A Discovery*, and language reform is given more prominence. The only significant reference occurs in the context of the submissions made to St. Leger in 1541–2: '[W]hen the Irish had once resolved to obey the king, they made no scruple to renounce the pope. And this was not only done by the mere Irish, but the chief of the degenerate English families did perform the same.'[35] Davies was well aware of the state of religious practice in Ireland. There can be no doubting his knowledge of and antipathy towards the Catholic church. Prior to 1603 an accommodation of sorts had been made with the Catholics. The administration tolerated recusancy, in order to maintain a foothold in Ireland without any more expensive military intervention. The need for these compromises disappeared after the Nine Years War when Sir Arthur Chichester became Lord Deputy in 1604. Davies acted for the state in the *Robert Lalor* case, which involved a charge of premunire, and he enforced religious conformity by issuing mandates to Catholic officials to attend Protestant services.[36] The March 1605 Proclamation declaring all persons in the realm to be free, natural and immediate subjects of the king was followed four months later by a proclamation ordering all seminary priests and Jesuits to leave Ireland and the laity to attend divine service in accordance with law.[37] Furthermore, Davies believed that the established church, which had 'no more demonstration of religion than amongst Tartars or canniballs', was incapable of converting Catholics to the state religion.[38] Michael Mullett argues that 'in 1612 it was only through the deliberate omission of the subject of the "State Ecclesiastical" that the Solicitor-General John Davies could maintain that: 'the clock of the civil Government is now well set, and all the wheels thereof do move in order; The strings of this Irish Harp, which the Civil magistrate doth finger, are all in tune … and make a good Harmony of this Commonweale.'[39]

This gap in Davies's analysis becomes all the more surprising in the light of the philosophical basis that informed his understanding of the nature of the common law. In his *Report of Cases* first published in 1615, Davies argued that the common law had evolved over centuries from the traditional customs of the people of England, which attained the force of law, and that it was 'connatural' to the people of England who 'cannot possibly be ruled by any other law'.[40] Notwithstanding this essentialist view of the nature of the common law, in *A Discovery* he argued that it could be imposed on the people of Ireland so as to make them grow civil and become English. He clearly recognised the distinct nature of Irish society: barbarous, uncivilised and with a legal system which he believed was conducive to 'mischief'. Davies proposed to eliminate the Brehon tradition, Ireland's 'connatural' legal system since the eighth century. What he did not address was how the common law might become the law of Ireland, when there were such fundamental differences between the two countries. Of these differences, the greatest was the fact that Ireland was predominantly Catholic. Protestantism was fundamental to the English polity and English ideas of self, and English statute law was peppered with anti-Catholic legislation. In the light of Ireland's unique language and manners, the four centuries of strife that preceded Davies's arrival in Ireland, the distinct constitutional status of the country and the exceptional degree of confessional difference, Davies's project for the uniform imposition of the common law so that Ireland's Catholics could 'grow civil and become English' was highly ambitious.

Yet, barely thirty years later, Davies's programme was virtually complete. In 1641, Patrick Darcy, the Catholic Confederate and lawyer, affirmed that the common law of England and the statutes and legal customs of Ireland were the constituents of legal authority in Ireland. Ireland was a separate kingdom under the English crown and the English parliament had no authority in Ireland.[41] Darcy's *Argument* was enormously influential and in particular his views on the independence of Irish parliament from legislative interference by its London counterpart continued to resonate, for example in the writings of Sir William Domville in his Disquisition of 1660 and in William Molyneux's *The case of Ireland's being bound* in 1698.[42]

The law in histories of the Restoration

This is a strangely neglected topic. In most histories of this period the law is perceived as incidental, in a very few its importance is acknowledged and rarely is it the central focus of investigation. There are significant studies relating to the law in the Tudor and early Stuart periods, and Toby Barnard examined the question for Cromwellian Ireland.[43] Thereafter, there is very little until the historiographical debates around the penal legislation following the Jacobite wars. Since Catholics constituted the largest proportion of the population of Ireland, Catholics and the law ought to be the object of particular study in the histories of this period.

There is some important scholarship relating to the roles played by Catholics in the courts and the legal profession. Colum Kenny has examined the legal basis for the exclusion of Catholics from the profession at various times over three centuries.[44] Hazel Maynard has analysed the demographic profile of Irish attendance at the four Inns of Court in London in the context of the changing political, social and economic environment over the period.[45] She also analysed two hundred Catholic admissions to the London Inns in the period 1660–89.[46] Gerald Simms explored the Jacobite period in detail in what is essentially a political and military history.[47] But he noted the important roles played by Catholic lawyers as additions to the bench under Tyrconnell's policy of catholicisation, as advisers and emissaries, in negotiating the terms of the Treaty of Limerick, and as legislators. The Patriot Parliament of 1689 was an almost entirely Catholic body which passed thirty-five acts in six weeks; this would have been impossible without the input and support of the fifty-three lawyers who were members. Much of the historiography of this period has been biographical and focused on the careers of individual lawyers; somewhat surprisingly, Catholics tend to predominate. Liam O'Malley focused on the career of the Catholic lawyer Patrick Darcy, the author of *An Argument*, whose analysis of the legal status of the Kingdom of Ireland under the English crown and the relationship between the parliaments of England and Ireland was of lasting importance.[48] Raymond Gillespie explored the *History of the Irish Confederation and the War in Ireland*, written by the Catholic lawyer Richard Bellings as a metaphor for social conditions in the 1670s.[49] Harold O'Sullivan explored some aspects of the land settlement and showed how the Old English lawyer John Bellew secured substantial land grants for the earl of Carlingford, which in turn enabled Bellew to save part of his own estate in Louth and retain his transplantation estate in Galway.[50] James McGuire focused on Richard Nagles's somewhat reluctant political career, which saw him intimately involved in the radical legislation of the Patriot Parliament.[51] Eoin Kinsella has shown how a lawyer could combine a commercial and political vocation in his study of the career of Col. John Browne, another prominent member of the Patriot Parliament, a Catholic lawyer who amassed a huge estate and was deeply involved in James II's military campaign.[52] Kenny, Maynard and these biographical works are concerned for the most part with legal professionals, and there is no doubt they contribute to our understanding of Catholic life in the period. But we know relatively little of how Catholics who were not lawyers experienced the law in the Restoration, notwithstanding that Catholics clearly come within the scope of many of the general surveys and studies of the period.

The international context

It is clear that the historiography of this period cannot be understood in an Irish vacuum. The law in Ireland was not an insular phenomenon. It was a primary tool of conquest, and making law was the clearest expression of the will of the monarch and his administration. The text of every act of the Irish parliament was enacted by the king. Proclamations derived their legal force from the authority of the crown's prerogative rights. In 1660, Ireland was a member of the Stuart's composite monarchy, and could not escape the influence of events in the other two kingdoms. And while Charles II and James II were kings of Ireland, they was also kings of Scotland and most importantly of England, and the priorities of England always outweighed the consequences in Ireland. Given the central role of the English monarchy, parliament and administration, events in England played a major role in forming how Ireland's Catholics experienced the law. Tim Harris's two volumes of social and political history acknowledge the importance of the interaction of events in the three kingdoms, and though most weight is inevitably given to events in England, there are substantial analyses of concurrent developments in Scotland and Ireland.[53] The traffic was not one-way. Events in England affected the other kingdoms, but events in Scotland and Ireland had a direct bearing on politics in England. The particular value of Harris's work for this study lies in showing the close integration between events in England and their implications in Ireland, which in turn led to profound legal consequences. Harris provides a useful corrective to the idea that the Restoration was all about Charles II. His books are focused on understanding the causes and consequences of 1688–9 Revolution, the seeds of which predated the Restoration, in the unresolved and seemingly irreconcilable structural issues, economic political and religious, in each of the kingdoms which Charles II inherited. The king's priority was to retain his throne and in doing so he managed to keep these problems under control for the most part. For example, in Ireland the 1662–5 settlement had not solved the land question and Catholics were restricted in the practice of their religion. Harris argues that, although the unsettled period in the early 1670s, and Exclusion Crisis and the Popish Plot some ten years later, had important repercussions for Ireland's Catholics, the country was largely quiescent during Charles II's long reign. In the less capable hands of James II, the failure to manage these underlying structural issues almost inevitably led to disastrous consequences for the Stuart monarchy. In England and

Scotland James II's limited promotion of religious toleration came into sharp conflict with two centuries of Reformation, and fanned fears of absolute monarchy. Harris sees the Glorious Revolution as a truly revolutionary event in England, despite it being relatively bloodless. The consequences were otherwise in Ireland – O'Kelly's 'Wofull Revolution'[54] – where it had profound political and legal consequences.

Developments in Scotland directly or indirectly affected the course of the Restoration in Ireland, starting with the careful coordination of General Monck's interventions in late 1659 with Theophilus Jones in Dublin. Scotland provides a useful comparison to the Irish experience. In Scotland, the seventeenth century was seen as a 'grotesque interlude' between the Reformation and the Enlightenment, and the Restoration a period of particular opprobrium. As in Ireland, the Restoration in Scotland is a victim of scholarly neglect and historiographical misrepresentation and Scotland is still neglected, insofar as political thought is concerned.[55] There were strong geographic and cultural links between Ireland and Scotland, not least because of a common language spoken by 30 per cent of the Scots and perhaps 70 per cent of the Irish at the time of the Restoration. But there was no common legal system and Scotland did not witness the mass confiscation of Catholic estates which had occurred in Ireland under the Protectorate.[56] Most importantly, in Scotland only a tiny minority was Catholic; in contrast, Catholics comprised more than 70 per cent of the Irish population. Given the relatively small number of Catholics it is not surprising there is no significant study of Catholics and the law. Therefore although there were important geographic and cultural links between the two countries, events in Scotland had less effect in Ireland than might be expected. Because there were such significant differences in terms of religion, legal systems and land ownership, there was little overlap in the issues considered in this book, and rarely a commonality of interest.

Looking outside the Stuart kingdoms, there are important points of comparison and contrast with the treatment of Catholics in the seventeenth-century Dutch Republic.[57] At a constitutional level Protestantism (Calvinism) was the official public church, but not the church of the state as in England and Ireland. Catholics constituted a significant minority of the population (45 per cent) and potentially laboured under significant legal disabilities. They were barred from holding high public office in the magistracy and academia. Catholic nobility could not attend state assemblies, but in a mark of the many ambiguities that attended Catholic life in the Republic, their votes were exercised on their behalf. Legally, all ranks of the army and navy were open, and the right to bear arms and membership of militias depended on social status, not religion. Being a Catholic was no bar to membership of guilds, the professions or obtaining university degrees. The public expression of the

Catholic religion was restricted. Priests were considered potential agents of the enemy regimes in Spain and France and had to act with discretion, but were not prosecuted for saying mass. Occasionally, in times of threat from foreign powers, members of Catholic religious orders and apostolic vicars (there were no bishops) were banned, mainly for propaganda purposes; there was little enforcement, and no Catholic martyrs. This ambiguity continued in religious establishments. The operation of Calvinist churches was supervised by the state which owned them. Ostensibly, Catholics had to make do with hidden churches, but their existence was an open secret and their lavish decoration reflected the wealth of their congregations. Dutch attitudes to land ownership by Catholics, a profound source of contention in seventeenth-century Ireland, were particularly telling. Unlike Britain or Ireland, land was not a primary source of wealth, and Dutch economic fortunes derived primarily from mercantile activity. There were no property confiscations after independence from the Habsburgs in the 1580s; those who supported Spain could sell their property and emigrate. Catholic ownership of land was not seen as threat or regulated and restricted. In the Dutch Republic attitudes towards Catholicism were driven partially by a different economic environment and more importantly by a policy of pragmatic toleration. In some cases, the Dutch could not afford to offend their Catholic neighbours on whom they depended for political security. But more significantly, the Dutch believed that a policy of toleration fostered the common good. Social harmony and public order were seen as the foundations of economic prosperity, and prosecuting citizens for their religious beliefs fomented division and strife. Catholics and the administration were prepared to connive in compromises and practical accommodation to achieve this object.

Themes and sources

Rather than focus on the political or administrative record, usually produced by Protestants who were its principal agents, and which is reasonably well served, this study examines how Catholics engaged with and experienced English common law primarily through the eyes of Catholic clerics and Gaelic poets. It also examines how landed Catholics engaged with the courts and how Catholic lawyers fashioned careers outside the narrow bounds of the profession. This work focuses on the period 1660 to 1691, but much of what happened after 1660 had its roots in earlier periods, and the events of this time had a long resonance into later periods. Where necessary, therefore, this book will have regard to earlier or later periods so that some of the continuities in early modern Ireland are not overlooked. Given the nature of the surviving records, it is almost inevitable that any account will be tilted towards the male elite – landowners, religious leaders and members of the professions. However, even elite sources are not concerned exclusively with the affairs of their authors and can shine a light on the lives of ordinary Catholics. Therefore, notwithstanding their elite origins, it can be argued that at least some of the sources have deeper roots.

Oliver Plunkett is a good example, and Toby Barnard suggested that his correspondence 'offers some correctives to a view that otherwise would have to be constructed from hostile testimony'.[58] His mission and relative poverty placed him inevitably in close contact with his impoverished flock. At the same time he had a legal training and a deep understanding of the relationship between law and religion. He was much influenced by his cousin, the distinguished and influential lawyer Sir Nicholas Plunkett. Plunkett and his episcopal colleague John Brenan had experience of legislation directed against them personally and against the institutions and clergy under their care. In addition, in their pastoral roles they had frequent contact with the laity and understood the impact of the law on secular and religious life. They sought to protect their flock from the worst excesses of legislation, whether proposed or enacted, and at the same time avoid overt engagement in politics. Chapter 1 examines the strategy that Plunkett and Brenan adopted and evaluates their cautious and calculated tactics in dealing with the Dublin administration. The approach taken is largely chronological and extensive quotation is made from the letters.

Plunkett and Brenan's letters offer a unique insight into the lives and *mentalité* of two of the most interesting and important members of the Irish Catholic hierarchy in this period.[59] Plunkett's letters were translated, edited and published by John Hanly and most of Brenan's letters were transcribed and translated at the behest of Cardinal Moran.[60] Many more of Plunkett's letters survived than Brenan's; this is partly balanced by the fact that Brenan survived Plunkett for twelve years. It may be objected that the correspondence is one-sided, in that it only records the words and thoughts of the writers and not those of their correspondents, to which there are several answers. In his commentary on Plunkett's letters, Hanly made use of some of the letters *to* Plunkett that remain in Catholic archives.[61] Secondly, some of the correspondence is inherently one-sided; Brenan's *Relatios* are a particular example. Finally, the sense of the correspondence can be often readily apprehended notwithstanding the absence of the letters to or from the recipient. But most importantly, these letters give a vivid, immediate and very personal sense of the thoughts and fears of two archbishops at times of enormous stress; for that alone, for all of the risks of imbalance, they are invaluable.

Other clerics of the period chose less pastoral paths and distinctly different approaches, some as intellectual campaigners and others as political activists, and the wide range of their responses is considered in Chapter 2. John Lynch and Nicholas French left a more consciously literary legacy and wrote from exile. In contrast to Plunkett and Brenan their approach was forceful and confrontational, underpinned by detailed forensic analysis. The Dedicatory Epistle of John Lynch's *Cambrensis Eversus* is particularly useful, written shortly after Charles II's restoration.[62] Nicholas French's writings were extensive and detail how Charles II failed to legislate for the restoration of the lands of his loyal Irish Catholic subjects, or to provide for religious toleration.[63] Their work forms a middle ground; notwithstanding their robust critique, both were strongly loyal to Charles II, and took a long strategic view. It was otherwise in the case of bishops Edmund O'Reilly and John O'Molony as their loyalty to the Stuart regime was tested. They were activists who flirted with rebellion, and O'Molony considered a reordering of the constitutional relationship between Ireland and the Stuarts. In contrast to Plunkett and Brenan they left scant correspondence. Yet even from these relatively meagre resources, it is possible to construct something of the worldview of two of the more radical members of the Catholic Restoration hierarchy.

In 1660, the majority of the population spoke Irish, and of that majority most were not literate and left little written trace.[64] As a result, they have generally been ignored by historians, notably in relation to the law. Vincent Morley contends that the true nature of the culture of any society will remain obscure to those who, because of inadequate linguistic skills, cannot understand its language or read its texts.[65] He criticised historians who cannot engage with the popular culture of this and later periods because of their failure to appreciate the significance of orality, and the tenacity of the scribal community and manuscript culture in Ireland.[66] In a striking phrase, he concluded that ignoring the Irish language 'consigned the bulk of the Irish people to the role of non-speaking extras in the historiography'.[67] Chapter 3 therefore is an important part of this book and examines Irish language sources to establish the nature of Gaelic engagement with the law. In 2008 Michael Perceval-Maxwell reviewed the historiography of the Restoration land settlement and affirmed that virtually the only way of tapping into seventeenth-century Irish opinion was through poetry in Irish, and that the most representative poet of the period was Dáibhí Ó Bruadair.[68] It can certainly be questioned how typical the Gaelic poets were of the Irish-speaking majority population and Ó Bruadair might cavil at being considered representative. The fact that Ó Bruadair and his elite patrons were bilingual and could move with evident ease between the Gaelic- and English-speaking worlds demonstrates the degree of penetration of the English language and its law, even in the more remote parts of Ireland. And this undoubtedly distinguishes him from the people who only spoke Irish. While his haughty disdain was diagnostic of his poetic calling, he ended his days among the common people in abject poverty. And his ability to move between English and Irish culture does not deny his deep roots in the latter. Ó Bruadair makes no claim to be a spokesman but his impulse to express himself in Irish reflects his profound understanding of Gaelic-speaking Ireland.

Other writers in Irish considered in this chapter provide greater context before and after the Restoration. These include the pre-Restoration poets of *Five Seventeenth-Century Political Poems,* edited by Cecile O'Rahilly. From the Restoration period, in addition to Ó Bruadair, Chapter 3 considers the work of Séafraidh Ó Donnchadha, Diarmaid Mac Sheáin Bhuí Mac Cárthaigh and Seamus Dall Mac Cuarta. The work of Seán Ó Gadhra and Aogán Ó Rathaille after the Restoration bookends the period. The chapter also engages with some works in prose, the didactic *Párliament na mBan* and the less elevated worldview of the satirical *Pairlement Chloinne Tomáis.* The latter is compared with the astringent commentary in English of the lawyer Richard Belling's *History of the Late War in Ireland.*

It is important to note some methodological points in respect of Irish-language sources. Material for the study of the Restoration in any language can be sparse and scattered, and the challenges are even greater for the literary record in Irish. The output is relatively small, almost certainly due to the unsettled conditions and the decline in the fortunes of the traditional patrons. Bernadette Cunningham and Raymond Gillespie have noted the lacuna between the end of the Confederate and the Cromwellian period and the start of the eighteenth century. They speak of a lost generation 'born in 1620s and 1630s, which came of age during the wars of the 1640s and the Cromwellian regime of the 1650s'. They had experienced violent conflict at first hand, and had to live with the consequences of land settlement, but were 'strangely silent'.[69] Vincent Morley noted that 1660–90 was a relatively fallow period that 'falls between one high point for literary activity in the 1640s and 1650s (Céitinn, Haicéad, Feirtéir, the "Five Seventeenth-Century Political Poems" edited by Cecile O'Rahilly, etc.) and a new surge that took off in the 1690s and continued into the eighteenth century'.[70] There is little print output for this period and the economic and political conditions were not conducive to preserving manuscripts, which were infrequently copied and often lost or destroyed.[71] Thus there can be a concern that the surviving texts may not be significant or typical.

A second challenge relates to interpretation. We have seen that in the early modern period the Irish language was under threat from English. English loan words began to appear regularly in Irish poetry, evidence of the widespread use of English, particularly in legal and official communication. The language itself was also undergoing a transition from Classical to Modern Irish, with significant orthographic and grammatical changes. In this post-bardic world the poets of the period were negotiating a literary challenge; the poetic forms of complex metre and rhyme that they had inherited and in which they had been trained, were giving way to looser forms. This must have created doubts and uncertainties, which pose a challenge in exploring the mind of the late seventeenth-century *file*.[72] On the other hand, for the most part the *filí* do not shy away from forthright expression in relation to legal matters. Although subtleties might be missed, the broad thrust of the *file*'s argument tends to be vividly clear.

Thirdly, there is a challenge inherent in trawling these sources for matter of legal and constitutional significance. These works were composed following the literary conventions of the time, and for the individual purposes of the writers. Consideration of the law was rarely their primary purpose and they were never intended as compendia of Gaelic thought; to fillet them for forensic material risks decontextualising their original or true meaning.

At first sight, it may seem odd to privilege poetry over prose in this period. But in reality there is not a great deal of prose, and the Restoration is not unique in this respect. Breandán Ó Buachalla argued that poetry was the sole vehicle for the expression of Jacobite sentiment in the Gaelic-speaking world in the eighteenth century. When reviewing *Aisling Ghéar* Mícheál Mac Craith did not find the predominance of poetry as a medium of expression in Ireland to be exceptional. He contrasted Ireland with the many different media in the English world – broadsides, sermons, political tracts, medallions, glass ware, street demonstrations, effigies. 'Far from being unable to cope with the strain, however, Gaelic poetry was more than sufficiently elastic and flexible to accommodate and reflect all the nuances expressed in so many different media in the English world.'[73]

Irish poetry has to be understood as a literary construct. To fully understand it requires knowledge of Early Modern Irish, the literary conventions that underpin the poetry and the historical context in which it is written.[74] This may even extend to understanding the range of meaning of individual words and phrases, the importance of different forms and the significance and tensions inherent in their use, often within the same poem.[75] As in any historical endeavour, scholars with different approaches can draw very divergent conclusions from the same material.[76] The challenges are less when one leaves the era of bardic poetry as the next generation of poets moved to more demotic metres and idioms, but they are still considerable for an historian who is not also an Irish scholar. Fortunately, there are excellent modern scholarly translations of the late seventeenth-century poetry and prose which have been used for this book.

Finally, a word of caution might be expressed about the plausibility of using Gaelic prose and poetry as an indicator of the Irish *mentalité* in respect of public events and politics. In 2002 Joep Leerssen argued that because

Gaelic 'literature functioned in an oral or at best handwritten form ... native Ireland had no public space' and that the 'hidden Ireland was a culture without a public sphere'.[77] As a consequence, he argued that 'Gaelic Ireland was atomized into many separate small-scale communities without the wherewithal to form a society, without the joint continuum of a public sphere'.[78] This view was fiercely contested by, among others, Vincent Morley and Breandán Ó Buachalla, who argued there was a vibrant politicised culture among the Gaelic literati, rooted in oral and manuscript resources. 'Morley's contention is that the failure to take proper account of these two factors in the elaboration of an Irish-language public sphere in rural Ireland has led to a radical misunderstanding of the political and cultural experience of the majority of the island's inhabitants from the seventeenth to the nineteenth century.'[79] This is a highly contentious debate.[80] In support, Morley and others have shown the vitality of scribal culture, not least in respect of more than 250 manuscript copies of Tuireamh na hÉireann and its importance as a key text in shaping identities and historic memories.[81] Ó Buachalla explored more than six hundred Jacobite poems, both in Irish and Scottish Gaelic, many of them not in print.[82] There is abundant evidence in the Gaelic poets of the Restoration for a high degree of awareness not only of political developments, but a mature sense of how legal concepts and processes influenced daily life in the ownership of land, the practice of religion and the life and liberty of the person. Whether the level of awareness by the intellectual elite penetrated to all of Gaelic Ireland can probably never be known.

Because of the paucity of law reports, any general assessment of the operation of the court system must remain conjectural. Such reports as do survive offer tantalising insights into its operation and reception.[83] For Catholics, there was a broad range of possible responses. Those who infringed the law experienced the courts in terms of penalties and punishments. In the field of civil law, Catholics had no option but to engage with legal processes, regardless of their attitude to the courts. Commercial transactions and family settlements were fashioned within the common law framework, and in the absence any viable alternative, resort to the courts was required to enforce rights of personal property. Ownership and use of land was regulated by common law concepts of title and tenure, and interests in land were always a fertile source of legal disputes. Catholics had a particular interest in litigation connected with land because of the unprecedented hardship they suffered under the confiscations of the Cromwellian era. In 1663, a unique opportunity arose to seek redress in the Court of Claims and Chapter 4 explores how Catholics used the court to recover their estates against an overwhelmingly hostile administration. Notwithstanding that court reporting was in its infancy in the period, there is a significant body of material that records how Catholics fared in the Court of Claims. The short-lived court made some of the most important decisions favouring Catholic litigants in this period, and is very well documented. The principal record of the court, a manuscript in Armagh edited by Geraldine Tallon, is an exceptionally important source for the Restoration.[84] Not strictly court reports, the submissions made and the evidence adduced provide a wealth of information relating to the mainly Catholic claimants. It is striking how little use has been made of this material since the Irish Manuscripts Commission published it in 2006. A record of the decrees of the court, Egerton MS 789 in the British Library, has also been edited and published, and complements the Armagh manuscript.[85] Since there were so many cases, it is challenging to assess the mass of evidence from the individual facts and circumstances in each individual case. The approach taken here is to examine the cases of some smaller landlords which are indicative of the processes followed by the court, and then to trace some of the larger judgments, which are significant in their own right, and frequently have related narratives showing how the Catholic owners fought to recover their lands before and after the sittings of the court. Of course there is a risk that the selected cases are not representative of the universal experience, but they account for about 20 per cent of Catholic claims, and it is clear that some tentative conclusions can be drawn. A number of cases are examined to show how the cost of litigation was a significant deterrent to engaging with the courts, and how religious identity could be flexible, depending on the personal circumstances of the landowner. Finally, a statistical analysis provides some more general conclusions.

The law and legal process cannot be understood without regard to the practitioners who were familiar with its principles, practices and systems. Chapter 5 explores how three Catholic lawyers could exploit the law in different ways for their own opportunities and self-advancement. It also suggests that, notwithstanding professional skill and status, legal practitioners were as vulnerable as many lay Catholics to the law's vicissitudes. It is clear that many Catholic lawyers exploited the law in order to make a living or protect and enhance their family and financial interests. Notwithstanding their reservations about the anti-Catholic bias in the legal system, they embraced the law and its possibilities. In many families the profession of the law was a tradition, if not an imperative. There are many possible approaches; biographical studies illustrate the complex interactions between various individuals and the larger forces that shaped their careers. The careers of some of the more significant practitioners are relatively well documented and understood. Rather less is known about lawyers who did not exercise their profession in the courts, or in Dublin, and three case studies are explored. As with all case studies, these individuals are not fully representative of the universal experience, but they complement the evidence supplied by other studies.

Sir John Walshe is a significant figure as a Munster lawyer whose career was played out on a regionally restricted stage. His career up to 1660 has been examined by Bríd McGrath and Micheál Ó Siochrú.[86] After 1660, he served as Ormond's seneschal, but the title of the office does little justice to the complexity of the relationship between the lawyer and his client. Sir William Talbot had no formal legal qualifications and worked primarily as a land agent. His family were prominent Leinster lawyers and politicians but William has not attracted much attention from historians of the period. Finally, Gerald Dillon was a lawyer from Connacht who represented both Catholic and Protestant clients. Dillon rose to high office nationally, participated in the negotiation of the Articles of Limerick, and chose to accompany James II into exile. Éamonn Ó Ciardha has written a short biographical study, and he appears incidentally in histories of Jacobite Ireland, particularly in relation to the Articles of Limerick.[87] Otherwise he is little noted.

Manuscript sources are particularly useful in exploring the careers of these lawyers. There are relatively few references to Sir John Walshe in the State papers, but the detail of his career after the Restoration can be gleaned from his extensive correspondence with the duke of Ormond in the Carte papers in the Bodleian Library. An insight into the constitutional political and religious thought of Sir William Talbot, tested at a time of great controversy, can be gleaned from his observations on the Popish Plot, preserved in the papers of Bishop William King in Trinity College Dublin. A great deal about Gerald Dillon's career at the bar can be understood from the Chancery Bill Books in the National Archives of Ireland.[88] Other aspects of his career can be traced in the remnant of Dillon's own papers in the Westport Estate Papers in the National Library of Ireland.[89] The survival of Dillon material in these papers is fortuitous, and while it is possible they do not afford a comprehensive view, there is sufficient breadth of material in the collection when correlated with other sources to provide a reasonably reliable picture of Dillon's life and times.

Conclusion

Apart from military force, the imposition of the common law was the most powerful instrument of the English administration in the conquest and control of Ireland. Sir John Davies was its most articulate advocate and traced the universal extension of the common law to the proclamation in March 1605 declaring all persons in the realm to be free, natural and immediate subjects of the king, and not subjects of any lords or chiefs. Davies imagined that the common law would pervade almost all aspects of life as it did in England; potentially the consequences were profound. Gaelic concepts of communal property and territory would be replaced by a system that was individualistic and profit based. The foundations of personal private property and the market economy were framed by common law concepts. For Catholics, the common law became of increasing importance in the seventeenth century, particularly in relation to land ownership and the practice of religion. But how and to what extent could a legal system founded on English custom gain acceptance in Ireland? And could a legal system which emanated from a polity founded on Protestantism accommodate a Catholic population? The subject of religion is a remarkable absence in Davies's *A Discovery*; this book shows that this was a crucial omission.

By 1660 Catholics had no option but to engage with common law processes and concepts. There was no alternative; the Brehon system had been overcome. But the appearance of acquiescence may not signify acceptance. Lawyers and the landowners may have engaged with the system, even if this engagement may not have always been satisfactory. Catholic prelates who were forced into hiding or exile and the dispossessed landowners who failed to secure a hearing in the Court of Claims had their allegiance to the Stuarts' legal system sorely tested. Arguably Irish speakers were least likely to be acculturated. Gaelic poetry shows a lingering disdain if not outright contempt for the common law. There was no one Catholic experience. Notwithstanding that the Cromwellian persecutions and confiscations had fostered unity in adversity, Catholic society was far from coherent and divisions and distinct points of view emerged quite quickly. The ethnic divisions in the 1640s resurfaced, particularly in regard to the land settlement. The Catholic church itself was riven with dissension. But while there was considerable diversity in Catholic opinion, the accession of the Catholic James II in 1685 created a commonality of purpose that had not been experienced among Irish Catholics since 1660.

The Irish parliament enacted legislation which was to have profound and enduring consequences. The administration issued hundreds of proclamations which had pervasive effect. The land settlement, restraints on the practice of religion and periods of persecution ensured that Catholics had particularly intense encounters with the acts and ordinances of the period. Yet references to the role of the law in studies of the Restoration are scant, and few acknowledge its centrality. Catholics are not the object of particular study in the histories of the law for this period. Since Catholics constituted the largest proportion of the population of Ireland, there is a major lacuna in the historiography. This book is not a history of the law in this period. Rather the object of this book is to explore and illustrate some aspects of how Irish Catholics engaged with and experienced the common law during the Restoration. This is a vast topic and the book does not aspire to be comprehensive. For example, with the notable exception of Chapter 4, which deals with the Court of Claims, the topics chosen for exploration admit very little about the role of women.

This book endeavours to take up the challenge of an interdisciplinary approach through a series of case studies. The next chapter examines how Archbishops Oliver Plunkett and John Brenan responded to the challenges posed by the law between 1670 and 1690. They were uniquely exposed to the effects of the law, and were particularly conscious of the consequences of legal initiatives for the laity. As leaders of the Catholic community they acted as mediators with the administration and were often the objects of persecution.

Notes

1 Thomas Phillips to the secretary of state, the earl of Salisbury, 19 May 1605, *CSPI 1603–6*, p. 275.

2 Apart from the common law, Catholics could have been subject to Catholic canon law and the Protestant ecclesiastical courts. Justice was administered in the superior courts and in other fora such as admiralty, presidency, manor and borough courts, petty and quarter sessions. The records for these other courts are largely absent, and in a study of this scope it would be impossible to adequately discuss their operation.

3 David Ibbetson, 'What is legal history a history of?' in *Law and History, Current Legal Issues 2003*, vol. 6 (Oxford, 2004), pp. 33–4. It could be argued that a further distinction should be drawn between the law as such and the political and administrative decisions that are enacted in legislation. But that is to discount the almost symbiotic relationship between the law and political decisions, which are framed by what is possible under the law and are shaped by legal concepts.

4 Emphasis added. Michael Lobban, 'Introduction: The tools and the tasks of the legal historian' in *Law and History, Current Legal Issues 2003*, vol. 6 (Oxford, 2004), pp. 1–2.

5 L. M. Friedman, *A History of American Law* (New York, 1985), pp. 11–12.

6 F. H. Newark, 'Notes on Irish legal history' in F. J. McIvor, *Elegantia Juris: Selected Writings of F. H. Newark* (Belfast, 1973), p. 203. W. N. Osborough, 'Preface' in W. N. Osborough (ed.), *Studies in Irish Legal History* (Dublin, 1999), p. vii.

7 Janet Sinder, 'Irish legal history: An overview and guide to the sources', *Law Library Journal* 93 (2001), pp. 231–60. Nothing has changed in that respect in the intervening years.

8 The Irish Legal History Society's mission is to encourage the study and advance the knowledge of the history of Irish law, especially by the publication of original documents and scholarly works relating to the history of Irish law, including its

institutions, doctrines and personalities, and the reprinting or editing of works of sufficient rarity or importance. http://www.ilhs.eu/, accessed 19 July 2023.

9 W. N. Osborough, 'In search of legal history: A map for explorers', *Long Room* 35 (1990), pp. 28–38.

10 Niamh Howlin and Kevin Costello (eds), *Law and Religion in Ireland 1700–1970* (Cham, 2021).

11 John F. McEldowney and Paul O'Higgins, 'The common law tradition and Irish legal history' in John F. McEldowney and Paul O'Higgins (eds), *The Common Law Tradition* (Dublin, 1970), pp. 13–25, at p. 14.

12 Patrick Walsh's review of Michael Brown and Seán Patrick Donlan (eds), *The Laws and Other Legalities of Ireland, 1689–1850* (Farnham, 2011) in *Journal for Eighteenth-Century Studies* 36 (2013), p. 449.

13 Ted McCormick, in the context of eighteenth-century Ireland, reviewing Brown and Donlan's *The Law and Other Legalities* in *History* 331 (July 2013), pp. 452–4.

14 Raymond Gillespie, *Seventeenth-Century Ireland* (Dublin, 2006), p. 46.

15 The critical edition referenced here is Sir John Davies, *A Discoverie of the True Causes Why Ireland Was Never Entirely Subdued, [And] Brought Under Obedience of the Crown of England Until the Beginning of His Majesty's Happy Reign (1612)*, ed. James P. Myers (Washington, DC, 1988). In his Introduction to the facsimile edition John Barry noted 'the creative artist is revealed by the occasional vivid metaphor, and by the elegant prose' (Shannon, 1969), p. viii. Davies's earlier tract *Lawes of Ireland* (1608/9) illustrates the development of his thought. It examines the constitutional status of the Irish parliament and is remarkable for a detailed description of the Brehon law lately supplanted by the common law throughout Ireland. See Hiram Morgan, '"Lawes of Irelande": A tract by Sir John Davies', *The Irish Jurist* 28–30 (1993–5), pp. 307–13.

16 Davies, *Discoverie*, pp. 69–124.

17 *Discoverie,* pp. 70–1.

18 *Discoverie*, pp. 78–9.

19 *Discoverie*, p. 109.

20 *Discoverie*, pp. 124–224.

21 For a detailed consideration of how ideas of commonwealth influenced Davies's thought, see D. Alan Orr, 'Sir John Davies's agrarian law for Ireland', *Journal of the History of Ideas* 75 (Jan. 2014), pp. 91–112.

22 *Discoverie*, pp. 125–6.

23 'Actions' in the legal sense. *Discoverie*, p. 126.

24 *Discoverie*, p. 205.

25 *Discoverie*, p. 136.

26 *Discoverie*, pp. 171, 174, 181–4, 187–90, 199.

27 *Discoverie*, p. 211.

28 *Discoverie*, p. 138.

29 11 Mar. 1605. Robert Steele (ed.), *A Bibliography of Royal Proclamations of the Tudor and Stuart Sovereigns 1485–1714,* (2 vols, Oxford, 1910), vol. 2, *Ireland and Scotland*, p. 17.

30 Thomas Phillips to the secretary of state, the earl of Salisbury, 19 May 1605, *CSPI 1603–6*, p. 275.
31 *Discoverie*, p. 217.
32 Hans S. Pawlisch, *Sir John Davies and the Conquest of Ireland* (Cambridge, 1985), pp. 3–10.
33 *CSPI 1603–6*, p. 275.
34 Pawlisch, *Sir John Davies,* p. 3.
35 *Discoverie*, p. 202.
36 4 May 1606, Davies to the secretary of state, the earl of Salisbury, *CSPI 1603–6,* pp. 465 and ff.
37 4 July 1605. Steele, *Bibliography of Royal Proclamations*, p. 17.
38 Davics to Salisbury, 20 Feb. 1604, *CSPI 1603–6*, p. 143.
39 Michael A. Mullett, *Catholics in Britain and Ireland, 1558–1829* (Basingstoke, 1998), p. 64.
40 Sir John Davies, *A Report of Cases and Matters in Law Resolved and Abridged in the King's Courts in Ireland* (Dublin, 1762), pp. 3–6.
41 *An argument* was delivered to a conference committee of the Irish House of Commons and Lords on 9 June 1641 and published at Waterford in 1643.
42 P. H. Kelly (ed. and intro), 'Sir William Domville, "A disquisition touching that great question whether an act of parliament made in England shall bind the kingdom and people of Ireland without their allowance and acceptance of such an act in the kingdom of Ireland"', *Analecta Hibernica* 40 (2007), pp. 17–72. Patrick Hyde Kelly (ed.), *William Molyneux: The case of Ireland's being bound by acts of parliament in England, stated Dublin, 1698* (Dublin, 2018).
43 For example, Brendan Bradshaw, *The Irish Constitutional Revolution of the Sixteenth Century* (Cambridge, 1979); Hans S. Pawlisch, *Sir John Davies and the Conquest of Ireland* (Cambridge, 1985); T. C. Barnard, *Cromwellian Ireland* (Oxford, 1975).
44 Colum Kenny, 'The exclusion of Catholics from the legal profession in Ireland, 1537–1829', *IHS* 25 (1987), pp. 337–57.
45 Hazel Maynard, 'Irish membership of the English Inns of Court, 1660–1699: Lawyers, litigation and the legal profession' (PhD thesis, University College, Dublin, 2006).
46 Hazel Maynard, 'The Irish legal profession and the Catholic revival, 1660–89' in James Kelly, John McCafferty and Charles Ivar McGrath (eds), *People, Politics and Power* (Dublin, 2009), pp. 28–50.
47 J. G. Simms, *Jacobite Ireland* (London, 1969).
48 Liam O'Malley, 'Patrick Darcy – Galway lawyer and politician, 1598–1668', in D. O'Cearbhaill (ed.), *Galway, Town and Gown, 1484–1984* (Dublin, 1984), pp. 90–109.
49 Raymond Gillespie, 'The social thought of Richard Bellings' in Micheál Ó Siochrú (ed.), *Kingdoms in Crisis: Ireland in the 1640s* (Dublin, 2001), pp. 212–28. Bellings to Ormond, 1 June 1661, Bodl., Carte MS 214, ff. 292–3.
50 Harold O'Sullivan, *John Bellew: A Seventeenth-Century Man of Many Parts, 1605–1679* (Dublin, 2000).

51 James McGuire, 'A lawyer in politics: The career of Sir Richard Nagle, c. 1636–1699' in N. M. Dawson (ed.), *Reflections on Law and History* (Dublin, 2006), pp. 18–31.
52 Eoin Kinsella, *Catholic Survival in Protestant Ireland, 1660–1711* (Woodbridge, 2018).
53 Tim Harris, *Restoration: Charles II and his Kingdoms, 1660–1685* (London, 2005) and *Revolution: The Great Crisis of the British Monarchy, 1685–1720* (London, 2006).
54 Charles O'Kelly, *Macariae Excidium,* cited in Harris, *Revolution,* p. 422.
55 See chapter 1 of Clare Jackson, *Restoration Scotland, 1660–1690: Royalist Politics, Religion and Ideas* (Woodbridge, 2003) for a comprehensive historiographical review, and in particular pp. 1–5. A notable Irish contribution is Jane H. Ohlmeyer (ed.), *Political Thought in Seventeenth-Century Ireland* (Cambridge, 2000).
56 There had been some confiscations, not on religious grounds, but because the owners were Royalists.
57 See Declan M. Downey, 'Accommodations with the Protestant state and church: A comparative study of respective Dutch and Irish Catholic experiences' in John Bergin, Eoin Magennis, Lesa Ní Mhunghaile and Patrick Walsh (eds), *New Perspectives on the Penal Laws: Eighteenth-Century Ireland, Idir an dá chultúr,* special issue no. 1 (Dublin, 2011).
58 Toby Barnard, 'Conclusion' in Coleman A. Dennehy (ed.), *Restoration Ireland: Always Settling and Never Settled* (Aldershot, 2008), p. 185.
59 There is a wealth of material concerning more overtly political figures such as Archbishop Peter Talbot and Fr Peter Walsh who are outside the scope of this study.
60 *The Letters of St. Oliver Plunkett*, ed. John Hanly (Dublin, 1979). P. Power (ed.), *A Bishop of the Penal Times, being the Letters and Reports of John Brenan, Bishop of Waterford (1671–93) and Archbishop of Cashel (1677–93)* (Cork, 1932).
61 Hanly, *Plunkett*, p. xiii.
62 John Lynch, *Cambrensis Eversus*, ed. and tr. Matthew Kelly (3 vols, Dublin, 1851–2), vol. 1.
63 French's most important works can be found in *The Historical Works of the Right Rev. Nicholas French D.D.,* (2 vols, Dublin, 1846).
64 The extent of the Irish-speaking population can only be estimated. Windele suggested that two-thirds of the population spoke Irish in 1730: John Windele, 'Present extent of the Irish language', *Ulster Journal of Archaeology* 5 (1857), pp. 243–5, quoted in Tony Crowley, *Wars of Words: The Politics of Language in Ireland 1537–2004* (Oxford, 2005), p. 72. Windele did not make clear how he arrived at the fraction of two-thirds.
65 Vincent Morley, *The Popular Mind in Eighteenth-Century Ireland* (Cork, 2017), p. 309.
66 Morley, *Popular Mind*, p. 310.
67 Morley, *Popular Mind*, p. 2.

68 Michael Perceval-Maxwell, 'The Irish Restoration land settlement' in Dennehy, *Restoration Ireland*, pp. 19–20. In the same way, in 1996, Breandán Ó Buachalla demonstrated in his magnum opus *Aisling Ghéar*, that poetry was the sole vehicle for the expression of Jacobite sentiment in the eighteenth-century Gaelic-speaking world.
69 Bernadette Cunningham and Raymond Gillespie, 'Lost worlds: History and religion in the poetry of Dáibhí Ó Bruadair' in Pádraigín Riggs (ed.), *Dáibhí Ó Bruadair: His Historical and Literary Context* (London, 2001), pp. 18–19.
70 Correspondence with author, 5 Aug. 2015.
71 See e.g. Breandán Ó Conchúir, 'The manuscript transmission of Ó Bruadair's poetry' in Riggs, *Dáibhí Ó Bruadair*, p. 49.
72 Poet in Irish, pl. *filí*.
73 Mícheál Mac Craith, '*Aisling ghéar: Na Stíobhartaigh agus an t-aos léinn 1603–1788* by Breandán Ó Buachalla', *Eighteenth-Century Ireland / Iris an Dá Chultúr* 13 (1998), pp. 166–71, at p. 166.
74 A knowledge of Modern Irish is not fully adequate to the task.
75 See Declan Kiberd, *Irish Classics* (Cambridge, MA, 2000), pp. 29–30.
76 See e.g. the different approaches taken to Eochaidh Ó hEódhusa's 1603 poem *Ionmholta malairt bhisigh*, by Kiberd, *Irish Classics*, pp. 15–17 – 'almost fully drained of the attendant irony' – and Marc Caball, *Poets and Politics: Continuity and Reaction in Irish Poetry, 1558–1625* (Cork, 1998), p. 94 – 'ironic banter'.
77 Joep Leerssen, *Hidden Ireland, Public Sphere* (Galway, 2002), p. 37.
78 Leerssen, *Hidden Ireland*, p. 37.
79 Michael Cronin, '*Ó Chéitinn go Raiftearaí: Mar a cumadh stair na hÉireann*, by Vincent Morley (Dublin, 2011)', *Dublin Review of Books*, March 2013, http://www.drb.ie/essays/half-the-picture, accessed 30 Nov. 2016.
80 'Introduction' in James Kelly and Ciarán Mac Murchaidh (eds), *Irish and English: Essays on the Irish Linguistic and Cultural Frontier, 1600–1900* (Dublin, 2012), pp. 41–2.
81 See e.g. Eamon Darcy, 'The social memory of Oliver Cromwell in Ireland' in Martyn Bennet, Ray Gillespie and R. Scott Spurlock (eds), *Cromwell and Ireland: New Perspectives* (Liverpool, 2021), p. 234.
82 Breandán Ó Buachalla, *Aisling ghéar: Na Stíobhartaigh agus an t-aos léinn 1603–1788* (Baile Átha Cliath, 1996). Vincent Morley, 'The popular influence of Foras Feasa ar Éireann' in Kelly and Mac Murchaidh, *Irish and English*, pp. 96–115. See also Darcy, 'Social memory', p. 234.
83 For example, the trial of Oliver Plunkett in London in 1681 (Chapter 1), the trials of Sir John Fitzgerald of Clonlish (Chapter 3) and the book of the pleas of the Crown at Longford in 1687 (Chapter 5).
84 The manuscript is in the Armagh Public Library. *Court of Claims, Submissions and Evidence, 1663*, ed. Geraldine Tallon (Dublin, 2006).
85 *19th Annual Report of the Deputy Keeper of the Public Records*, 1887, app. V, pp. 41–87, Abstract of the decrees of the court of claims for the trial of innocents.

86 See Bríd McGrath, 'A biographical dictionary of the membership of the Irish House of Commons 1640–1641' (2 vols, Ph.D. thesis, Trinity College Dublin, 1998), esp. pp. 295–6 and Micheál Ó Siochrú, 'Sir John Walsh' in *DIB*, vol. 9, pp. 739–40.

87 Éamonn Ó Ciardha, 'Garret (Gerard, Gerald) Dillon' in *DIB*, vol. 3, pp. 288–9. Eoin Kinsella, *Catholic Survival in Protestant Ireland, 1660–1711* (Woodbridge, 2018).

88 NAI SR.2/4/5–7, now only available on microfilm, MFGS/57/001–3.

89 NLI, Westport Estate Papers, Collection List No. 78, compiled by Brigid Clesham and Wesley Geddis. These papers are an exceptionally important source for the understanding of wealthy landed Catholics in Connacht in the late seventeenth and early eighteenth centuries. There are a further 63 boxes of Westport papers in NLI which are listed but not calendared and relate to the eighteenth century and later; personal communication from Librarian, 29 Mar. 2018.

1

Accommodating the law: Oliver Plunkett and John Brenan

In any case, when the wind is favourable we must hoist the sails and make progress; when the gale arises we shall lower them and retire to some quiet little port beneath some mountain or cliff[1]

Nothing is known about the metropolitan of this province, and should he be taken, woe to him ... although everyone of sense knows his innocence; but innocence does not suffice in these countries ubi sedes est Satanae[2]

Most of the Irish Catholic bishops and clergy were in exile under Cromwell, and those who returned found a depleted and pauperised church in 1660. Almost half the Irish dioceses had no bishop in the period 1660 to 1690. The reasons are complex and included the persecution of clergy, a lack of suitable candidates due to the depredations of the Commonwealth, the fear of retaliation by the London authorities and the inability of the people to support a bishop due to poverty. At the end of the 1660s, Patrick Plunkett was the only active Catholic bishop in Ireland, but in 1669 four archbishops including Oliver Plunkett were appointed.[3] John Brenan was appointed bishop of Waterford in 1671.

Family and formation

Oliver Plunkett, a cousin of Patrick, was archbishop of Armagh (1669–81) and John Brenan was bishop of Waterford (1671–93) and archbishop of Cashel (1677–93). Plunkett was a member of the Old English gentry and Brenan came from a Kilkenny burgher family.[4] But Brenan's family had long lost the 'O' and assimilated with their Old English neighbours.[5] Plunkett and Brenan knew one another since they had shared an adventurous trip to Rome in 1647 with Fr PierFrancesco Scarampi to study for the priesthood, and they were ordained together in 1654. They generally shared the same viewpoint, although Brenan was aware that Plunkett was a proud man with a strong personality and could be overzealous.[6] They could not return to

Cromwellian Ireland and so both taught in Rome; Plunkett was professor of theology for 12 years and Brenan taught philosophy and theology for 15. Their many years in Rome familiarised them with the protocols and policies of the Vatican, and facilitated easy correspondence with Rome after their return to Ireland. Plunkett's period as archbishop ended after 12 years when he was executed in 1681; Brenan survived as bishop and archbishop for 22 years.[7]

Correspondence

Plunkett's correspondence from 1669 to 1681 is preserved principally in the archives of Propaganda Fide in Rome, and in Downside Abbey and Westminster Cathedral.[8] Brenan's correspondence from 1672 to 1692 is also preserved in the archives of Propaganda.[9] A large part was with the Internuncio in Brussels and another significant part was with the secretary of Propaganda in Rome. Their correspondence does not follow a regular pattern, perhaps because of the vagaries of preservation, but more likely because of the conditions under which it was written. There is a significant gap in Brenan's correspondence after the proclamation of 27 October 1673 that banned Catholic bishops and regular clergy, until calmer conditions were restored in 1675. It is more difficult to explain another gap of 18 months which followed, or why he should be writing in March 1677 'From my place of refuge in Ireland', when Catholics in Ireland were enjoying a period of respite and he was about to be appointed to Cashel.[10] The gap in Brenan's correspondence between October 1678 and April 1680 must reflect the proclamation of October 1678 expelling clerics. Plunkett's arrest and trial provoked renewed correspondence, but Brenan was cautious: 'It behoves us to make use of little paper and few titles when writing in these times. I have written several letters but received no answer, and perhaps it is better it should be so.'[11] Brenan noted in September 1680 that he was still cautious about writing: if a letter were found, every effort would be made to pursue the writers and 'give them a taste of the prison'.[12] But Plunkett was irrepressible. His pen, ink and inkstand were taken from him in Dublin Castle, yet he managed to send a last letter to the Internuncio on board the ship that took him to London.[13] He was held in solitary confinement and incommunicado for six months, and his next letter was in May 1681, seeking financial support to pay for conveying witnesses to and from London.[14] Brenan's correspondence is reasonably regular from 1681 until 1687; there is a four-year gap until 1691, reflecting the upheaval following the Williamite revolution. In February 1691, he noted that correspondence was 'especially difficult, when this kingdom is pestered with a very formidable heretical army under the Calvinistic Prince of Orange'.[15] Even after the fall of Limerick, he was still corresponding, and apologising for not writing 'due to the malignity of the past times, ... nor does the present state of affairs make the letter writing more secure'.[16]

Cultivating the viceroy

For Catholic clerics, Restoration Ireland was a constantly evolving challenge. There was significant anti-Catholic legislation, but the degree of enforcement depended on a variety of factors. The English and international political situation could precipitate hostile responses and the actions of the Catholic clergy or laity, whether in Rome or Ireland, could be perceived as provocative. Plunkett and Brenan did not contest the writ of English common law in Ireland; their primary concern was how legislation and new ordinances were created and applied in practice, according to the policy adopted by the Lord Lieutenant or Lord Deputy following policy dictated in London.

The dismissal of Edward Hyde from his post as Lord Chancellor in 1667 and the removal of James Butler as Lord Lieutenant in 1669 signalled a significant change of policy. With the king's approval, Peter Talbot was appointed archbishop of Dublin and Plunkett's arrival in Ireland in early 1670 coincided with a period of toleration. Between 1669 and 1671, four archbishops and seven bishops were appointed to repair the damage done by the Remonstrance controversy and Peter Taaffe's mission to Ireland – in effect a new hierarchy had been created.[17] There is nothing in Plunkett's letters to show that he received any formal instructions from Rome as to how he should approach his mission, but it is abundantly clear that his strategy was to cooperate with, and not oppose, the Dublin administration. He believed that cultivating good relations was the key to moderating the effects of the law, and reducing the likelihood of new disabling legislation, religious or secular. He knew that he was in an inferior position from a legal and political point of view but believed that his social standing and superior education allowed him to confidently meet the members of the administration as equals. He had the example of his formidable cousin, the lawyer Sir Nicholas Plunkett, who moved with ease and assurance in the highest circles.[18]

En route to his diocese, he sought to cultivate good relations with the administration in London, and had an audience with the Catholic Queen Catherine, who was known for her support of Catholic clergy and causes, and trusted that Plunkett would be well-disposed towards the king.[19] He was no sooner in Ireland than he was plunged into the dangerous maelstrom of church–state relations, and Plunkett quickly relied on his superior social connections.[20] He also had to deal with the doubts of his colleagues in the archdiocese who objected to his appointment. Plunkett wrote an extensive memorandum, claiming that his eminent social position as a member of the Plunkett family would ensure he was not *persona non grata* with the king, and therefore he could serve the Catholics of Ireland well.[21] It was clear to the new primate that the success of his mission to Ireland depended on royal approval at the highest levels.

In the light of his subsequent deep knowledge of, and involvement in, secular matters, his first letter from Ireland to the secretary of Propaganda must be treated with some scepticism: 'As for temporal affairs, I do not wish to know anything of them, and to this effect I exhort the others also, and if I am exiled or if I must suffer, it will be for the administration of the sacraments.'[22] In this respect he differed markedly from Peter Talbot who, together with his brother Richard, was deeply involved in attempts to restore Catholic privileges. But it did not take long for Plunkett to note the civil and religious restrictions on Catholics and that secular affairs could not be neatly excluded from religious. He reported to Rome: 'the obstacles to promoting the faith are the penal laws against the priests and laity, who are excluded from every government position unless they renounce the jurisdiction of the pope'.[23] In the climate of the time he was forced to adopt a disguise and in a remarkable passage written two years after his arrival, he recalled: 'In the time of Robartes … who was my enemy and persecuted me, I went under the name of Captain Browne, with my sword, my wig and my pistols, a situation which lasted only two or three months. In the houses which I entered and in the inns, I used to kiss the women, I used to sing.'[24]

But he quickly changed his opinion of Viceroy Robartes and commented to Brenan on the effect of the change of guard in the viceregal court when Robartes was dismissed.[25] Plunkett plunged into contact with his successor Berkeley, whose instructions from the English court included a degree of toleration for Catholics. Berkeley preferred to deal with Plunkett, rather than Peter Talbot, whom he held at a distance notwithstanding his powerful connections.[26] A week later Plunkett wrote to Brenan about his intimate relations with the new viceroy and his family, which Brenan recorded: 'The Archbishop of Armagh is very much in the favour of the new viceroy and has had audience of him twice, spending two hours with him on each occasion.' Lady Berkeley, the viceroy's wife, his daughters and members of his household were Catholic and exerted considerable influence: 'Mass is often said in the palace, something unheard of in a century, and all this is in private.'[27] He clearly held an elevated view of his own merit in Berkeley's eyes, and urged the secretary of Propaganda to ensure that the other bishops did not meddle in political affairs, which he regarded as his own responsibility.[28]

Plunkett was beginning to learn of another challenge, namely how to deal with recalcitrant clerics who caused legal difficulties for his fellow bishops. In May 1670 he sent Brenan a full account of the trial of James Lynch, archbishop of Tuam, who had been accused of *lèse-majesté* on the evidence of an Augustinian, Fr Martin French. French's superior and a Fr Dillon, who had disciplined French, were also charged with premunire, the offence of asserting or maintaining papal jurisdiction. Lynch was acquitted, but subsequently charged with premunire, again on the evidence of French. Lynch was once again acquitted, the jury of two Catholics and ten Protestants (one of the latter being 'a gentleman of upright conscience') had been locked away for twenty-four hours to consider their verdict. Plunkett had been given an account of the trial by his cousin Sir Nicholas Plunkett, who had 'advised me never to excommunicate any priest of bad life, but to suspend him from saying Mass and hearing Confession, and in this way I should not incur premunire'.[29] In the same letter Plunkett related another case in which George Codden, a Franciscan, had accused Plunkett's vicar-general Patrick Daly and another Franciscan of *lèse-majesté* before a criminal justice, because Codden would not submit to Daly's discipline. Plunkett had met Codden who 'seem[ed] … more fit for the lunatic asylum than the cloister'.[30] In this case the judges held a high opinion of the accused and rejected the accusations. It would seem from these cases that, notwithstanding a malicious prosecution, members of the hierarchy and clergy could get a favourable verdict from upright jurymen or sympathetic judges.

In June 1670 he told Brenan that he had to leave Armagh in a great rush to minister to the viceroy's first secretary, who, though ill, presented Plunkett with a 'complete pontifical outfit'. He recognised the animus between the viceroy and Archbishop Talbot, and suggested Brenan write 'a strong letter to Archbishop Talbot not to leave his diocese, and send me the letter to deliver to him'.[31] Plunkett also sought to build relationships with the Protestant church and he mentioned to Brenan that the Church of Ireland primate James Margetson had received him with all due respect and that schools with Catholic masters were now to be allowed; all this he put down to the viceroy who 'has been pleased on several occasions to speak of me in the presence of others with great esteem'.[32]

Plunkett sought to build Berkeley's confidence. In June 1670, he sent him the proceedings of a meeting of the four archbishops and bishops Plunkett of Meath and Phelan of Ossory. Berkeley continued to rely on Plunkett for information concerning troublesome church matters, and in June 1670 Plunkett went to Berkeley 'by the secret door' to negotiate the contents of a declaration of loyalty to be made at the meeting of the bishops.[33] He continued to maintain a close interest in the religious convictions of the members of the administration, and was able to enlighten Brenan about the manoeuvres at the English court that resulted in Berkeley's appointment.[34] Notwithstanding Plunkett's excellent relations with Berkeley, drawing on his experience from the Lynch case, Sir Nicholas Plunkett advised him that in addition he should cultivate good relations with as many Protestant gentlemen as possible, in case Plunkett found himself before a Protestant tribunal.[35]

Plunkett favoured an unorthodox approach and worked closely with the administration to deal with the problem of tories in Ulster.[36] In September 1670 he met with groups of tories from Tyrone to persuade them to abandon raiding and robbery and leave the country. Plunkett arranged pardons and safe-conducts for fifteen, and the viceroy gave them 400 scudi to defray their travel expenses to allow them take up military service in France or Flanders.[37] Unknown to Plunkett, Peter Talbot and others roundly criticised him for this service to the administration and after receiving complaints Plunkett had to respond to Rome to explain his actions.[38] Plunkett was given a pension of £200 per annum on Berkeley's recommendation for this service, but payment was stopped in late 1671. Officially the reason given was a deficit in the Treasury but Plunkett thought that in reality Peter Talbot had sowed the 'cockle in the wheat'.[39]

In the light of Peter Talbot's hostility, it is ironic that Plunkett acted as advocate with Berkeley in February 1671 when Talbot and others who were accused of exercising foreign jurisdiction. Hypocritically, Talbot had asked for help and Plunkett travelled to Dublin where Sir Nicholas Plunkett joined him, and both made the case for the accused before Berkeley and the Privy Council.[40] During that visit, Plunkett and Talbot attended a meeting to raise a fund from Catholic landowners for Richard Talbot's mission to London to recover the lands of dispossessed Catholics.[41] Two months later Plunkett wrote to Brenan, concerned that he and Talbot might be summoned to London to respond to allegations that the meeting had sought to levy the Catholic clergy to fund the campaign led by Richard Talbot.[42] But Berkeley's relations with Plunkett were such that he wrote to assure him that, if he was obliged to send him to London, he should not have the slightest fear because of the recommendation Berkeley would send of him to the king.[43]

After his dealings with Talbot, Plunkett may have been encouraged to help James Lynch, the archbishop of Tuam, who was plagued again by charges of premunire laid by Fr Martin French in April 1671. Plunkett brokered a temporary peace between French, Lynch and the superior of the Dominican order. Lynch, however, was still to face the judges on assize, and Plunkett noted Sir Nicholas Plunkett's tactic of briefing the judges before they travelled. This appears to have been persuasive, and Lynch and the other defendants were acquitted.[44] Once again the influence of this prominent Catholic lawyer on Protestant judges must be noted.

Plunkett also had to deal with disputes within the church. Although divisions between secular and religious priests were not pronounced in his period as primate, he was involved in the settlement of a dispute about questing rights (the right to seek alms from a local population) in the diocese of Meath in May 1671.[45] Of much longer term consequence was the questing rights dispute in four northern dioceses in Louth, Fermanagh and Down between the Franciscans and Dominicans, which he decided in favour of the latter.[46] The outcome was never accepted by the Franciscans and the number of disputes Plunkett subsequently endured with Franciscans is noteworthy. He was alert to the dangers posed by Franciscan provocation of the authorities, and he counted some of his greatest enemies among members of the order, such as Peter Walsh and John MacMoyer, one of the principal witnesses at his trial.

Trouble came not only from the laws which had been enacted by parliament and from some Catholic clerics, but also from edicts by provincial presidents. In December 1670 Plunkett noted that Catholics in Ulster were generally left untroubled by 'the earl of Charlemont, president of this province', and Plunkett had built a good relationship with him. Charlemont seems to have assisted Plunkett when he dismissed Terence Kelly, 'a man of infamy for his thirty-year public concubinage', by thwarting Kelly from citing Plunkett in the civil courts for premunire. He also gave Plunkett a life-interest in 'a fine house'.[47] It was otherwise elsewhere: in Munster '[t]he earl of Orrery ... issued an edict against the meeting of Catholics for Mass' and '[t]he president of the province of Tuam had also begun to molest the Catholics of the city of Galway'.[48] There was further trouble in Munster in August 1671, when Plunkett suspected that a troublesome Franciscan was stirring up disturbance and division in Limerick and might have provoked Orrery to issue a decree prohibiting the celebration of mass in Limerick and Cork.'[49] Plunkett suspected that strained political relations between Orrery and the viceroy were at the heart of this, particularly when, in September 1671, Orrery acted provocatively and published a decree 'ordering all Catholic ecclesiastics and laity to cease to reside in that city'.[50] Perhaps because of the attitude of the provincial presidents, Plunkett maintained his close relationship with the viceroy. In September 1671, Berkeley was annoyed to learn that Rome proposed to appoint ten new bishops to Irish dioceses, among whom was Fr Patrick Duffy. Plunkett took a dim view of Duffy: 'I regard him as unfit. He is a great drinker, a great man to swear scandalously, and he is not outstanding either by birth or by reason of learning.'[51] Plunkett was summoned, and predictably he mollified the viceroy. In relation to the bishops, Berkeley said 'he would close his eyes', except for Duffy, who Berkeley thought 'should use his talents elsewhere'.[52]

By September 1671 Plunkett had two years' practical experience of dealing with the intricacies of the legal limits of the power of the papacy in Ireland. When he first came to Ireland he had no understanding of the effect of the premunire laws, notwithstanding that he had studied civil and canon law for three years after his ordination in 1654.[53] Therefore it is not surprising to find that he took a particular interest in the origins and effects of the law and sent a long letter to the Internuncio on the topic.[54] In theory, no Catholic could avoid the law, for it rejected papal jurisdiction: 'whoever speaks, acts or writes in favour of the pontifical jurisdiction even in spirituals' was exposed. The penalty was exile and confiscation of all fixed and moveable property. Similarly, the role of the king in spiritual matters had been fixed by law: 'Also whoever says the king is not head of the church or whoever says the pope is head of the church incurs the same penalties. And whoever refuses to swear that the king is head of the Church is incapable of holding all public offices.'[55] Anyone who gave aid to a person who committed premunire was liable to the same penalties. The premunire law had gone through various stages of development, starting with Edward III's exclusion of papal influence in conferring benefices but had taken its most virulent form under Elizabeth I. Although Plunkett noted that it was not enforced 'with such great severity' in the time of James I or Charles I, or in the time of the present king, the clergy were always at risk of a mischievous suit: 'whenever a rascal charges a cleric before the courts, it is only with the greatest difficulty that the infliction of some penalty can be avoided'. He cited the Lynch and other cases as examples.[56]

In this letter Plunkett also traced how English legislation came into force in Ireland under Poynings's Law, and how the Elizabethan version of premunire, having been made law in England, only became Irish law when passed in an Irish parliament on a day when Catholics were absent due to a religious holiday. Later he noted how changes in the law in England could not apply in Ireland until the Irish parliament met.[57] He did not expect the imminent English parliament to make any laws which would affect Catholics in Ireland, not least because of a lack of jurisdiction: 'this country is under its own laws and parliament and is not subject to the decrees of the English parliament'.[58] But he also understood how legislation of the Irish parliament was not always required, since the latest developments in the English parliament could be followed by proclamations in Ireland.[59]

During the first two years of his primacy, Plunkett tested and pursued his policy of cooperation with vigour and considerable success. Three months after his arrival he could claim to have held two synods, ordained two men and confirmed 10,000 people.[60] Throughout this period, one sees Plunkett's remarkable relationship with Berkeley, as he sought to manage the effects of the premunire laws, to avoid provocation and to use their good relationship to mitigate the damage from troublesome cases.

The law and managing the church

Brenan had been appointed to the see of Waterford in May 1671 and Plunkett lost no time in introducing him to Berkeley and, through the good offices of Sir Nicholas Plunkett, to the Protestant bishop of Waterford, Hugh Gore, who received him.[61] Once again we see Sir Nicholas Plunkett's uncanny ability to negotiate with and influence Protestant grandees. Brenan found a church decayed by decades of legal persecution. He wrote that the last bishop had been exiled, there had been no bishop for 22 years after his death and the clergy were for the most part impoverished.[62] Church buildings were few and poorly built: 'All the ancient churches, now in the hands of the Protestants are stone buildings. The Catholic oratories are almost all houses of straw.'[63] Religious practice was constrained by a lack of clergy. Many of the diocesan clergy remained abroad after ordination, unwilling to return to a life of privation and persecution. Priests who did return often had charge of more than one parish. Many of the priests were old, and the rest very young; notwithstanding their youth they had to be sent to parishes because of the shortage of clergy.[64] Members of the clergy were often poorly educated, and so impoverished they relied on cattle dealing or agriculture to supplement the pittances afforded them by their parishioners.[65] Brenan made significant efforts to regularise matters for clergy and laity when the opportunity arose. In 1672 he confirmed 15,000 people, some as old as 60, who could not have been confirmed in earlier periods due to the absence of bishops.[66]

In Armagh, Plunkett took an exceptional interest in education, and he mentioned the dearth of Catholic schools and the dangers of sending Catholic children to Protestant schools in a report written only a month after he came to Ireland.[67] He was pleased to report to Cardinal Barberini in 1671 that, after the closure of the Jesuit school in New Ross, he invited one of the teachers to help him set up a school in Drogheda in which there were 150 general students, and 25 secular priests studying moral theology.[68] Plunkett relied on his strategy of cooperation and Berkeley's good offices to protect his schools.[69]

Whatever the merits of the Drogheda school for laymen, it was no substitute for the kind of religious education that Plunkett had experienced in his own clerical formation. He analysed this educational deficit in a report to Rome and attributed particular difficulties to the legal situation: 'On account of the penal laws here we cannot have schools with any stability.' Something of this is reflected in the Gaelic text, *Comhairle Mhic Clamha ó Achadh na Muileann* (The Advice of Mac Clave from Aughnamullen) which is part poetry and part prose.[70] It is believed to be the work of a Tyrone priest, Eoghan Ó Donnghaile (1649–c.1724).[71] The *Comhairle* takes the form of the pseudo-advice of John Mac Clave, a parish priest deposed by Plunkett, and its theme is the lack of learning among the Catholic clergy. Essentially satirical, *Comhairle* affirms Plunket and Brenan's frequent observations on the deleterious effect on the quality of the Catholic clergy due to the legal limitations on clerical education.

The economic damage caused by dispossession had consequences: 'Only three catholic gentlemen in all Ulster have recovered their estates and property'. Seminarians could not be sent to foreign universities, especially to Rome, where they would get the most reliable education. Plunkett sought support to send six of his most intelligent young priests to Rome for this foundation in education but approval does not seem to have been forthcoming.[72]

Essex: negotiating ambiguity

To Plunkett's great disappointment, by January 1672 there were rumours that Berkeley was to be replaced by Arthur Capel, earl of Essex, as a consequence of political changes in England.[73] At this time, John O'Molony was appointed bishop of Killaloe, much to the displeasure of Ormond. As a consequence, O'Molony hesitated to return to Ireland from France. Again, Plunkett intervened with Berkeley and received his assurance that he had no order from the king to disturb O'Molony, regardless of Ormond's views. Plunkett gave some tactical advice to the Internuncio for O'Molony: 'Once he is in possession of his diocese, it will be difficult to disturb him unless because of some serious crime. … As experience shows, and the laws themselves have it, it is much more repugnant to eject a guest than not to admit him in the first place.'[74]

In February 1672, the king issued the Declaration of Indulgence which suspended the penal laws against English and Irish Catholics and had several distinct political objectives, including providing a measure of toleration to dissenters and securing an alliance with France against the Dutch. Ireland was merely incidental in this, but in April Plunkett noted the ruling's immediate implementation by Berkeley.[75] Brenan also signalled his approval to the Internuncio but at the same time was shrewdly observing the political manoeuvres from the side-lines. Berkeley was losing support; he had made powerful enemies in the earls of Ranelagh and Ossory, and his position as viceroy was under threat. On the other hand, Peter and Richard Talbot were favoured in London. In April 1672 Brenan wrote to the Internuncio: 'The viceroy has now renounced the friendship of the Archbishop of Armagh and of [Colonel] John Patrick, and has been reconciled with the Archbishop of Dublin and his brother, who will seek to procure for him a continuation in his office of Viceroy.'[76] But this was to no avail, and noting Berkeley's imminent departure, and notwithstanding his change of allegiance to the Talbots, Brenan commented that the church was indebted to him as he had always showed himself friendly to Catholics.[77]

Plunkett was concerned the progress made under Berkeley was now at risk.[78] In fact Essex's appointment was due to several political objectives, of which the most important was Charles II's need to demonstrate to parliament that he intended to secure the Protestant interest and thereby procure funding for the war with France. Notwithstanding this, the suspension of the penal laws gave Plunkett some cause for hope, and there were good reports from the queen's chaplains Phillip Howard and Patrick Maginn.[79] So when Essex summoned Plunkett in August 1672, the fact that he was with him for two hours and found him courteous was considered highly significant, given Essex's public reputation as a devout Anglican. Plunkett could not yet know that the king had given Essex private instructions which 'allowed him the discretion to apply the oaths of allegiance and supremacy as he saw fit, to ensure catholic appointments to commissions of the peace, to determine an appropriate policy for religious toleration, and, crucially, to come to some accommodation with the catholic clergy'.[80] It was surprisingly easy, therefore, for Plunkett to insinuate his strategy of cooperation in the fracture between the public and private policies. The new viceroy asked to be advised when synods were to be held so that they would not be misinterpreted.[81] 'I hope that he will live up to the good reports we have had of him' was Plunkett's somewhat rueful aspiration. He concluded his report to Brussels: 'I assure you that during his term of office I shall keep my province and clergy safe from persecution as I have done under the previous regime.'[82]

In September 1672 Brenan recorded how the penal laws affected daily religious observance in Waterford. Generally the Catholic clergy were free to perform their church duties, except on Sundays, when Protestants attended church, and following a ruling by the Protestant magistrate, Catholics were prohibited from any assembly, nor allowed to walk through the city.[83] He too had formed a good impression of Essex: 'The new Viceroy is a lover of justice and is respected; he is supposed to be favourable to the Catholics.'[84] And there were further positive developments in September 1672 regarding the Oath of Supremacy when Plunkett reported: 'In virtue of a recent letter of the king, Catholics are permitted to hold offices and appointments without taking the oath that the king is the head of the Church: the new viceroy intimated this to Sir Nicholas Plunkett.' Catholics could become justices of the peace and would be able to trade freely and become freemen of town and city councils.[85] It seemed that the gains made under Berkeley would be maintained, but caution was required. In November 1672, Plunkett summarised the tactical approach he preferred: 'In any case, when the wind is favourable we must hoist the sails and make progress; when the gale arises we shall lower them and retire to some quiet little port beneath some mountain or cliff.'[86]

The political wind was beginning to take an adverse turn. The relatively benign regime in Ireland was not to survive, and the Declaration of Indulgence backfired. Political events in England triggered a series of developments which had adverse consequences for Ireland's Catholics. An unusual proclamation in January 1673 made clear that the king had no intention of upsetting the land settlement.[87] Brenan watched developments in London anxiously: 'We continue to enjoy great toleration here ... if progress be not hindered by the present Parliament in London.'[88] Charles II was in no position to argue with parliament, since he needed financial support to fund the Dutch war. Brenan's concerns were justified when the House of Commons forced the king to withdraw the Declaration of Indulgence in February 1673. In March, the English Commons demanded the recall of Prince Rupert's commission to examine the Irish land settlement and passed a new Test Act. Catholics were to be removed as justices of the peace. Peter Talbot was expelled 'for his notorious disloyalty and disobedience and contempt of the laws', and he was subsequently charged with premunire and raising money contrary to law.[89] Plunkett noted the hostility of the English parliament and the new rules restricting Catholics. He understood that these were English changes, and could not apply directly in Ireland until the Irish parliament met, which was not expected in 1673.[90] The fact that the duke of York publicly acknowledged his Catholicism by refusing to take the oath under the Test Act did nothing to calm matters.[91] In April Brenan noted: 'the English Parliament adopting strong and repeated petitions to the King that all our clergy should be banished from the kingdom by public edict from Ireland as they were expelled from London'. He felt the situation was exacerbated by the actions of the divided Catholics themselves, and that 'adversaries are whispering to the King all sorts of calumnies'.[92] A week later Brenan noted: 'The Archbishop of Dublin writes to me that he is obliged to retire to France for some time, by order of the King, privately conveyed to him.'[93] In September 1673 Plunkett told the Internuncio that the Irish bishops had held neither synods nor provincial councils, and he bewailed the rashness of Talbot in Dublin, who had 'gave considerable provocation to the earl of Essex, our wise and prudent viceroy'.[94]

There is little in the subsequent letters that throws light on Plunkett's continuing relationship with Essex, who had moved to distance himself from any pro-Catholic sentiment. A proclamation of October 1673 ordered the banishment of Catholic bishops and regulars, and the closure of religious houses and schools. Notwithstanding the rising tide of anti-Catholic sentiment, Essex sought to have Plunkett excluded from the effect of the proclamation, because of his role in subduing tories, and urged his brother Sir Henry Capel to have Plunkett exempted.[95] This might be seen as the apogee of Plunkett's good relationship with Essex, but there was to be no exemption from the proclamation.[96]

On the run

Plunkett reported the result in Ireland: 'The bishops have all been put under ban ... [o]nly the parish clergy remain, leaderless and like the scattered twigs of a brush.' The situation in London was ominous: 'The House of Commons also wished to deprive Catholic peers of a vote in parliament ... that no Catholic should live within five miles of London, and should have some distinctive mark as the Jews have in Rome.' Plunkett's forebodings of November 1672 had come to pass. In a major departure from his policy of cooperation he defied the law and did not register to leave Ireland. He no longer had any influence over events and his plan was to weather the storm.[97] Plunkett joined his old colleague Brenan in hiding and in December 1673 he wrote the first of a series of letters from 'a hide-out in Armagh diocese' where they shared a hut in The Fews, with little support from the laity.[98] In this climate of fear, they could not rely on the secular clergy for financial or moral support: 'the priests give nothing to bishops or ordinaries, nor will they even approach them'. Physical conditions were very difficult: 'I count myself fortunate now and again to obtain a little barley-bread and the house ... is made of straw and is roofed in such a way that from the bed we can see the stars, and at the head of the bed every small shower or rain refreshes us.'[99] Plunkett was devastated to report that '[a]ll the convents and novitiates had been disbanded and the novices are scattered'.[100] The school was levelled to the ground in November 1673, despite all Plunkett's efforts.

The position continued to deteriorate, and in January 1674 Plunkett wrote about the implementation of the 1673 proclamation. The bishops and religious who had reported for deportation had been unable to travel, and expected to be treated favourably until they could board ship. These included James Lynch the archbishop of Tuam, Patrick Plunkett the bishop of Meath and John O'Molony the bishop of Killaloe. On 10 January 1674, a further proclamation had been issued, in effect ordering the bishops and religious to leave or else face prison.[101] Those who had not submitted their names for exile would be treated with even greater severity. Even Plunkett, the bishop of Meath, 'was cited to embark despite the fact that Ormond had procured him a letter of favour from the king'.[102] In fact he was allowed stay in Dublin, perhaps because of his advanced age.[103] Another, more severe edict was expected comprising 'an order to all magistrates and lieutenants to send out the police around the houses in the cities and in the country to seek out bishops and religious' and Plunkett went on to describe how he and Brenan set out in appalling weather to find safer shelter. Both suffered terribly from travelling in the January cold and physical ailments were taking their toll. Not many bishops and religious had yet been arrested, but Plunkett expected 'that the time will come when I shall hear there is a lack of space in the prisons, so full will they be'. He was also aware of developments in England, where Catholics in the armed forces were under pressure. Catholics were being forced from London, and members of the Cabal Privy Council were at risk of impeachment. Plunkett was highly attuned to the significance of events in Scotland and England and it was remarkable that, even from his Armagh hideout, he was able to keep abreast of ominous developments and could quote Vergil: 'We are in greater fear and trembling now that "our neighbour is on fire etc."'[104] He reported that in Scotland it would be *lèse-majesté* to hear mass; the punishment was to be drawn and quartered. Although there were some Catholic families in mainland Scotland, such as the Gordons in the North-East, there was particular concern for the 4,000 Catholic families in the Hebrides. In England there was to be a new oath for all the Catholics of London, including a provision that the Pope was a heretic. The penalties for refusal to take the oath included forfeiture of three-quarters of the property of the offender. Restrictions were imposed on the royal family. There was discussion in parliament about the forced rearing of Catholic children as Protestant and the castration and life-imprisonment of priests. As usual, Plunkett forensically noted that '[t]hese edicts and proclamations and decrees of theirs do not at present include Ireland, because it is not named by the king in them but I am sure that, as usual, we shall not be forgotten'.[105] His comments were prophetic, and in April 1674 there was a new proclamation, 'more severe than previous edict', reviving the proclamation of the previous year.[106] In some respects the new proclamation reflected the lack of effective enforcement of the October 1673 edict. Essex blamed the lack of military force, but Plunkett, always alive to the interplay between enforcement and provocation, blamed these new measures on the Franciscans seeking alms as if there had been no proclamation against regular clergy, and on the bishops who had stayed openly in Dublin too long.[107] The other bishops were in very straitened circumstances because 'the wealthy for fear of the edicts and penal laws will not give us lodging in their homes and the … people who are prepared to take us in have no bread, not even oaten bread'.[108] Later that month Plunkett noted that, although the secular clergy had not been the subject of the proclamations, they would be left without leadership because the hierarchy had been singled out. He feared that Peter Walsh, who was said to be returning to Ireland with Ormond, would step into that vacuum and create trouble with remonstrances, as he had done in 1666. Plunkett was clear-eyed (and eerily prophetic) about what might ensue: 'As for me, I shall try out what kind of rooms they have in the prisons before I abandon my flock, nor shall I leave until they drag me with the rope around my neck to the ship.'[109]

In a rare letter to Fr Peter Creagh, the agent for the Irish clergy in Rome, Plunkett noted how strictly the law was being applied.[110] He himself had a close shave with the enforcers who had accidentally come upon his hideout.[111] He was seriously concerned what would happen should he be arrested. He was perennially short of money, but conditions were even more acute because of the recent famine that had impoverished the laity who were in no position to support the clergy.[112] He noted that, up to then, 'soldiers, bailiffs and police have not been very active or concerned about carrying out the edicts'. But because of the poverty of Catholics and Protestants, he was concerned what might happen if rewards of £20 were offered for the capture of a prelate; he thought the reward might be difficult to resist and few would escape. As a consequence he feared he could not support himself while in prison or afford to go into exile.[113] Notwithstanding that he was in hiding, Plunkett remained in contact with political developments, and continued to espouse a cautious, low-profile approach to forestall any further measures against the church.[114] He feared that Franciscan insouciance might provoke parliament which was due to meet in November.[115] It was only towards the end of this period that his letters turned again to the Viceroy's reaction; the last of his letters from hiding feared that the friars' activities would provoke Essex.[116]

The tempest moderated?

The end of the Anglo-Dutch war enabled Charles II to prorogue the London parliament and its constant demands for anti-Catholic measures.[117] These English political developments had direct Irish consequences; Plunkett was glad of the respite and his next recorded letter was from Dublin. Only Peter Talbot had left Ireland, entirely due to his political activities. Plunkett and Brenan emerged from hiding into a Catholic community where the hierarchy was still reasonably intact and the religious orders still troublingly active. It was his constant concern that, while the secular clergy were amenable to his jurisdiction, the religious orders were not. In March 1675 he once again decried the behaviour of the Franciscans, who had not only re-established their convents, but also proposed to hold a chapter to elect their provincial. He regarded this as extremely provocative, and feared a return to internal exile, particularly in the light of recent developments in London. Therefore, since he could not act effectively himself, he asked Propaganda to ensure that no chapter was held and that the provincial be appointed, not elected.[118] Five months later, his concern had not abated. There were fears of a new parliament, in which case he felt: 'we are finished. This parliament would issue rigorous edicts and would force our people to take oaths against our faith, and whoever protested and refused to swear would lose all his possessions.' He noted that the viceroy had behaved with discretion towards the Catholics; this was more than could be said of the Franciscans whose conduct had been offensive. He urged: '[i]n circumstances such as the present it is necessary to walk prudently and with fear' and he instanced two of the clergy who had fallen foul of the law. The vicar apostolic of Killala was imprisoned for life where he had no food or means of sustenance, had been fined £100 and his possessions confiscated, while the former provincial of the Franciscans had been imprisoned for the last 18 months. Not every case against a cleric was won by the administration however; the vicar-general of Derry, Luke Plunkett, had been accused of *lèse-majesté*; 'but the informers were unable to prove anything; the judge, who is a friend of Sir Nicholas Plunkett, had him released and acquitted, to the confusion of the informers'.[119]

Brenan took stock in a long report to Rome in September: 'The Catholic people … by the Penal Laws … are, on account of their religion, oppressed in manifold ways, being shut out from holding any office, public or private, in the kingdom, nevertheless the greater part of them bear all this in a Christian manner.' He noted the effect of the 1673 edicts on the hierarchy. The English House of Commons had demanded that the archbishop of Dublin should be banished, the archbishop of Tuam had been exiled and the bishop of Killaloe had left of his own accord in response to a request to establish an Irish College in France. Apart from Tuam, none of the other bishops had been arrested and very few of the religious molested. In relation to education, he reported that 'in virtue of the Penal Laws, no Catholic is allowed to be a schoolmaster, and thus our young people have to be taught by Protestant masters'. There was at least some respite from the travails of the last two years: 'At present, the tempest, such as it was, is greatly moderated, so much so that the edicts and persecution are almost forgotten.' But Brenan was far from sanguine and echoed Plunkett's concerns that the religious orders, especially the Franciscans, were back in the community and opening public chapels. He thought that the Irish parliament believed that, when new bishops were appointed by Rome, they would disturb the Protestants 'not only in the religion which they profess but in the possession of the temporal goods which they enjoy'. For Protestants, the protection of the land settlement was an even greater priority than their religious freedom. In Brenan's view, parliament's fears were fuelled by the malign doctrines of Peter Walsh, in his numerous pamphlets: 'full of rancour against the Pope and the Bishops'.[120] Plunkett was also wary of the force of international events on domestic matters; in July 1676 he feared that war with France would force the king to call a parliament in England that would issue new measures against the Catholics. For once his fears were groundless and clearly he had no inkling of Charles II's secret peace treaty of February 1676 with Louis XIV; in fact a period of relative calm followed.[121]

Ormond's reinstatement as Lord Lieutenant in May 1677 and the moderation in persecution may have given encouragement to Plunkett's enemies. Plunkett's strategy of cultivating good relations with the administration led to accusations of collaboration by dissenting clerics in his diocese. Brenan was quick to defend him, and in August 1677, he argued that Plunkett's familiarity with officials in the government was useful in dealing with vexatious accusations brought against him. Brenan thought that, without this familiarity, there was no doubt that Plunkett would be exiled, like the archbishops of Dublin and Tuam.[122] Three months later, in October 1677, Brenan wrote optimistically to Rome: 'Our affairs here are taking a favourable turn; we are living without disturbance and without fear.'[123] The statutes of the synod held in Ardpatrick in August 1678 contained a number of politico-legal provisions. Plunkett's attitude to tories had hardened, despite the fact that he seems to have been prepared to help the well-known raparee Patrick Fleming leave Ireland in early 1678.[124] The priests of the province were ordered to 'preach against the robbers commonly called tories, and all who favour and receive them'.[125] Plunkett publicly expressed his loyalty to the Crown and at the synod the priests were ordered to 'pray unceasingly the divine majesty for the well-being of our most serene King Charles II'.[126] For his part, Brenan had held synods in 1672, when conditions 'could hardly be called hard', and in 1676 and 1677 when 'persecution slumbered'.[127]

The Popish Plot

Brenan's optimism of October 1677 and the professions of loyalty to Charles II at the Ardpatrick synod were to be dashed on 8 October 1678 when an order was made for the arrest of Archbishop Peter Talbot after Titus Oates had appeared before the English Privy Council in September and alleged a 'Popish Plot'. Talbot was imprisoned in Dublin Castle and all the archbishops, bishops and vicars-general and religious were ordered to leave the country by 20 November.[128] Plunkett laid the responsibility squarely on Talbot himself, for returning to Ireland, where he had always fomented trouble, and quoted Matthew 26: 24: 'it would have been better for us if that man had not been born!'[129] A storm was about to engulf Plunkett. He noted: 'There are certain men under arrest in London on suspicion of conspiracy against the king and for communication with foreign princes, and for the murder of a gentleman in London. As regards the conspiracy against the person of the king it is purely imaginary.'[130] He was relieved he had not been named by person in the edict and intended to go on the run with Brenan. But he feared the resumption of a parliament in Dublin, and the edicts it might promulgate.[131]

By May 1679 he was in hiding for the second time, writing to Rome that: 'Matters here are going from bad to worse because of a public edict. Forty scudi are promised to whoever captures a prelate or Jesuit, and twenty to whoever brings in a vicar general or friar. Police, spies and soldiers go hunting night and day.' In Ulster the secular clergy were being harassed by Presbyterians, and 'many of them do not dare to appear by day'.[132] On the same day Plunkett wrote to the Internuncio of his fears for his own liberty and seeking practical advice and directions as to where he might choose his exile.[133] Tanari's cynical reply deliberately gave no instructions to Plunkett; he did not want to create the impression that provision would be made for Plunkett if he were exiled, and he preferred to keep pressure on him to remain with his diocese. A month later Propaganda approved Tanari's course of action, on the grounds of expense and to ensure that the diocese was not completely abandoned.[134] In reality Rome was abandoning Plunkett to his own fate by refusing to provide him any comfort that he would be welcome if forced to flee Ireland.

At this point, Plunkett believed that he was being pursued because he had not obeyed the proclamation, and that his punishment would be exile. Six months later, still in hiding, he was slightly more optimistic: 'we should not despair of a better situation than in the past'. He seemed to believe that the Popish Plot had no bearing on him personally and was a marginal event, driven by events in England: 'it is becoming progressively clear that this plot, this shedding of much Catholic blood, was thought up by Presbyterians, people who are hostile to both monarchy and hierarchy'.[135]

Plunkett's arrest, trial and execution

All that was to change, because a Popish Plot without an Irish dimension was not credible. An anonymous note given to the duke of York in October 1679 implicated Col. John Fitzpatrick, Patrick Tyrrell the bishop of Clogher and Plunkett in a plot to bring a French army to Ireland and precipitated Plunkett's arrest on 6 December 1679.[136] The process of gathering evidence to implicate him began; it took three months to mature. No one, including Plunkett himself, seemed to think he might be at mortal risk. From prison in Dublin Castle he himself wrote in January 1680 that there was little evidence against him.[137] Although Plunkett's strategy of cooperation with the administration no longer carried any weight with the Lord Lieutenant, nevertheless Ormond was far from convinced there was an Irish dimension to the plot, and he had always 'responded as moderately as he could' and followed orders from England 'as humanely as possible'.[138] Neither was he impressed by the quality of the witnesses in the case: 'the extravagant villainy and folly of the discoverers'.[139] Notwithstanding that his friend of over thirty years was in prison, Brenan also felt there were still some signs of hope.[140]

The king's Whig opponents, led by the earl of Shaftesbury, were looking for evidence of an Irish dimension that would bolster Oates's accusations, and gradually opportunistic witnesses from Ulster began to emerge. In all about twenty witnesses were found, chief of whom was the Franciscan John MacMoyer, who not only carried a series of grudges arising from Plunkett's attempts to discipline him, but who had also given warnings to Ormond as far back as 1676 about Plunkett's plan to facilitate a French invasion force.[141] Ormond had ignored these warnings in 1676, but the toxic conditions in 1680 left him with no choice. In June 1680 Brenan, the only archbishop at large, was writing about the public anger inflamed by the false testimony given by the witnesses against Plunkett.[142] As ever the Internuncio was sanguine, even supine. He reported to Rome that, even though there were now witnesses, since there was no conspiracy, the truth would prevail.[143]

Plunkett was tried in Dundalk in July 1680 for treason and exercising papal jurisdiction; it was clear that he was facing capital charges. The jury was packed. It should have been drawn from the population of Dundalk which was confessionally mixed, but Plunkett reported that MacMoyer, the principal witness against him, petitioned that no Catholics be included. Plunkett did not object; he knew MacMoyer lacked local credibility. As ever, shortage of money was a problem, and while preparing to defend himself, Plunkett was put to considerable expense. Life in prison was uncomfortable, and compromised by his poverty. In the event, and regardless of the confessional profile of the jury, the principal witnesses failed to appear and his trial was put back. He was still exposed, however: 'In accordance with the law here, I have to present myself before three criminal sessions before I can be released.'[144]

During the hiatus in Plunkett's trial, the bishop of Cork was in prison, the bishop of Killaloe in hiding and the bishop of Limerick remained free only because of his great age. Notwithstanding all this, Brenan wrote: 'The government is moderate, nor do we see that rigour which is felt in England.'[145]

MacMoyer, Plunkett's principal accuser, went to London to convince the authorities that no Irish jury would convict and in October 1680 Plunkett knew that he was to face trial in London. Ormond had done all he could but was in no position to resist his transfer to London, since he was regarded as unduly favourable to Catholics. Further informers had emerged and Plunkett was short of money, requiring him to sell or pawn personal property, even his chalice and cross. In contrast the House of Lords and the Privy Council in England sought extra witnesses who would be paid from the Treasury. Plunkett was now clearly worried about the charges he himself might face but at the same time about three of his colleagues: 'Bishop Tyrell, Father Luke Plunkett and Dr. Drumgoole have been declared guilty of lèse-majesté by the grand jury. This is rather strange – in virtue of a trial held even without the presence of the accused, and without hearing their side, sentence is pronounced.' This did not augur well for his own trial.[146]

A 'royal order' was procured and Plunkett was escorted by 'a body of the royal guards' and brought to London.[147] He was held in Newgate under difficult conditions; in November he petitioned the Lords to be allowed his servant and board while in prison but this was denied.[148] On 12 February 1681, the grand jury of Westminster brought in a verdict of *Ignoramus*: there was insufficient evidence against Plunkett for him to be put on trial.[149] This was the second time that Plunkett had faced a court without conviction, but he was not released. The reasons have not been detailed but Plunkett's prominence told against him and the prosecution believed that more cogent witnesses could be prepared for a later hearing. The grand jury eventually found a true bill against him in March. At his arraignment on 3 May 1681, Plunkett argued that he should not be tried in England for offences alleged to have been committed in Ireland, to which the presiding judge rejoined that the trial was legal since it had been ordered by parliament.[150]

The details of Plunkett's trial in London have been examined elsewhere and do not require repetition here.[151] Brenan related how Plunkett was given thirty-five days to arrange the witnesses and documents required for his defence.[152] He sent his servant to Ireland with a letter, begging friends to contribute the funds required to defray the cost of his trial. No support seems to have come from his indigent family in Ireland; rather it was the financial and moral support of English Catholics who 'did for me all that even my brother would do'.[153] A letter he sent to Brussels on 16 May urgently seeking funds to pay his witnesses' expenses did not receive a favourable response.[154] Tanari, the Internuncio, pleaded 'the poverty of the country'.[155] Only five of thirty potential witnesses agreed to travel, and great obstacles were encountered in procuring copies of defence documents.[156] Defence witnesses were reluctant to travel to London because of the expense, and more pertinently because of the risk they would be imprisoned, since in principle Catholics were barred from the city. Their safe-conduct passes arrived in Dublin on 6 June, two days before the trial. They were further delayed by storms which prevented them reaching London within the thirty-five days allowed. Plunkett requested an extension of ten days, because a special messenger had been sent ahead to say that the witnesses' arrival was imminent. But the extension was not granted and the trial went ahead as scheduled. In accordance with contemporary practice, Plunkett's capital trial was held without counsel, evidence or witnesses for the defence, and the charges, evidence and witnesses for the prosecution were announced only on the day of the trial. The vociferously hostile crowd supported the partisan judges who were prepared to admit hearsay evidence, contrary to legal authority.[157] The fact that most of the witnesses against Plunkett were Irish Catholics was one of the greatest ironies and dangers of the trial. Had he cultivated some of the Ulster clergy as assiduously as the Dublin administration, there might have been fewer witnesses against him. The jury was handpicked and the judges at best uncaring of legal nicety and generally hostile. Plunkett was tried for premunire and treason and condemned on 8 June 1681; in the circumstances it is perhaps not surprising that he was not more vigorous in his own defence.[158] Several days later he petitioned the king for a retrial on the grounds that he was 'unexpectedly brought to his trial destitute of all means to make his just defence and exposed naked to the malice of his accusers'.[159] No response is recorded and the king refused to intervene.[160] Of the three viceroys whom Plunkett had served, Berkeley was dead and Robartes remained silent: only Essex approached the king for a pardon on the basis of the witnesses' perjury.[161] Echard recorded: 'Upon which the king in a passion said, "Why did you not attest this at his trial? It would have done him good then. I dare not pardon anyone"'.[162] In contrast, on the scaffold, Plunkett pardoned all those who had a part in his trial. Plunkett was no match for Shaftesbury's intrigues and had been sacrificed by the king to secure the Stuart succession.

While awaiting his execution, Plunkett summarised his religious and political philosophy in a long, remarkable letter to his confessor:

> it is objected why do we not obey the king's edicts? It is an axiom in the civil law, *Mandante consule silet decretu' pro consulis*.[163] Christ is the consul, the king the proconsul. The consul says *spritus santus posuit vos Regere Ecclesiam Dei* and *pasce oves meas*.[164] The proconsul says leave your flocks go far from them and *nolite Regere* or *pascere oves vestras*.[165] For he who is far from the Flocks cannot feed them. Are we to obey men, rather than God. Shall we despise the Consul and hear the proconsul's contrary commands.[166]

Plunkett had done everything he could to avoid placing himself or his church in conflict with the state, but when that conflict was thrust upon him, he had no doubt where his duty lay. He contested the legitimacy of the state's actions but more importantly he proclaimed the superiority of divine law, and believed his death would prove an inspiration to all Catholics.

After Plunkett

Brenan had no doubt concerning the irregularity of Plunkett's trial.[167] Plunkett was executed on 1 July and on 14 August 1681 Brenan wrote that Plunkett had been murdered, and that all other bishops must be in dread: 'for wicked men are not wanting to accuse them though innocent, and rewards and pardons are held out to stimulate such perjurers'. He expressed his own fears of what might occur if he were arrested.[168] In fact, Brenan survived as archbishop for another 12 years by maintaining a low, elusive, profile. But the worst appeared to be over. Although bishops were concealed, in prison or at risk of exile, none had actually been forced to leave Ireland. Brenan acknowledged that the administration in Ireland was more moderate and less oppressive than in England.[169] By May 1682, Plunkett's accusers were in disarray. An early report after the trial stated: 'I am told that three of the witnesses that swore against Plunkett are gone distracted.'[170] MacMoyer seems to have changed allegiance, and in December 1681 he was accused of warning certain members of the Ulster clergy to leave Ireland or they would suffer the same fate as Plunkett. As a consequence he was in prison.[171] Henry O'Neill retracted the evidence against Plunkett before his own execution in March 1682.[172] Catholics took comfort from this and Brenan noted 'we now begin to breathe and hope more than during these four years past'. In addition he was able to report that informers had lost all credibility.[173] But Brenan was innately cautious, and he feared that the appointment of new bishops would be provocative. He noted that, before his recent departure for London, the viceroy had sought information about the number of bishops. Ormond had left his son, Lord Ossory, in charge and Brenan had no idea what future laws might hold and thought it wiser to suspend new appointments.[174]

A year later, in February 1683 he reported: 'We are enjoying somewhat greater liberty than formerly', but with customary caution hoped that 'the too great confidence of some indiscreet persons [whom he did not identify] may not deprive us of it'.[175] However the times were still unsettled, and when the terror associated with the Plot started to subside, in 1683 some Catholic religious started to 'insolently' re-emerge, such as the Dominican friars and nuns at Burrishoole. Ormond was in no mind to allow the law to be flouted and ordered that they be brought to trial.[176] The persecution was not over, the times were far from tranquil and Brenan maintained a low profile.[177] He feared an accidental flare-up of old troubles, and as always he watched the administration closely. It was particularly worrying at a time when Catholic gentlemen were on trial in Cork for conspiracy against the king; in the event they were found not guilty.[178]

Brenan was delighted by the accession of James II. He was neutral in respect of the various interest groups that surrounded the new king, but inclined towards Tyrconnell. He wrote to Brussels that there was a calmer atmosphere under the new king, and looked forward to better times. He was hopeful for the new parliament to be held in England in May 1685.[179] James II raised the hopes of the Catholic interest, and in June Brenan reported 'a calm season with a good prospect of things favourable to our holy religion, and comforting the afflicted'.[180] But the hierarchy was cautious. When the bishops met in July they sent messages of goodwill to the new king, and asked that Tyrconnell be given authority to protect the public exercise of religion against all authority. Bishops Maguire and Tyrell had gone to London to pursue this policy, but Brenan feared they had overstepped their instructions.[181] In October, Brenan complained that he had not a single line from Maguire and Tyrell. He reminded the Internuncio that, since 1678, Catholics had been deprived of all public offices, and the clergy 'assailed by the fury of our adversaries'. Now he was able to report that '[m]atters have proceeded peacefully and we hope for further consolation' and he believed that 'affairs will go on gradually to great advantage, and to the confusion of the enemies of the King and Government'. Catholics were now in public offices and administration – 'things not known nor seen for the past hundred and fifty years. *Benedictus Deus*.'[182] Brenan admired Tyrconnell's hasty zeal, a view not shared by the editor of his letters.[183] As always, Brenan was concerned about the effect of the law on religion and education, but he could report that a provincial synod was held and some schools had reopened.[184] Notwithstanding this, education for lay students remained problematic. In principle Catholic schools were illegal, so that children were still forced to attend Protestant establishments.[185]

Brenan noted the transformation that had overtaken Catholic affairs since James II's accession and the appointment of Tyrconnell. The Protestant archbishop of Cashel, Thomas Price, had died in August 1685 and his revenues were to be used to pay stipends to Catholic bishops.[186] Now, almost the whole army was Catholic, as were the judiciary and magistrates. Bishops and clergy could wear ecclesiastical dress in public and the religious orders appeared everywhere in their habits, and had begun to repair monasteries and convents. But there were still inconveniences for Catholics. For example, the Protestant archbishops had a public court jurisdiction, which Catholics were obliged to attend for matrimonial disputes. Mostly, however, the Catholic archbishops privately regulated these issues.[187] There was no record of any further correspondence from Brenan until 1691. By then, the battle of the Boyne had been lost, but the battle of Aughrim and the fall of Limerick were still to come. His dioceses of Waterford and Cashel were in Williamite hands. In February clerical promotions were the subject of some of his last recorded letters.[188] He was involved in the negotiation of the Treaty of Limerick, and would have been aware of the dreadful slaughter at Thomond Bridge and the failure of the Jacobite defence.[189] His last letter catalogued the decay of the Catholic hierarchy: 'In this kingdom there are at present only two Bishops ... the Archbishop of Cashel and the Bishop of Ossory.'[190] The hierarchy had returned to the state it was in 30 years earlier. Brenan died peacefully in 1692 or 1693 and is buried alongside the literary historian Geoffrey Keating in Tubrid, Co. Tipperary.[191]

Conclusion

Neither Plunkett nor Brenan were revolutionaries who sought to liberate Ireland's Catholics from the law which so oppressed them. Instead their strategy was to be watchful, to cooperate, to conciliate and to avoid provocation. Plunkett had studied civil and canon law, he had learnt a good deal of the common law from his cousin and for very practical reasons had an avid interest in the application of the law. He believed that, with his knowledge and connections, he could outwit the worst aspects of its rigour. It is ironic therefore that, of all the members of the hierarchy who suffered under the law during the Restoration, Plunkett was the most notable victim. There were other potential targets. It is not surprising that Peter Talbot should fall victim and die in prison; he had a reputation for conspiracy and meddling and was the most politically active member of the hierarchy. Patrick Tyrrell, bishop of Clogher had been arrested and charged with high treason in October 1680 based on evidence given by Plunkett's accuser John MacMoyer. John O'Molony, bishop of Killaloe, who was believed to have been involved in the 1667–8 French plot, remained at large throughout the period and could have just as readily been a victim.[192] For a period of time Plunkett's strategy of cooperation with the administration was successful, but he was unable to contend with the English political forces arrayed against him and he failed spectacularly. Perhaps Plunkett was simply unlucky to get caught. It may also be the case that Plunkett's prominence as primate made him the most obvious target, and once the existence of a plot was 'proven', nothing could have saved him. Certainly, neither of his viceregal colleagues in collaboration, Robartes nor Essex, did anything useful to help.[193] The king prioritised the Stuart succession over any intervention to extricate him.

It could be argued that Plunkett courted a martyr's crown. By the second decade of the seventeenth century, the cult of martyrdom was fully established in Ireland, and Plunkett can hardly have avoided its influence.[194] As he left Rome in 1669, he was warned he might have to die for his faith and was 'inflamed with the desire of his shedding his blood for Christ'.[195] However it seems more likely that, faced with no choice, he embraced the fate provided for him by God's will. Having been condemned, he told his nephew 'I die most willingly, and being the first among the Irish, with the grace of God, I shall give good example to the others, not to fear death.'[196] He was clear where his duty lay; he told his confessor Maurice Corker that in a contest between the state and the church, the latter must always prevail. 'But they will kill us? Quid inde.[197] By our deaths the number of Catholics will not be diminished but rather augmented.'[198] To this end, Plunkett asked to be interred with the Jesuits who sacrificed their lives at Tyburn, and the copper plate on his coffin referred to his having suffered martyrdom with constancy.[199]

In some respects, Plunkett's character has been obscured by hagiography but his determined and powerful personality shines vividly through his letters. It can be argued that Plunkett's character contributed to his downfall. His self-confidence may have led him to believe that the worst that could befall him was a period of exile, followed by his return to Ireland, as was the experience of his cousin Bishop Patrick in 1664. Mooney suggested that the tragedy of his life might be traced to the fact that his training, outlook and temperament were at odds with the people in his Ulster diocese. He also showed that Plunkett's accusers were educated in Rome, and his fate cannot be attributed to locally educated unreconstructed clerics opposed to Tridentine reform.[200] Hanly, who must have understood his character as well as anyone, thought: 'It is possible that he might not have died as he did if he were less conscientious as a reforming bishop.'[201] It would be a travesty to over-simplify the many steps of Plunkett's route to the scaffold, but the proximate causes are reasonably clear. His disciplinary disputes with MacMoyer lead directly to the witnesses who gave evidence against him, and ultimately to his ignominious execution. Plunkett was always prepared to cooperate, but perhaps in retrospect his faith and adamantine personality can be perceived as his greatest strength, and gave him the courage to face his final violent encounter with the law with great composure and grace.

Irish clerics had a range of options in the exercise of their ministry. Plunkett and Brenan had chosen to leave the stability of Roman academic life for the challenges of leading a flock traumatised by years of war and oppression. Their strategy of accommodation occasionally involved taking a more active tactical role, but their cautious approach could not survive the tide of brutal external events. Plunkett's life was swept away by the politics of the Popish Plot and Brenan lost all agency in the aftermath of the Jacobite disaster. Other clerics of the period chose different paths, some as intellectual campaigners and others as political activists, and it is to these we now turn.

Notes

1 Plunkett to Fr John Paul Olivia, 2 Nov. 1672, *The Letters of St. Oliver Plunkett*, ed. John Hanly (Dublin, 1979), p. 351.

2 Brenan to secretary of Propaganda, 14 Aug. 1681, P. F. Moran, *The Life of Oliver Plunkett, Archbishop of Armagh: [A Compendium of the Author's Memoirs of him]* (Dublin, 1861), pp. 370–1.

3 Plunkett to Armagh, Peter Talbot to Dublin, William Burgatt to Cashel and James Lynch to Tuam. See Plunkett's memorandum on the Irish episcopate, c.1668, in Hanly, *Plunkett*, pp. 22–3.

4 Power outlines something of Brenan's background, P. Power (ed.), *A Bishop of the Penal Times, being the Letters and Reports of John Brenan, Bishop of Waterford (1671–93) and Archbishop of Cashel (1677–93)* (Cork, 1932), p. 6. On the other hand, Ó Ciardha states that nothing is known of his parents: Éamonn Ó Ciardha, 'John Brenan' in *DIB,* vol. 1, pp. 799–800.

5 Catherine Breathnach, 'Archbishop John Brenan (1625–1693), his life and work' *Tipperary Historical Journal* (1993), pp. 148–9.

6 'of a hot disposition', Brenan to Cardinal Protector of Ireland, 30 Mar. 1672, and 'touchy and of a hot disposition', Brenan to Internuncio, 4 Apr. 1672: Moran, *Life*, p. 222. 'Touchy and hot-tempered': Raymond Murray, 'St. Oliver Plunkett' in *DIB,* vol. 8, p. 192.

7 Brenan survived long enough to be one of the clerical leaders involved in the negotiation of the Treaty of Limerick.

8 Plunkett's letters were translated, edited and published by Hanly, who was Postulator of the Cause of St Oliver Plunkett from 1968 to 1975. Despite this understandable bias, his edition of the letters is indispensable. As might be expected of a significant religious figure, there is considerable hagiography relating to Plunkett: Moran, *Life*; Emmanuel Curtis, *Blessed Oliver Plunkett* (Dublin, 1963); Desmond Forristal, *Oliver Plunkett in his own Words* (Dublin, 1975). See also Murray, 'St. Oliver Plunkett' in *DIB,* vol. 8, pp. 191–3, and John Hanley, 'Oliver Plunket' in *ODNB,* accessed 18 Dec. 2018. Tomás Ó Fiaich's short biography, *Oliver Plunkett, Ireland's New Saint* (Dublin, 1975), is comprehensive, fair and remarkably candid. Neither does Canice Mooney pull his punches in relation to Plunkett's personality: see 'Accusations against Oliver Plunkett', *Seanchas Ard Mhacha* 2 (1956–7), pp. 119–40 for an unsentimental assessment. A modern biography is overdue.

9 Brenan is much less well served than Plunkett. Most of Brenan's letters were transcribed and translated at the behest of Cardinal Moran and published by Power. This edition of the letters, although short, is as indispensable as Hanly

is to Plunkett. Other letters can be found in Moran. Catherine Breathnach's short article contains a wealth of useful material. See also Ó Ciardha, 'John Brenan'.

10 Brenan to Internuncio, 30 Mar. 1677, Moran, *Life*, pp. 252–3.
11 Brenan to Internuncio, 20 Apr. 1680, Power, *Brenan*, p. 69.
12 Brenan to unidentified recipient, 12 Sept. 1680, Moran, *Life,* p. 279.
13 Plunkett to Internuncio, 24 Oct. 1680, 'from on board ship in the Irish Sea', Hanly, *Plunkett*, p. 560.
14 Plunkett to Canon Gregory Joyce in Brussels, 16 May 1681, Hanly, *Plunkett*, p. 564.
15 Brenan to unidentified recipient, 2 Feb. 1691, Power, *Brenan*, p. 97.
16 Brenan to Internuncio, 11 Sept. 1692, Power, *Brenan*, p. 99.
17 Benignus Millett, 'Survival and reorganization 1650–95' in P. J. Corish, *A History of Irish Catholicism* (5 vols, Dublin, 1968), vol. 3, part 7, p. 22.
18 In the years to come there were to be many examples of Sir Nicholas's powerful influence with Protestant officials.
19 Plunkett to Cardinal Barberini, 30 Dec. 1669, Hanly, *Plunkett*, p. 55.
20 Plunkett to Brenan, 18 Apr. 1670, Hanly, *Plunkett*, p. 70. Before his return to Ireland, Brenan was agent for the Irish clergy in Rome, and Plunkett first wrote to him 20 Mar. 1670, Hanly, *Plunkett*, p. 66. Brenan was consecrated bishop 6 Sept. 1671 in Rome, and was in Ireland within a few months, Hanly, *Plunkett*, p. 217. Plunkett's last letter to him in Rome was 22 Mar. 1671, Hanly, *Plunkett*, p. 178.
21 Plunkett to secretary of Propaganda, July–Aug. 1669, Hanly, *Plunkett*, p. 35.
22 Plunkett to secretary of Propaganda, 4 May 1670, Hanly, *Plunkett*, p. 79.
23 Plunkett to secretary of Propaganda, 1 Nov. 1670, Hanly, *Plunkett*, p. 145.
24 Plunkett to Internuncio, 2 Apr. 1672, Hanly, *Plunkett*, p. 301.
25 Plunkett to Brenan, 6 May 1670, Hanly, *Plunkett*, p. 81.
26 Berkeley 'had known and distrusted Talbot in exile': Aidan Clarke, 'Peter Talbot' in *DIB*, vol. 9, p. 246. Talbot seemed to resent Plunkett's relationship with Berkeley.
27 Plunkett to Brenan, 14 May 1670, Hanly, *Plunkett*, p. 83; a reflection of the King's own marriage to a Catholic.
28 Plunkett to secretary of Propaganda, mid-May 1670, Hanly, *Plunkett*, p. 92.
29 Plunkett to Brenan, 14 May 1670, Hanly, *Plunkett*, pp. 86–7.
30 Codden was to be sent away, but he still remained in the diocese in 1672, to Plunkett's dismay: Plunkett to Internuncio, 20 Dec. 1672, Hanly, *Plunkett*, p. 359. Codden would later give evidence against Plunkett in 1681; however, the evidence was not used in court.
31 He was already planting the seed of the primacy dispute that subsequently erupted between Armagh and Dublin.
32 Plunkett to Brenan, 14 June 1670, Hanly, *Plunkett*, p. 93.
33 The declaration promised to report any rebellion to the king and to encourage loyalty among the laity. It may have helped Berkeley undermine Ormond's efforts to support Peter Walsh's Remonstrance. See Liam O'Rourke, 'Catholicism

and the Church of Ireland under the viceroyalty of Arthur Capel, first earl of Essex, 1672–77' (M.Litt. thesis, National University of Ireland, Maynooth, 2010), p. 34.
34 Plunkett to Capt. Poulton, 15 June 1670, Hanly, *Plunkett*, p. 94; to newly elected Pope Clement X, 20 June 1670, p. 106, and to Brenan 22 June 1670, p. 110.
35 Plunkett to Brenan, 17 Aug. 1670, Hanly, *Plunkett*, pp. 127–8.
36 The hierarchy wanted to maintain law and order and the laity had been warned to give no aid to tories by the synod of Dublin in June 1670. This was at the same time as a proclamation offering a reward for the apprehension of named tories was issued: 1 June 1670, James Kelly and Mary Ann Lyons (eds), *Proclamations of Ireland 1660–1820* (5 vols, Dublin, 2014), i, p. 239. Among the most notorious tories at the time were Redmond O'Hanlon in Ulster, Dudley Costelloe in Connacht and the Brennans in Leinster.
37 Plunkett to secretary of Propaganda, 27 Jan. 1671, Hanly, *Plunkett*, p. 160.
38 Talbot had been complaining since July 1670 to Rome about Plunkett's involvement. He charged that Plunket had made a laughing stock of the Catholic clergy, by ordering them to round up tories: Hanly, *Plunkett*, pp. 157–8.
39 Plunkett to Internuncio, 15 Nov. 1671, Hanly, *Plunkett*, p. 277. In Aug. 1672, Plunkett was less circumspect, and told the Internuncio that Peter Talbot had spread a rumour that Plunkett was being paid a large salary from Rome and so the royal pension was stopped: 1 Aug. 1672, Hanly, *Plunkett*, p. 318.
40 Plunkett to Internuncio, 7 Feb. 1671, Hanly, *Plunkett*, p. 163.
41 Plunkett and the Ulster clergy declined to contribute; Ó Fiaich attributes this to Plunkett's dislike of Peter Talbot. Ó Fiaich, *Oliver Plunkett*, p. 54.
42 In England it was believed that parliament wanted him brought to London so that he might be charged with promoting Catholicism: Cathaldus Giblin, 'Catalogue of material of Irish interest in the collection "*Nunziatura di Fiandra*", Vatican Archives: Part 2' *Collectanea Hibernica* 3 (1960), pp. 7–130, at p. 63.
43 Plunkett to Brenan, 22 Mar. 1671, Hanly, *Plunkett*, p. 178.
44 Plunkett to Internuncio, 28 Sept. 1671, Hanly, *Plunkett*, p. 253.
45 Plunkett to secretary of Propaganda, 10 May 1671, Hanly, *Plunkett*, p. 189.
46 Plunkett to the clergy of the dioceses of Armagh, Clogher, Down and Dromore, 11 Oct. 1671, Hanly, *Plunkett*, p. 272.
47 Plunkett to secretary of Propaganda, 23 Feb. 1671, Hanly, *Plunkett*, p. 166. After the Restoration, William Caulfeild was appointed governor of the fort of Charlemont for life, and created a viscount, Lord Charlemont, in 1665. There was no presidency in Ulster.
48 Plunkett to Brenan, 30 Dec. 1670, Hanly, *Plunkett*, p. 152. It is not clear to whom Plunkett referred as the president of Tuam; this may be Lord Kingston who shared the Connacht presidency with Berkeley.
49 This appears to be the first mention in Plunkett's letters of mass being said in the open. Plunkett to Internuncio, 9 Aug. 1671, Hanly, *Plunkett*, p. 218. This

was not new for Orrery. Five years earlier, the Jesuits reported that Orrery's harassment forced them to withdraw to the countryside: Vera Moynes (ed.), *Irish Jesuit Annual Letters 1604–1674* (Dublin, 2019), p. 937.

50 Limerick. Plunkett to Internuncio, 28 Sept. 1671, Hanly, *Plunkett*, p. 253.

51 Plunkett to Internuncio, 16 Mar. 1671, Hanly, *Plunkett*, p. 176. Throughout early 1671, Plunkett continued to rail against Duffy's appointment, most notably in a letter to the Internuncio, 7 June 1671, Hanly, *Plunkett*, p. 202. Notwithstanding Plunkett's objections, Duffy was appointed bishop of Clogher in 1671. He died in 1675.

52 Plunkett to Internuncio, 29 Sept. 1671, Hanly, *Plunkett*, p. 258.

53 Timothy Corcoran, 'Blessed Oliver Plunkett and his Irish Jesuit schools' *Studies* 30/119 (Sept. 1941), pp. 415–24, at p. 416. P. F. Moran, 'Blessed Oliver Plunkett' in *The Catholic Encyclopedia* (New York, 1911). Accessed 18 July 2023 from http://www.newadvent.org/cathen/12169b.htm. Murray, 'Oliver Plunkett', p. 191.

54 Plunkett to Internuncio, 30 Sept. 1671, Hanly, *Plunkett*, pp. 265–6. Hanly suggests it was drafted with the help of Sir Nicholas Plunkett: p. 263.

55 Hanly, *Plunkett*, p. 265.

56 Plunkett to Internuncio, 30 Sept. 1671, Hanly, *Plunkett*, pp. 265–6. The Lynch case is discussed above.

57 Plunkett to secretary of Propaganda, 19 Mar. 1673, Hanly, *Plunkett*, p. 370.

58 Plunkett to secretary of Propaganda, 26 Sept. 1673, Hanly, *Plunkett*, p. 379.

59 Plunkett to secretary of Propaganda, 12 Nov. 1673, Hanly, *Plunkett*, p. 386.

60 Plunkett to Cardinal Protector of England, 18 June 1670, Hanly, *Plunkett*, p. 103.

61 Plunkett to Internuncio, 15 Nov. 1671, Hanly, *Plunkett*, p. 277. By 1671, every diocese had a bishop or vicar general: Raymond Gillespie, *Seventeenth-Century Ireland* (Dublin, 2006), p. 240.

62 *Relatio*, 6 Sept. 1672, Power, *Brenan,* p. 28. In fact, Bishop Patrick Comerford had died in 1652.

63 *Relatio*, 18 June 1672, Power, *Brenan,* p. 23. Brenan was taking some licence here; Protestant worship was often conducted 'either in a dirty cabin or in a common alehouse': Richard Mant, *History of the Church of Ireland* (2 vols, London, 1840), vol. 1, p. 667 quoted in Simms, *NHI*, vol. 3 p. 435.

64 Report to prefect of Propaganda, 28 May 1672, Power, *Brenan,* p. 21.

65 *Relatio*, 6 Sept. 1672, Power, *Brenan*, p. 30.

66 Brenan to Propaganda, 28 May 1672, Power, *Brenan*, p. 22.

67 Plunkett to secretary of Propaganda, Apr. 1670, Hanly, *Plunkett*, p. 74.

68 Plunkett to Cardinal Francis Barberini?, 30 May 1671, Hanly, *Plunkett*, p. 199.

69 Plunkett to Cardinal Barberini, 30 May 1671, Hanly, *Plunkett*, p. 199. See also Timothy Corcoran, *State Policy in Irish Education A.D. 1536 to 1816* (Dublin, 1916), p. 84.

70 J. Duffy (ed.), 'Comhairle Mhic Clamha ó Achadh na Muileann', *Clogher Record*, 5 (1963–5), pp. 307–47

71 Bernadette Cunningham, 'Language, literature and print in Irish, 1630–1730' in *The Cambridge History of Ireland* (4 vols, Cambridge, 2018), ii, p. 447.
72 Plunkett to Internuncio, 27 Sept. 1671, Hanly, *Plunkett*, pp. 247–8.
73 Plunkett to Internuncio, 20 Jan. 1672, Hanly, *Plunkett*, p. 288.
74 Plunkett to Internuncio, 20 Jan. 1672, Hanly, *Plunkett*, p. 288.
75 Plunkett to Internuncio, 2 Apr. 1672, Hanly, *Plunkett*, pp. 301–2. John Miller, *Popery and Politics in England 1660–1688* (Cambridge, 1973), p. 117.
76 Brenan to Internuncio, 4 Apr. 1672, Moran, *Life*, pp. 223–4.
77 Brenan to Prefect of Propaganda, 28 May 1672, Power, *Brenan*, p. 22.
78 Plunkett to Internuncio, 20 Jan. 1672, Hanly, *Plunkett*, p. 288.
79 Plunkett to Internuncio, 14 May 1672, Hanly, *Plunkett*, p. 305.
80 John Gibney, 'Arthur Capel' in *DIB*, vol 2, p. 317.
81 Early in 1673, the Superior of the Jesuit mission advised Essex that he intended to carry out a purely pastoral visit, to which the viceroy assented: Moynes, *Jesuit Annual Letters*, pp. 989–90.
82 Plunkett to Internuncio, 16 Aug. 1672, Hanly, *Plunkett*, pp. 321–2.
83 Brenan, *Relatio*, 6 Sept. 1672, Power, *Brenan*, pp. 26 and 32–3. This regime was not applied outside the city or on weekdays.
84 Brenan to Prefect of Propaganda, 6 Sept. 1672, Power, *Brenan*, p. 26. Power believed that Essex had been appointed with a brief to pursue a less tolerant policy towards Catholics.
85 Plunkett to Internuncio, 30 Sept. 1672, Hanly, *Plunkett*, p. 336. This is a reference to the power given to the Lord Lieutenant to dispense with the requirement that Catholics elected to corporations take the oath of supremacy: Gibney, 'Arthur Capel', p. 317. Essex had a friendly relationship with Nicholas Plunkett: O'Rourke, 'Essex', p. 43.
86 Plunkett to Fr John Paul Olivia, 22 Nov. 1672, Hanly, *Plunkett*, p. 351.
87 24 Jan. 1673, *Proclamations*, i, p. 297.
88 Brenan to unidentified recipient, 22 Feb. 1673, Power, *Brenan*, p. 38.
89 Aidan Clarke, 'Peter Talbot' in *DIB,* vol. 9, p. 246. Talbot had instructed his nephew Walter Dungan, a Catholic JP in Kildare, to arrest John Byrne, a Dominican.
90 Plunkett to secretary of Propaganda, 19 Mar. 1673, Hanly, *Plunkett*, p. 370.
91 He was forced to resign as Lord High Admiral and flushed out as an open Catholic.
92 Brenan to unidentified recipient, 22 Apr. 1673, Power, *Brenan*, p. 40. Talbot had been a strong opponent of the Remonstrance and pursued remonstrant clergy.
93 Brenan to unidentified recipient, 30 Apr. 1673, Power, *Brenan*, p. 43.
94 Plunkett to Internuncio, 26 Sep. 1673, Hanly, *Plunkett*, p. 379.
95 Essex to Sir Henry Capel, 13 Oct. 1673, William P. Burke, *Irish Priests in Penal Times* (Waterford, 1914), p. 47.
96 Essex also sought to protect some half-dozen friars whom he had encouraged to foment conflict with the secular clergy: Essex to Ormond, 14 Nov. 1673, Osmund Airy (ed.), *Essex Papers* (London, 1890), pp. 137–8.

97 Plunkett to secretary of Propaganda, 12 Nov. 1673, Hanly, *Plunkett*, p. 386. Most of the Irish Jesuits adopted similar tactics. They did not dare appear in public and only two left the country in 1674: Moynes, *Jesuit Annual Letters*, pp. 991, 992.
98 The winter of 1673/4 was particularly severe.
99 Plunkett to pro-secretary of Propaganda, 15 Dec. 1673, Hanly, *Plunkett*, p. 389. This was the first of Plunkett's letters 'from a hideout in Armagh'; the last was in Oct. 1674.
100 Plunkett to pro-secretary of Propaganda, 15 Dec. 1673: Hánly, *Plunkett*, p. 390. The Jesuit school in Cashel had been forced to close a year earlier, and an attempt to reopen the New Ross school in Aug.1673 fell victim to the October proclamation: Moynes, *Jesuit Annual Letters*, pp. 988, 991.
101 Plunkett to Internuncio, 27 Jan. 1674, Hanly, *Plunkett*, p. 398. There is no record of a proclamation on 10 Jan. 1674; the second proclamation was issued on 27 Apr. 1674, *Proclamations*, i, p. 316.
102 Ormond's support is surprising; although one of Plunkett's nephews was married to Ormond's niece. Plunkett had led the opposition to the Remonstrance in 1666.
103 He was born in 1603. It is not clear who procured the letter but it is unlikely that Ormond was not involved.
104 Vergil, *Aeneid* 2.l.311.
105 Plunkett to Internuncio, 12 Feb. 1674, Hanly, *Plunkett*, p. 402.
106 27 Apr. 1674, *Proclamations*, i, p. 316. Plunkett to Internuncio, 4 May 1674, Hanly, *Plunkett*, p. 404.
107 Probably a reference to bishops who registered their intention to leave but lingered in Dublin.
108 Plunkett to Internuncio, 4 May 1674, Hanly, *Plunkett*, p. 404.
109 Plunkett to secretary of Propaganda, 26 May 1674, Hanly, *Plunkett*, p. 408. Brenan had left Ulster for his own diocese and was in hiding in the Knockmealdown Mountains.
110 Plunkett to Fr Peter Creagh, 26 May 1674, Hanly, *Plunkett*, p. 410.
111 Plunkett to Internuncio, 10 June 1674, Hanly, *Plunkett*, p. 413.
112 E.g., Essex to Arlington, 18 Apr. 1674: Airy, *Essex Papers*, p. 214. Three months later Plunkett noted that 'the poor have begun to eat horse-flesh': 5 July 1674, Plunkett to Internuncio, Hanly, *Plunkett*, p. 420.
113 Plunkett to Internuncio, 10 June 1674, Hanly, *Plunkett*, p. 414. In England a reward of £5 had been offered for anyone catching a priest; this measure had not been introduced yet to Ireland: Plunkett to Internuncio, 5 July 1674, Hanly, *Plunkett*, p. 420.
114 Because of financial worries, he had given up his correspondence with his 'agents in Dublin, London and in the provinces of Cashel and Tuam', but he had received two letters from the Internuncio in the previous month. Plunkett to Internuncio, 15 Sept. 1674, Hanly, *Plunkett*, p. 426.
115 Plunkett to Internuncio, 15 Sept. 1674, Hanly, *Plunkett*, p. 428.
116 Plunkett to Internuncio, 18 Oct. 1674, Hanly, *Plunkett*, p. 438.

117 Plunkett to Internuncio, 18 Oct. 1674, Hanly, *Plunkett*, p. 438. The English Parliament did not meet again until Apr. 1675.
118 Plunkett to secretary of Propaganda, 5 Mar. 1675, from Dublin, Hanly, *Plunkett*, p. 440.
119 Plunkett to secretary of Propaganda, 11 Aug. 1675, Hanly, *Plunkett*, p. 452. Once again, Nicholas Plunkett's personal relationships with, and powerful influence on, the Protestant judiciary had been decisive.
120 *Relatio*, 20 Sept. 1675, Power, *Brenan*, p. 48.
121 Plunkett to pro-secretary of Propaganda, 16 July 1676, Hanly, *Plunkett*, p. 464. Plunkett took the opportunity to visit his colleague Brenan in Munster in September and wrote to the Internuncio urging that Brenan should retain the diocese of Waterford and be appointed to Cashel; 1 Oct. 1676, Hanly, *Plunkett*, pp. 475–6. During this visit, both Brenan and Plunkett came to the attention of the informer Eustace Comyne, and narrowly escaped arrest having attended a meeting with Ormond's seneschal John Walshe. There are 21 other letters from July 1676 to Aug. 1678 (nos. 175–97 in Hanly). They are mainly concerned with Jansenistic teaching, disciplinary matters, episcopal appointments, activities of the religious, and financial concerns, both personal and concerning the Irish episcopate generally.
122 Report by Brenan to unidentified official, 5 Aug. 1677, Power, *Brenan*, pp. 54–5. See also Ó Fiaich, *Oliver Plunkett*, pp. 62–3.
123 Brenan to secretary of Propaganda, 14 Oct. 1677, Power, *Brenan*, p. 57.
124 Plunkett to Fr Manus Quin, 31 Jan. 1678, Hanly, *Plunkett*, p. 501. See P. G. Murray 'A previously unnoticed letter of Oliver Plunkett's' *Seanachas Ard Mhacha* 8 (1975/76), pp. 23–33, for a full exploration of the background to this letter, and Plunkett's dealings with Fleming.
125 Decree No. 1, Plunkett to Internuncio, Hanly, *Plunkett*, p. 517.
126 Decree No. 26, Plunkett to Internuncio, Hanly, *Plunkett*, p. 519.
127 Power, *Brenan*, p. 9.
128 16 Oct. 1678, *Proclamations*, i, pp. 392–5.
129 Plunkett to Internuncio, 24 Oct. 1678, Hanly, *Plunkett*, p. 528.
130 A reference to Sir Edmund Godfrey, murdered 17 Oct. 1678.
131 Plunkett to Internuncio, 24 Oct. 1678, Hanly, *Plunkett*, pp. 527–9. He seems to have been exceptionally well informed: Oates first presented his claims to the House of Lords on 31 Oct. 1678. See John Gibney, *Ireland and the Popish Plot* (Basingstoke, 2009), p. 6.
132 Plunkett to secretary of Propaganda, 15 May 1679, Hanly, *Plunkett*, p. 530.
133 Plunkett to Internuncio, 15 May 1679, Hanly, *Plunkett*, p. 532.
134 10 June and 1 July 1679. See Giblin, '"*Nunziatura di Fiandra*", part 2', p. 72.
135 Plunkett to Internuncio, 30 Nov. 1679, Hanly, *Plunkett*, p. 538.
136 The circumstances surrounding Plunkett's arrest are explored thoroughly by John Brady in 'The arrest of Oliver Plunkett' *Irish Ecclesiastical Record* 81 (Feb. 1954), pp. 81–92, and 'Why was Oliver Plunket arrested' *Irish Ecclesiastical Record* 83 (Jan. 1955), pp. 41–7.
137 Plunkett to Internuncio, 17 Jan. 1680, Hanly, *Plunkett*, p. 542.

138 Michael Perceval-Maxwell, 'James Butler' in *DIB*, vol. 2, p. 142.
139 Ormond to Ossory, 10 Apr. 1680, Gibney, *Popish Plot*, p. 81.
140 Brenan to Internuncio, 20 Apr. 1680, Power, *Brenan*, p. 69.
141 According to Plunkett, MacMoyer was a notorious drunkard who led a dissolute life. He was an associate of the tories, for which he had been tried in Armagh in 1678 and fined. None of this would ingratiate him to Plunkett who attempted to discipline him. See Plunkett to Internuncio, 15 July 1680, Hanly, *Plunkett*, p. 556. In exceptionally strong language, Ó'Fiaich described MacMoyer's hostility to Plunkett as 'consuming hate': *Oliver Plunkett*, p. 120. A full analysis of Plunkett's relationship with MacMoyer is in Tomás Ó Fiaich, 'The fall and return of John Mac Moyer' *Seanchas Ard Mhacha* 3 (1958), pp. 51–86.
142 Brenan to Internuncio, 30 Jun. 1680, Moran, *Life*, p. 278.
143 8 Jun. 1680. Giblin, '"*Nunziatura di Fiandra*", part 2, p. 76.
144 Plunkett to Internuncio, 25 July 1680, Hanly, *Plunkett*, p. 555.
145 Brenan to unidentified recipient, 12 Sep. 1680, Moran, *Life*, p. 279.
146 Plunkett to Internuncio, 21 Oct. 1680, Hanly, *Plunkett*, p. 560. Tyrell was from Clogher, Plunkett the vicar-general of Derry and Drumgoole became vicar-general of Armagh. It was around this time that Plunkett is said to have ministered to his fellow prisoner Peter Talbot, before he died in Dublin Castle.
147 Brenan wrote an undated *Narrative* of Plunkett's trial, which can be found in Moran, *Life*, pp. 294–6, 299–300, 322–4, 347–50.
148 Plunkett to House of Lords, 8 Nov. 1680, Hanly, *Plunkett*, p. 563. Although he did not know it at the time, the death of his much-revered cousin and legal adviser, Sir Nicholas Plunkett on 25 Dec. 1680 was a further blow to Plunkett.
149 HMC, *Ormonde MS*, NS. vol. 5, p. 580. See also J. G. Simms, 'The restoration, 1660–85' in *NHI*, vol. 3, p. 433. A similar verdict was recorded in respect of Sir John Fitzgerald of Clonlish on the same day. Unlike Plunkett, Fitzgerald was released.
150 An ironic echo of the argument made 40 years earlier, in Apr. 1641.
151 See, e.g., Alice Curtayne, *The Trial of Oliver Plunkett* (London, 1953). C. P. Curran, 'The trial of the primate' in *Blessed Oliver Plunkett Historical Studies* (Dublin, 1937), pp. 123–32, and James Comyn, *Irish at Law* (London, 1983), pp. 4–11, look at the legality of the trial. Gibney's *Popish Plot* examines the political background comprehensively and details the various strands of evidence against Plunkett.
152 Dec. 1680, Moran, *Life*, p. 295.
153 Plunkett to his cousin Fr Michael Plunkett, 22 Jun. 1681, Hanly, *Plunkett*, p. 574.
154 16 May 1681, Plunkett to Canon Gregory Joyce, Hanly, *Plunkett*, p. 564. Plunkett was looking for 640 scudi or crowns.
155 Curtayne, *Trial*, p. 183. This is difficult to reconcile with Tanari's account of 17 May 1681 of the 20,000 scudi he dispensed to the subjects of the king of England who were refugees in Flanders: Giblin, '"*Nunziatura di Fiandra*",

part 2', p. 80. Plunkett was condemned on 6 June and Tanari sent 200 scudi which had been collected in Belgium to Plunkett on 28 June 1681. He thought the timing opportune, since Plunkett must have been in great want: Giblin, '"*Nunziatura di Fiandra*", part 2', p. 68. The day after Plunkett's execution, Tanari, unaware of what happened, believed that political intervention might save Plunkett from the gallows. He thought that money he received from the Pope for Plunkett might be used to relieve Plunkett 'when he is sent into exile after his long term in prison'. Giblin, '"*Nunziatura di Fiandra*", part 2', p. 86.

156 Brenan's *Narrative* Moran, *Life*, pp. 295–6. Passes were issued for the witnesses to travel, but the names on the passes don't appear to have survived. *CSPD 1680–81*, p. 313. They may have been Edmund Fay from Meath, Anthony Murry, Paul Neale, James Doorgan, and Cornelius Tully from Louth, referred to by John Plunkett in an affidavit as potential witnesses who had decided against travelling to London until safe passes for their egress and regress were obtained. *CSPD 1680–81*, p. 318.

157 Curran, 'Trial of the primate', pp. 127–9.

158 Ó Fiaich, *Oliver Plunkett*, p. 91.

159 Plunkett to Charles II, soon after 8 June 1681, Hanly, *Plunkett*, p. 565.

160 As did the duke of York, despite the petition of his mother-in-law, the duchess of Modena: Gibney, *Popish Plot*, p. 149. Queen Catherine, whom Plunkett had met in 1670 on his way to Ireland, was in no position to plead on his behalf, having been threatened with impeachment in 1679.

161 Essex had a guilty conscience, having joined Shaftesbury in arguing for the existence of an Irish element to the Popish Plot.

162 Laurence Echard, *History of England* (3 vols, London, 1718), vol. 3, p. 631, referenced in Moran, *Life*, p. 345. See David Dickson, *New Foundations Ireland 1660–1800* (Dublin, 2000), p. 20; Gibney, *Popish Plot*, p. 149, and Hanly, *Plunkett*, p. 587.

163 The proconsul's command is silenced in the face of a command from the consul.

164 The Holy Spirit has placed you to rule the church of God and feed my sheep.

165 Do not rule or feed your sheep.

166 Plunkett to Fr Maurice Corker, 24 June 1681, Hanly, *Plunkett*, p. 577.

167 Part of Brenan's *Narrative* 'can be shown to be not entirely accurate': Ó Fiaich, 'Fall and return', p. 55. The *Narrative* can be found in Moran, *Life*, pp. 294–6, 299–300, 322–4, 347–50.

168 Brenan to secretary of Propaganda, 14 Aug. 1681, Moran, *Life*, pp. 370–1. In fact, Plunkett was the last Tyburn martyr.

169 The bishops of Cork and Kildare were in prison; not accused of conspiracy, but of overstaying after the edict of exile. The bishop of Kildare would probably be allowed go to Germany, and the bishop of Cork exiled. The bishop of Limerick was so old he was allowed remain. The whereabouts of the bishop of Killaloe were not known. Brenan to unidentified recipient, 15 Oct. 1681, Power, *Brenan*, p. 71.

170 Newsletter to John Squier, Newcastle; 2 July 1681, *CSPD 1680–81*, p. 340. It is not clear who Squier was. He was the recipient of newsletters on many other occasions: see *CSPD* from 1680 to 1687.
171 Ormond to Sir Leoline Jenkins, 6 Dec. 1681, *CSPD 1680–81*, p. 605. Ó Fiaich, 'Fall and return', p. 81.
172 Curtayne, *Trial*, p. 231. His recantation is printed in full in Moran, *Life*, pp. 314–16.
173 Brenan to secretary of Propaganda, 1 May 1682, Moran, *Life*, pp. 313–14. The acquittal of Sir John Fitzgerald of Clonlish which Ó Bruadair celebrated in *Searc na Suadh (Love of Sages),* was one instance. See poem no. XXXVI in John C. Mac Erlean (ed.), *Duanaire Dháibhidh Uí Bhruadair: The Poems of David Ó Bruadair,* part 2 (Dublin, 1913), p. 265, 16 May 1682.
174 Brenan to secretary of Propaganda, 1 May 1682, Power, *Brenan*, p. 72.
175 Brenan to unidentified recipient, 8 Feb. 1683, Power, *Brenan*, p. 74.
176 Ormond to Arran, 30 Aug. 1683, Burke, *Irish Priests*, p. 59. Gillespie situates this in the wider context of Ormond being seen to bear down on Catholics as much as Presbyterians in the wake of the Rye House Plot: *Seventeenth-Century Ireland*, p. 268.
177 Brenan to Propaganda, 4 Oct. 1683, quoted in Breathnach, 'Archbishop Brenan', p. 156.
178 Brenan to unidentified recipient, 14 Apr. 1684, Power, *Brenan*, p. 77.
179 Brenan to Internuncio, 17 Mar. 1685, Power, *Brenan*, p. 79.
180 Brenan to unidentified recipient, 6 June 1685, Power, *Brenan*, pp. 80–1.
181 See Giblin, '"*Nunziatura di Fiandra*", part 2', p. 103.
182 Brenan to Internuncio, 12 Oct. 1685, Power, *Brenan*, pp. 82–3.
183 Power, *Brenan*, p. 83.
184 Report on Diocese of Cashel, 6 Nov. 1687, Power, *Brenan*, p. 85. Report on diocese of Waterford and Lismore, 9 Nov. 1687, Power, *Brenan*, p. 91.
185 Report on Diocese of Waterford and Lismore, 9 Nov. 1687, Power, *Brenan*, p. 93.
186 £300 to the primate; £200 to the archbishops of Dublin and Cashel and the bishop of Clogher; £150 each to other bishops; Power, *Brenan*, p. 89. *CSPD Jan. 1686–May 1687,* p. 421.
187 Report on Cashel diocese, Nov. 1687, Power, *Brenan*, p. 87.
188 Brenan to Internuncio, 2 Feb. 1691, 11 Sept. 1692. Power, *Brenan*, pp. 97–9.
189 On 25 Sept. 1691 Brenan was a member of the group of Irish peace representatives who dined with Ginkel, and then crossed into Limerick: John T. Gilbert (ed.), *A Jacobite Narrative of the War in Ireland, 1688–1691* (Shannon, 1971).
190 Brenan to Internuncio, 20 Sept. 1692, Power, *Brenan*, p. 100.
191 1692, Power, *Bishop*, p. 19; 1693, Ó Ciardha, *DIB,* vol. 1, p. 800.
192 This was certainly the opinion of O'Molony's biographer James Hogan in *Studies: An Irish Quarterly Review* 9/35 (Sept. 1920), p. 427.
193 Berkeley died in 1678.
194 Alan Ford, 'Martyrdom, history and memory in early modern Ireland', in Ian McBride (ed.), *History and Memory in Modern Ireland* (Cambridge, 2001), pp. 43–66.

195 Moran, *Life*, p. 20.
196 Plunkett to Michael Plunkett, 22 June 1681, Hanly, *Plunkett*, p. 572.
197 What then?
198 Plunkett to Fr Maurice Corker, 24 June 1681, Hanly, *Plunkett*, p. 577.
199 Moran, *Life,* p. 343.
200 Canice Mooney, 'Accusations against Oliver Plunkett', pp. 119–20.
201 Hanly, *Plunkett*, p. xix.

2

Challenging the law: clerical critics

Laws and civil contentions, more savage than the sword, grind us to the dust; and, after narrowly escaping the steel of our enemies, we are now the victims of their enactments.[1]

It is indeed a most wonderful conveniency to dispossess the Ancient Proprietor who Fought for the King, and give his Estate to a Fanatic Soldier who Fought for Cromwell.[2]

To think that now in my 65th year I should bend the knee is not likely.[3]

Sir, These Kingdoms are of Opinion, Popery will break in upon them, and it were a pity to disappoint them.[4]

This chapter examines the attitudes to the law of some other members of the hierarchy, who did not share Plunkett's non-confrontational approach. A notable contrast can be drawn between the intellectual approach of Archdeacon John Lynch of Tuam and Bishop Nicholas French of Ferns on the one hand, and the activist bishops Edmund O'Reilly and John O'Molony on the other. Like Plunkett and Brenan, Lynch and French accepted the constitutional framework within which the common law operated. Lynch questioned the legitimacy of the law-making of the English and Irish parliaments, which had operated outside the terms of the constitutional framework, with predictably deleterious results. French was more concerned with the nature of the output of parliament, tainted by cupidity, and contrary to natural and divine law. On the other hand, O'Reilly and O'Molony had little time for legal analysis, and were quite prepared to defy and even subvert the constitutional framework.

Both Lynch and French left Ireland in 1652–53, and never returned. They wrote from an external perspective, and were not subject to the limitations and exigencies of day-to-day correspondence. In exile, Lynch could write freely and felt an obligation to do so: 'I, however, being far from my native land, and out of the power of her governors, prefer the danger of public remonstrance to criminal silence.'[5] Similarly, in French's attack on Ormond he wrote: 'The greatness of his person cannot terrify me from appearing for my country, and country-men, nor from speaking clearly, freely and plainly the truth.'[6] They both wrote histories – *Cambrensis Eversus* was a rebuttal of the historical writings of Gerald of Wales and French wrote of more recent events. They could take a longer and more considered view than Plunkett and Brenan's correspondence. The Dedicatory Epistle of Lynch's *Cambrensis Eversus*, written shortly after Charles II's restoration, expresses deep disappointment at the King's failure to restore religious toleration or confiscated estates, but not without hope of future redress.[7] French's writings are extensive and from a different perspective also detail how Charles II failed to legislate for the restoration of the lands of his loyal Irish subjects, or to provide for religious toleration.[8]

There were many significant figures among the clergy and hierarchy in this period. In particular the political and religious thought of Peter Walsh and Peter Talbot have been much explored. Edmond O'Reilly and John O'Molony are less well noted. Like Lynch and French, they spent a great deal of their lives in France, but unlike them, very little survives of their writings. What remains shows an interventionist and more aggressive aspect of the hierarchy in the second half of the seventeenth century, and they form a useful contrast to Plunkett and Brenan's more conciliatory approach. Most of O'Reilly's career predated the Restoration and he left little literary trace. But a letter of 1660 and his Report to Rome after he left Ireland in 1661 paint a vivid picture of clerical life at that time and chronicle his attitude to the intersection between legal authority and religious obligation.[9] The Nunciature in Brussels was charged with the supervision of the Irish church and aspects of O'Reilly's relations with the Dublin administration can be gleaned occasionally from the Internuncio's correspondence with Rome.[10] Ó Fiaich has chronicled his defiant personality, his loyalty to the church and his surprisingly obsequious submission to Ormond in 1665.[11] O'Molony left scant correspondence and was another maverick, 'the most dangerous (because the wisest) of all', according to the earl of Essex.[12] In 1681 he too wrote a report to Rome after he left Ireland.[13] Letters he wrote in 1686 and 1689 illuminate his political thought, and James II's former secretary of state Melfort noted his conditional loyalty to the Stuarts during his presence in the French court.[14] Even from these relatively slight resources, it is possible to construct something of the worldview of two of the more radical members of the Restoration hierarchy.

John Lynch

Lynch (c.1599–1677) was made archdeacon of Tuam c.1631, and left Ireland for France in 1652–63, after Galway fell to the Cromwellians. He never returned to Ireland and died in Brittany in 1677.[15] *Cambrensis Eversus* (1662) was written in the 1650s and is his most important text. It is a refutation of the works of Giraldus Cambrensis and more recent Protestant historians of Ireland, and a defence of the Old English in the Confederate wars.[16] Cunningham argues that it 'bear[s] the intellectual scars of the trauma of having lived through the mid-seventeenth-century crisis in Ireland'.[17] Like all his major works, it was written in Latin, in a high literary style with numerous allusions to classical literature and history. The choice of language suggests a European rather than merely Irish or English audience. It is based on a wide range of other works, in particular Keating's *Foras Feasa ar Éirinn*, and covers from the earliest times to the mid-1650s.[18] Its Dedicatory Epistle was written in 1662, and so provides a useful insight into Irish Catholic attitudes in the very early days of Charles II's reign.[19] Much of the text was given over to an analysis of political developments before and after Charles's accession. It did not dwell overmuch on the past: 'Past miseries strike our hearts and senses less forcibly than the present, which make a more grievous impression, and are more difficult to be borne.'[20] But Lynch made plain the present state of the country 'for while your other kingdoms are delirious with joy, Ireland alone grieves and mourns, groaning deeply'.[21] At the outset, he made his royalist credentials clear, when he described himself as: 'A most loyal subject of your Majesty, as well as an ardent lover of my country'. In the same paragraph he stated the purpose of his work: 'to vindicate and restore to its ancient splendour the character of my nation'.[22] He took a lively interest in legal matters and a chapter of *Cambrensis* is devoted to the refutation of Giraldus's suggestion that the Irish were a nation without laws. Lynch also stressed the importance of the law in more recent events. Although the structure is not explicit, it is possible to discern how Lynch carefully formulated the elements of his argument.[23]

His first proposition, fundamental to his entire argument, is that sovereignty is vested in the people, who will only obey a just king; an unjust king has no rights over the people. The relationship between the king and his subjects is contractual; subjects will diligently serve the king who protects them and guarantees their legal rights.[24] In the past, the Irish made war against English kings whose sovereignty they did not acknowledge.[25] But because of his descent from the old Irish kings, James I was the first English king whose sovereignty was fully acknowledged in Ireland, and to whom all Irishmen owed loyalty.[26] Notwithstanding the iniquities which had been visited on the Irish, they did not consider themselves released from their obligation of loyalty, which had been amply demonstrated. Rather it was incumbent on the king to reciprocate. In this way, loyal Irish subjects can be reconciled to English common law. For Lynch, what mattered was not the particular legal system and structures under which the subjects lived; rather it was the just administration of the law. It is striking to note his alignment with Sir John Davies (at least in this respect), whom he quoted approvingly.[27] His purpose is to demand a just response from the king to the sacrifices of his Irish subjects who have observed their part of the contract by securing his restoration. Lynch claimed he had: 'exerted to the utmost my powers of language, to confirm your title to the kingdom of Ireland, in defence of which my countrymen lately rose in arms for you, and lavishly sacrificed their treasures and their blood'.[28]

He then set out his second proposition: the constitutional contract has not been honoured by the king, because 'laws and civil contentions, more savage than the sword, grind us to the dust; and, after narrowly escaping the steel of our enemies, we are now the victims of their enactments'.[29] It might seem strange that Lynch was so heavily engaged in these matters relatively early in the king's reign, but the events of 1660–62 gave him good cause. Charles II's Proclamation of 1 June 1660 maintained that Ireland was still in rebellion. It was based on 'the information of the Lords and Commons now assembled in Parliament' – the Convention Parliament of England.[30] Lynch objected that the Irish people were 'brought before the bar of the English Parliament for condemnation or acquittal' and that this was a violation of a fundamental constitutional principle that had always governed legal relations between England and Ireland.[31]

The next step in his argument is to contest the constitutional validity of the English parliament, which had been responsible for the catastrophic civil wars: 'the Parliament itself, the representatives of the whole nation, converted the whole kingdom into one universal scene of indiscriminate and frenzied plunder, conflagration, and massacre'. The ensuing chaos culminated in the execution of Charles I and he accused the English parliament of judicial murder.[32] In the light of the dishonourable role played by the English parliament in the processes that ultimately led to the execution of the king, it was hypocritical for that parliament to exclude the Irish from the Act of Indemnity and Oblivion of 1660. He argued that 'all the murders committed in Ireland, by all the seditious bands, do not approximate even remotely in guilt to the murder of the King'.[33] Yet the English parliament was intent on denying a pardon to the Irish for lesser offences.[34] He concluded: 'The intemperate remonstrances of these English would persuade your Majesty to reward their perfidy, and to punish our loyalty: a paradox that was never heard of.'[35]

He applied the same argument to the confiscation of Irish land. He accepted that confiscation was appropriate in certain circumstances: 'The laws of just and lawful war do, I allow, transfer the property of the vanquished to their conquerors'. But these circumstances did not pertain in Ireland. For its own venal purposes, the English parliament had decided on the guilt of all Irish Catholics and their exclusion from the Act of Indemnity and Oblivion was the foundation stone for the confiscation of Irish estates. He argued that the parliamentarians were mere criminal thieves: 'Rebellion against a King, treachery to allies, are not wars but robberies.' And therefore the parliamentarians should not be rewarded because they 'apply the laws of a just war to the robberies by which they have so long and so grievously harassed us'. Furthermore, the profession of religion was turned into a capital crime, under which Catholics were at risk of losing their lives.[36]

Having disposed of the legitimacy of the London parliament, the next step in his argument was to consider the constitutional validity of the parliament that had met recently in Dublin. Catholics had no hope of using constitutional and legal means to right the wrongs inflicted on them because they were now excluded from the legislative process. It was likely that there was not a single Catholic in the parliament held in Dublin in May 1661.[37] Different standards were applied in Ireland and in England: 'Would not the English fly to arms at once, if Irishmen alone deliberated and voted in the English Parliament, and confiscated English property, and made it their own?' The new parliament could not be impartial, and was evidently bent on serving its own interests.[38]

He reinforced his argument concerning the unrepresentative nature of law-making in Ireland when he reviewed the 1649 peace treaty that Ormond had negotiated, to which the king had been a party and which had never been implemented.[39] He pointed out that 'one of the conditions of the peace concluded with your Lieutenant in Ireland was, that the Parliament which was to be held in the first instance should be free'. Instead, the recent parliament had the effect of 'hurling our nobles from their ancient opulence and power, and transferring their places to cobblers, weavers, smiths, quarrymen, pedlars, girdle-makers, and others of the same servile rank, [who] anxiously desire to make Ireland a theatre and arena of slavery'.[40] It was contrary to the 1649 peace that Catholics were prevented from participation.[41] He argued that this was entirely novel as never in Irish parliamentary history had Catholics been forced to take the Oath of Supremacy.[42]

Without conceding the validity of its membership, the next stage in his argument was to examine the legislation of the parliament. He argued that the anti-Catholic legislation was contrary to the 1649 peace and 'cannot now be justified by any plea of necessity or expediency, when the Catholics have given repeated and unequivocal proofs of their loyalty'.[43] He had no difficulty in diagnosing the underlying cause: 'The Commons … fear that they themselves may not be allowed to retain – as the service-money of their sedition, the salary of their rebellion, the wages of their murder and robbery, and the reward of their impiety – those estates inherited by Catholics from ancestors who held them as the emblems of their nobility.'[44]

Thus, the London and Dublin parliaments lacked constitutional legitimacy and their enactments were doubly flawed, being neither in accordance with the 1649 peace nor justified by any claim of supervening necessity. It was clear that the terms of the contractual relationship between the king, expressed by his enactments in parliament, and his Catholic subjects were fundamentally breached.

In the final step of his argument, Lynch resorted to the king's royal prerogative. He moved away from questions of guilt or innocence, instead exhorting the king to exercise his benevolence towards the Irish.[45] He turned away from the iniquities of the recent parliament to address the king directly and remind him of the responsibility owed to his loyal supporters: 'You have not hesitated to relieve those who shared your own fate in exile, and no one experienced a harder fate or bore it with greater fortitude than you.'[46] He desperately clung to the hope that the king would ensure the enactment of the terms of the Gracious Declaration of November 1660.[47] Again he argued against the iniquity of rewarding the parliamentarians at the expense of the native Irish and Old English. He reminded the king of the history of confiscation.[48] He warned of the danger when his wishes were thwarted by the administration in Dublin which had taken an independent stance and disregarded his directions.[49] He cited a very concrete example: 'Your Majesty's letters patent secured to the old citizens the right of free trade in their native towns: your ministers not only refuse that right, but will not allow them to sleep within their native walls without written permission from the governor.'[50] He summarised: 'The force of your authority they not only nullify and contemn; your very laws are subjected to revision.'[51]

In the final part of the Dedicatory Epistle, Lynch urged the king to restore individual liberties, to take advice from at least one knowledgeable Irish peer and above all to restore the free practice of religion.[52] He reiterated the fundamental loyalty of Ireland's Catholics.[53] The last paragraph is a valedictory prayer to the king, emphasising the critical importance of a properly constituted parliament enacting wise laws.[54] The conclusion of the Dedicatory Epistle reflects the tenor of the work as a whole. It is a forensic analysis, infused with national feeling and religious ardour.

Cambrensis was published in Latin, and did not have a wide circulation because many copies were burnt in the Great Fire in 1666. Nevertheless there was a copy in the library of Peter Creagh, which he left in Rome when he went to Ireland in 1676.[55] Ó Ciosáin argues that Lynch's reputation developed in the eighteenth century and was enhanced when *Cambrensis* was translated in the nineteenth. It was an influential text, admired and quoted by Catholic historians.[56] The Dedicatory Epistle presents a lucid statement of the contractual principle that underpinned the relationship between the monarch and the nation. Like all contractual relationships, it consisted of reciprocal obligations, and was conditional on the satisfaction of the fundamental terms by both parties. Notwithstanding the failure to meet Catholic expectations of redress after the Restoration, it is also a strong statement of loyalty to the Crown, which had a contractual and moral obligation to provide restitution.

Lynch's focus was essentially constitutional and his primary focus was on parliaments as an expression of the king's will. The London and Dublin parliaments lacked legitimacy, and had failed to vindicate the interests of the king's Irish subjects. The London parliament was forever tainted as it had murdered its own sovereign. Moreover, it exceeded its jurisdiction in attempting to legislate for Ireland, and displayed its contempt for loyal Irish Catholics in their exclusion from the 1660 Act of Oblivion. The members of the English parliament should not be rewarded with Irish land. To turn the profession of religion into a crime compounded the offence. The Irish parliament lacked legitimacy because its membership was unrepresentative of Catholics, who formed the largest element in the population and had given every demonstration of loyalty. Instead it was only concerned with self-interest, and specifically the retention of estates illegally wrested from their original owners. Lynch sought to side-step these unworthy assemblies, which ignored the king's wishes and directions, by appealing to the monarch to exercise his prerogative and directly intervene in order to implement his Gracious Declaration and ensure the just administration of the law.

There was no intrinsic objection to English common law, and a legal system controlled by a properly constituted Irish parliament was the appropriate mechanism to reconcile the Irish people to the English Crown. He emphasised the critical importance of Catholic involvement in making and enforcing legislation, and placed his hopes in the king reforming the Irish parliament so that his friendly intentions and obligations towards his loyal Catholic Irish followers might take legislative reality. Lynch lived long enough (d. 1677) that subsequent events must have sorely disappointed him, but little evidence of this can be gleaned from his later writings, which related to pre-Restoration politics and church history.

Nicholas French

French (1603–78) was appointed bishop of Ferns in 1645 and became actively involved with the Catholic Confederates. He took part in confederate delegations to the Pope in the Vatican (1648) and to Charles IV, duke of Lorraine in Brussels (1651). He left Ireland in 1651 and at the Restoration had hopes of returning. In 1666 his recall to Ireland was mooted, to attend a meeting of the Irish clergy which was called to debate the Remonstrance, the declaration by Irish Catholics that their religion did not impair their loyalty to the king, and that the papacy had no temporal power in Ireland. Peter Walsh saw it as a means of countering the Protestant argument that Catholics were inherently disloyal, could not be trusted with office and should not be restored to their estates. Ormond saw it as a means of identifying loyal Catholics and creating division within the Catholic interest generally. But the Vatican and the majority of the Irish clergy opposed it. It was clear that French would not sign it and was at risk of being arrested if he attended the meeting to discuss it.[57] He never did return and died in 1678.

After the Restoration, and during his exile, he wrote a sequence of pamphlets and books: *Vera Descriptio* (Cologne, 1667), *A Narrative of the Earl of Clarendon's Settlement and Sale of Ireland* (1668), *The Bleeding Iphigenia* (1674) and *The Unkinde Desertor* (1676). Amongst other matters, they analysed how Charles II failed to legislate for the restoration of the confiscated lands of his loyal Irish subjects and to provide for religious toleration. The *Vera Descriptio* is written in Latin and addressed to the Pope, to the intent that the Vatican would use its influence to improve the conditions of Ireland's Catholics.[58] In the course of a wide historical and political analysis it provides a legal exposition of the process whereby Irish Catholics were dispossessed during the Cromwellian period, and fared no better in the Restoration. Under Charles II the Cromwellian land settlement had been 'confirmed and transformed into an inviolable law by two acts of Parliament'.[59] Despite the terms of the 1649 peace, Irish Catholics were excluded from the general pardon for actions against the king in the 1640s. In addition, the legal persecution of Catholics had continued after the Restoration, notwithstanding that under the Commonwealth 9,000 Catholics had been sold into slavery, and the parliamentarians had slaughtered 50,000 innocents who 'the laws of nature and international law render immune from the cruelty and frenzy of war'.[60] French referred to a decree of 1663 under which priests and religious were outlawed unless they left the realm and the Catholic laity forbidden on pain of treason from offering hospitality or communicating with them.[61] An outstanding example of this pervasive anti-Catholic sentiment was the case of Catholic Irish soldiers who had served the king in his exile, but had now lost their positions because they could not subscribe to the Oath of Supremacy which required them to acknowledge the king as 'Ecclesiastical Primate' and that 'the Pope was denied to have any spiritual power in the three said realms'.[62]

A Narrative of the Earl of Clarendon's Settlement and Sale of Ireland followed a year later.[63] Unlike the *Vera Descriptio*, it is written in English and intended for an Irish and English readership, as were *The Bleeding Iphigenia* and *The Unkinde Desertor*. Unlike the latter, which are essentially polemics, *A Narrative* is a history, albeit highly partisan, of the land settlement. Rankin describes it as an embittered personal attack, in contrast to Lynch's 'careful attempts at rhetorical positioning – the flattering dedication to the King, the praise of his councillors, etc.'[64] Despite being 'one of the most racy and vigorous of Dr. French's productions', it is a closely observed analysis of the proclamations and legislation enabling the land settlement.[65] French traced the root of the matter to the proclamation of 1 June 1660 titled *Against the Rebels in Ireland*, which maintained that there was a fresh outbreak of rebellion, 'notwithstanding it was very well known at the time, there was not an Irish man in arms in any part of Ireland'.[66] Clarendon was not his only target. He noted the crucial intervention by Ormond in the House of Lords to exclude Irish Catholics from the 1660 English Act of Oblivion.[67] The conspiracy against Catholics continued when Broghill, Anglesey, Clotworthy and Mervyn 'brought forth that monstrous issue of their brain, which was exposed to the World under the Name and Title of His Majesties most Gracious Declaration for the Settlement of Ireland'.[68] The Declaration was enacted in the Act of Settlement which established for a fundamental law 'that the Irish Rebels were conquered by his Majesties Protestant Subjects in his Majesties absence', thereby laying the constitutional foundation for the claim that the Protestant interest in the land settlement should not be disturbed.[69] He argued that the Court of Claims established under the Act was fundamentally flawed in that the criteria for innocence were impossible to satisfy. Moreover the commissioners were parliamentarians who had most to lose, and the process dispensed with the basic tenet of natural justice that 'every man is to be held Innocent until he be convicted'.[70] The Act of Explanation prevented any further declarations of innocence, which French characterised as a 'grand breach of publick Faith, the Law of God, and Nations'. The fifty-four owners partially restored to their estates were simply a ploy in order 'to give some colour of Justice, to an action which is evidently repugnant to Magna Charta, and the Fundamental Laws of England (to condemn so many thousands before they are heard)'.[71] French claimed that Clarendon, 'a lawyer by his first profession', and Sir Heneage Finch, the solicitor general, had in effect been handsomely bribed to ensure the legislation protected the Cromwellian interest, and that the injustice of the Act was such that God visited the plague on the city of London in 1665.[72]

One by one, he carefully dissected the legal rights of the four categories of beneficiaries under the legislation. After a close reading of the Adventurers' Act he concluded that the Adventurers' claims, 'if they were examined by the strict Letter of the Law, would prove very defective and invalid, as being no ways pursuant to those Acts of Parliament upon which they pretend to be found'.[73] He next turned to Cromwell's soldiers. To the argument that it was now a matter of convenience to confirm the soldiers' titles, French argued: 'Ruat Coelum & fiat Justicia, is a Motto which better becomes a Lord Chancellor'.[74] In French's reading, they derived their title from their swords, used against both Charles I and Charles II, and concluded: 'I do not think any man will be so impudent as to justify this prodigious Title'. So far as the Protestant Irish '49 officers were concerned, they had far less right to be compensated with Irish land than the thousands of Catholic Irish officers who had served the king loyally, and merely because they were Irish had not been compensated. Finally, he denied the title of the associates and family of the king, whose only claim to Irish estates lay in their relationship with Charles II. The title of the duke of York over enormous Irish estates could not be justified merely because they were previously held by those who had been complicit in the murder of the king's father. If the regicides did not have good title, if followed that neither could the duke. 'The Land was given them by a Tyrant, for murdering the King, let the World judge of the goodness of their Title.'[75] York's acceptance of the land in effect validated the original Cromwellian confiscation.

French claimed Clarendon believed that 'the Protestant English Interest cannot be maintained in Ireland, without extirpating the Natives'.[76] He was prepared to concede: 'As for the Protestant Interest, I must confess his Majesties bound to maintain it in all his Kingdoms and Dominions, as far forth as the Glory of God requires, and the Law of Nations, and the several Constitutions of particular places will admit.'[77] But he could not concede that it was the promotion of the Protestant religion that had motivated the Act of Settlement. He contended that 'as to the present Settlement of Ireland, it is apparent to the World, that the Confiscation of Estates, and not the Conversion of Souls, is the only thing aimed at'. Neither could 'the New English Title to Land be well maintained, without destroying the old Title of the Natives'.[78] French pointed out that this had never been the practice in other English possessions; neither was it followed by Christian princes 'that followed the Law of the Gospel'.[79]

He defended the rights of Irish Catholics to retain their land. To the accusation that the Irish had been involved in an unlawful insurrection, he replied that the 'Usurped Powers' could find evidence of no more than 400 murders.[80] The Cromwellians themselves were guilty of murders and 'for want of Men did hang Women, not only without legal proof, but without probability that they could or would be guilty of killing Souldiers, or Innocent English'.[81] The loyalty of the Confederates to the royalist cause could not be doubted, and this had been acknowledged by the king in his Declaration. For Irish landowners the result was 'their Estates were kept from them by violence, and the un-resistible power of Cromwell's Army; but now they seem to be legally adjudged against them by two Acts of Parliament'.[82] Seven thousand former landowners who had never offended the king or his father had been dispossessed.[83] French laid the blame for all this on the king's advisers, most notably the first earl of Clarendon.

But the king was bound to exercise his royal prerogative.[84] Clarendon's fall and exile in 1667 provided a favourable opportunity for the exercise of royal mercy, and French hoped the king would reflect on the great injustice done to the Irish nation.[85] He developed his argument further, with reference to other considerations. How could the king not be mindful of the plight of innocent widows and orphans? Could the king not see that the Irish Catholics were a bulwark against English and Scottish Presbyterians, and that Ireland and England were natural allies against the Scots?[86] Finally, a just settlement for Ireland would reduce the temptation for foreign powers to meddle in Irish affairs to the discontent of England.

French's next publication, *The Bleeding Iphigenia* was prompted by the defection of the Jesuit scholar Andrew Sall to the Protestant church.[87] French prepared the book for publication in 1672, while waiting for an opportunity to return to Ireland. He claimed it was a book 'which the entire nation is longing for'. He must have sent advance details or a draft of the book to 'certain Irishmen distinguished for learning and position' who esteemed it highly. It took five months to write, secretarial costs were subsidised by Propaganda Fide and the printing costs were defrayed by wealthy Irishmen.[88] *The Bleeding Iphigenia* is another indictment of the Restoration settlement; this time French's target was Roger Boyle, earl of Orrery. French's belief was that '[i]t hath been a principal care, and study of some statesmen near the King, to oppress and overthrow the Catholics of Ireland, and at the same time to persuade his majesty, that we ought to be destroyed by Justice and Law'.[89] The discussion was by reference to the pamphlet dispute between Orrery and the Franciscan Peter Walsh, and is notable for French's use of biblical quotation and reference to legal philosophers to support his case. In the first part of the text he contrasts the legal pardon given to the Commonwealth rebels with the treatment of the loyal Catholic Irish. He defends the Irish 'rebellion' by reference to the doctrine of a just war: 'This doctrine in warranted by the law of nature (a more binding law than are the positive laws of men, which if repugne to that of nature are not laws)'.[90] He argued under this law a man may legally kill another in self-defence. This principle is extended to all of Ireland: 'Now if such defence is lawful for private men, how much more for a Commonwealth or Nation?'[91]

Notwithstanding the emphasis on legal analysis, the defence of the Catholic religion 'without which there is no salvation' was fundamental to French's thought. He found his authority in the Old Testament: 'this was the judgment of the pious and valiant Maccabees made of the war they undertook, and nobly pursued for their religion and laws, which they preferred before their wives and children, and all temporal things most dear unto them'.[92]

The remainder of the text is largely a rehearsal of the arguments made in the *Narrative* relating to the land settlement. He summarised by asking 'By what law are we thus treated, and destroyed, by that of god, or Nature, or Nations? All done against us, is against all those laws, and against the law of England too, a good law, by which no man is to be deprived of his lands and goods, but by a due course of law, the benefit of this law was denied us.'[93]

After Clarendon's fall and exile in 1667, French turned his attention to Ormond. *The Unkinde Desertor* was written in 1668, but not published until 1676. French had been persuaded to suspend the printing in the hope that Ormond would rectify the land settlement, and only when it was apparent that Ormond either could or would not do so, did French allow publication of his attack on the duke.[94] In the 1640s French had supported Ormond, but when Cromwell 'like a lightning passed through the land' Ormond had fled Ireland in 1650 and 'left the Catholics to the butchery' of the Protectorate in 1650.[95] French castigated his avarice, duplicity and hostility to Catholics, never more so than at the Restoration when, 'with Ormond, all was lawful that was not unprofitable'.[96] He concluded his introduction with a quotation from scripture: 'In the land of the holy he hath done wicked things, and he shall not see the glory of our Lord.'[97]

Much of the text is taken up with a relation of how Ormond conducted himself in the 1640s, and in particular his role in the surrender of Dublin to the English parliament in 1647. Chapter 9 deals with the king's grant of Sir Robert Lynch's estate to Ormond.[98] French invokes the supremacy of natural law, from which 'none can pretend exemption … so that this law binds as well the prince as the lowest man … a man's life, liberty, fame, lands, estates and fortunes are his own by the law of nature'.[99] For 'treason, rebellion and other crimes by way of attainder' the prince can take them away, but they cannot be so taken 'for convenience, or at his will or pleasure'. French asks rhetorically, what crime Sir Robert had committed? He could have had the benefit of the Act of Oblivion proposed in the 1649 truce, and had not engaged in any subsequent rebellion. The king's grant to Ormond was void under natural law and the law of the land. Therefore, 'in conscience he [Ormond] is bound to restore the said estate, because he holds it *male fide*; and the prince himself rightly informed is obliged in conscience to have the estate restored to the right owner'.[100] As for Sir Robert, so also for the Catholics of Ireland. In chapter 18, French reiterates his claim in the *Narrative* that Ormond was responsible for the exclusion of Irish Catholics from the Act of Indemnity in 1660. Subsequently, Ormond, Clarendon,

Orrery, Clotworthy 'and the rest of that holy Synagogue' drew up the Bill of Settlement, 'of an immense bulk, fraught with fair language and barbarous contents and proceedings'.[101] The effect of the Act was summarised and commented upon, and French hoped that the authors of this injustice '[i]f they have not a trembling in the head as Cain had, likely they will have a trembling in their hearts'.[102]

These three works were published in Louvain but printed in English and had a considerable impact. *A Narrative* was the shortest, and since Clarendon was its principal target, it is not surprising that he was aware of its contents. The Clarendon Papers mention a document, 'Short Animadversions on a libel intituled *A Narrative of the Settlement and Sale of Ireland*', without making clear the identity of its author.[103] Even twenty years after its publication, *A Narrative* could still cause upset at the highest levels in the Irish administration when a reprint went on sale in Dublin. Michael Boyle, the archbishop of Armagh, complained to Ormond that the effect would be 'to serve a turn and to make the people mad'. The Catholic bookseller William Weston explained to Boyle that a hundred copies had come from a London bookseller, William Grantham, and Boyle commented: 'There were many of them bought up here and gave great disturbance to the people.'[104] Several days later the Dublin Privy Council ordered that Weston and the Dublin printer Joseph Ray be arrested and all copies of the pamphlet seized. Only six could be found, one of which was sent to the secretary of state, the earl of Sunderland, so that he might pass it on to the king.[105] Ray was released and when Watson was examined he said disingenuously he 'did not conceave that there was any inconvenience in selling them' so 'publiquely uttered' them in his shop.[106] The Privy Council took a very different view and ten days later sent a warrant to London for Grantham's arrest.[107] *A Narrative* was reprinted, with some additions, under the title *Iniquity Display'd, or, The Settlement of the Kingdom of Ireland*, in 1704.[108] Not surprisingly, Carte denounced the anonymous pamphlet, which he attributed to Peter Talbot.[109]

The Bleeding Iphigenia was a more substantial publication, and provoked a strong and widespread reaction. Essex seems to have shown a copy to Charles II, drawing his attention to the passage that justified taking up arms in the defence of religion without the authority of the king. In 1686 *The Bleeding Iphigenia* was a title among a parcel of books from France which Henry Hyde, the second earl of Clarendon had seized on the grounds that they were 'in truth libels upon the late King and his Government and tend to the stirring up people against the settlement here'.[110] Peter Walsh wrote to French, and denounced the book as 'a plain justification of the Irish rebellion' of 1641.[111] Luke Wadding retained six copies of his predecessor's work in his library, and had given away sixty.[112] Ohlmeyer remarked how the Protestant historian Edmund Borlase noted with horror how French's *Bleeding Iphigenia* ('a virulent and scandalous piece') and other seditious Catholic pamphlets were readily available 'at home and abroad'.[113]

Unsurprisingly, Ormond bore the brunt of the reaction to *The Unkinde Desertor*, French's most substantial work. Perceval-Maxwell argued that after its publication, Ormond became identified in the minds of Irish Catholics with the failure to repeal the Cromwellian land settlement. He linked the book to Ormond's fear that Kilkenny Castle would be burned down, although the connection is far from clear.[114] In 1698, there was a copy in the library of William Daton, the Catholic bishop of Ossory.[115] French's attack on Ormond prompted a delayed reply from Clarendon in his *History of the Rebellion and Civil Wars in Ireland*, which was not published until 1719.

French challenged the legitimacy of the legislation of the parliaments and in particular the motives of the agents who had promoted the land settlement and continued to subvert the Catholic religion. For Lynch, the fault lay in the composition of the Dublin and London parliaments; for French it lay with the king's advisers, Clarendon, Orrery and Ormond, who were blinded by religious intolerance and had criminalised all Irish Catholics. Acting from self-interest and the imperative to protect the material welfare of their co-religionists, they had perfected a settlement that could not be defended under the laws of God, Nature or England itself.

Edmund O'Reilly

The forensic and analytical approach of John Lynch was not shared by his contemporary in Douai Edmund O'Reilly. This is probably not surprising, since according to Oliver Plunkett, O'Reilly was 'a man of a good mother wit, but no extraordinary learning'.[116] O'Reilly may have been radicalised by two years' imprisonment in Exeter for refusing to take the Oath of Supremacy on his way to Ireland after ordination in the 1620s – a harbinger of his later stubborn defiance.[117] He was appointed vicar general of the diocese of Dublin in 1636, but shortly afterwards returned to study on continent, until he returned to Dublin in 1641. Ó Fiaich surmised that he would have been sympathetic to the 1641 insurgents.[118] Gaughan suggests that when the Supreme Council of the Confederation was established in October 1642, O'Reilly's archbishop Thomas Fleming took up residence in Kilkenny to focus on national issues, and as a consequence O'Reilly was the practical ruler of the Dublin diocese during the Confederation 1642–48.[119] He had sided with the papal nuncio, Rinuccini, over Ormond during the late 1640s and was removed as vicar general in 1648. He was restored in 1650 and in 1651 he supported the project to place Ireland under the protection of the duke of Lorraine. He was arrested in 1653 and tried for his part in the 1642 capture of Wicklow Castle by insurgents. Although found guilty, through the intercession of influential friends he was not executed, and spent the next three years in jail, until he was banished in 1656. In 1657 he was appointed archbishop of Armagh, but not without controversy. Although not yet restored, the king objected that appointments were being made without his being consulted, and sent Richard Bellings to the Internuncio to enquire why the king's enemies were being preferred for promotion. In Peter Talbot's view O'Reilly was 'the best of that gang', in other words the least worst.[120] Between his appointment and arrival in Ireland in October 1659, his movements and opinions were monitored closely. In January 1658, his bitterness against Clarendon and Ormond was noted and, because he was considered indiscreet, there was a suggestion he might be closely observed in order to obtain useful information. In August, an informer relayed that together with others, he was plotting to encourage Irish soldiers to leave Charles's service in Spain and had arrived in England where 'if not prevented, will do no good'.[121] He was thought to favour the Cromwellians and oppose the Stuarts and was accused of seeking an accommodation with Cromwell in order to secure favourable terms for Irish Catholics.[122] Peter Walsh reported to the Stuart court that in 1658, armed with letters of introduction from the French chief minister, Cardinal Mazarin, he had met John Thurloe, Cromwell's secretary.[123] As a former supporter of the nuncio, and with his Cromwellian associations, it was little surprise that when O'Reilly eventually arrived in Ireland in late 1659, he was to have little influence with the Dublin administration. As early as March 1660, he was accused of disloyalty to the king and was obliged to conceal himself 'in hiding-places and caves'.[124] O'Reilly outlined his position in a characteristically defensive report to Rome on his activities since his arrival in Ireland. He had been accused of inciting rebellion and professed 'God is my witness that nothing was further from my thoughts'. He was said to be working against the king's interests, and carefully not pinning his colours to the Stuart mast. He replied that he 'only put before myself the glory of God, the increase of religion and obedience to the authority ordained by God (whosoever it might be), at least in those things which do not offend God'.[125] It was little wonder that in May the Jesuits feared a new persecution because of his resistance to Charles II's restoration.[126] At the same time reports from Paris warned Clarendon that O'Reilly would 'always act in the worst cause'.[127] The newly restored king had indicated he did not want to be in the awkward position of ordering O'Reilly's execution for *lèse-majesté,* and the Roman authorities feared his presence in Ireland was a hindrance at a crucial time when the future of Catholics in post-Restoration was being negotiated.[128] A campaign against him resulted in his being recalled to Rome in 1660.[129] His fellow priests rejoined that the case against him was essentially political and that he had carried out all his religious functions with zeal and at great cost.[130] O'Reilly not only faced difficulties with Rome, but also with Dublin because at much the same time the government issued an order for his arrest. O'Reilly complained to Peter Walsh that he had been singled out for unfair treatment, and that he alone had been exempted from the mitigation of the penal laws on the king's restoration. But Walsh advised him that nothing could be done for him, and that he should stay out of Ireland for three years.[131] Rome had ordered his return and Dublin his arrest; his position was untenable. After four turbulent years as primate, he left Ireland in 1661 and lived in Rome from 1662 to 1665.

O'Reilly's independent stance had not changed when in Rome and accordingly he felt that the church had to restore itself without aid from the authorities. In his 1662 report on the state of the church he urged that the Irish priests ministering on the continent be ordered to return to Ireland 'under an arbitrary penalty unless they obey'.[132] In similar vein, he urged the appointment of more bishops, regardless of the consequences: 'The church is not lessened by persecutions but increased.'[133] He clearly saw where his duty lay as between church and state and was not afraid to spell it out: 'Someone else may say: this would offend the king. I answer: Either the king honours and loves the Catholic faith or he does not. If he honours and loves it, he will give it connivance and hence it cannot be argued by the Puritans that what is done is done without his knowledge and consent. If he does not love it, it is not proper to await his consent: we must obey God rather than man.'[134] The precise extent of such loyalty as he was prepared to offer is difficult to gauge – his allegiance seems to have been determined only by the preservation and advancement of the faith. Ormond and Charles II always regarded him as disloyal but in 1660 he reported to Rome that others had accused him of 'working against His Most Serene Majesty, the King', which he flatly denied.[135] In his 1662 report to Rome, he memorably described life in Ireland in the early days of the Restoration:

> Our clergy live in much patience and misery as to worldly things; they visit the sick by night; they celebrate mass before and round about dawn, and that in hiding-places and recesses, having appointed scouts to look around and with eyes and ears agog to keep watch lest the robbers, that is, the soldiers should come by surprise ... while I was in Ireland I did not enter into the house of any catholic. I had made myself a small hut in a wood or in a mountainous district, one here, another there, so that no one should suffer for my sake.[136]

He noted that it was unlikely he would bend his knee to royal supremacy, given that he was now sixty-five and had been imprisoned for refusing to take such an oath thirty-four years earlier.[137]

On the face of it, O'Reilly seemed to relish the prospect of a clash with the administration, and therefore it is all the more surprising to find him negotiating his return to Ireland in 1665. He appeared to want an accommodation with Ormond, and his earlier defiance had withered to abject submission. He wrote to the Lord Lieutenant, seeking permission to return by agreeing to comply with all the instructions and commands of his nemesis: 'If otherwise, who am I, a worm not a man, the reproach of mankind, the vility of the people, a dead dog and a flea.'[138] Ormond allowed him to return in 1666 for the assembly of the bishops and clergy to consider the Remonstrance, which he was expected to support, but ultimately rejected.[139] When the assembly failed, Ormond initially imprisoned him and then he was deported.[140]

In 1666 there were reports of O'Reilly's involvement in a rebellion, supported by aid from France.[141] Preparations were being made in Brest for a French invasion fleet. Ormond was convinced that O'Reilly's presence in Ireland in June 1666 showed there was no intention to invade Ireland, but he kept him under close observation.[142] After the failure of the Remonstrance assembly, Ormond considered having O'Reilly tried for high treason, on the grounds of his involvement in the preparation of a French invasion, but thought better of it.[143] He still had lingering suspicions about O'Reilly's possible involvement in a plot and thought his expulsion might reveal the truth: 'My purpose is to send him back [to France] again, after sometime in which it may be discerned whether he had not some worse purpose in his coming.'[144] However all of the evidence against him is highly circumstantial, and there appears to be no direct evidence of his involvement. He died in France in 1669.

With understandable tact, Ó Fiaich described O'Reilly as a political failure. There were episodes in his life with varying degrees of obscurity which do not redound to his credit. These include his dalliance with Cromwellians which may have saved him from execution in 1653, his abject submission to Ormond in 1665 and the possibility he might have become Ormond's spy which baffled Ó Fiaich, his most devoted biographer. Plunkett did not hold a high opinion of him, and the feeling appears to be mutual – O'Reilly failed to recommend Plunkett for promotion to bishop. Perhaps his most enduring contribution to the Restoration church was as a cautionary example to his successor? O'Reilly's independent character and his defiant allegiance to Rome, rather than any political conviction, seemed to mark his actions. He put his religious obligations above all others and believed that in any conflict between the laws of God and royal authority 'we must obey God rather than man'.[145] Ironically, Plunkett was to express the identical sentiment as he awaited his execution in 1681.[146]

John O'Molony

John O'Molony (1617–1702) was educated in France and had strong connections with the French royal court. In 1920 the historian James Hogan argued that O'Molony was the 'moving spirit of the whole enterprise' to bring an expeditionary force of 20,000 men from France in 1666–67.[147] Irish exiles in France sought to exploit Louis XIV's declaration of war on England in 1666 to 'liberate' Ireland; the form of government after the liberation remained unclear. Hogan argued that O'Molony's activities in the mid-1660s had momentous long-term consequences and were the prompt for French interest in Irish matters that culminated in the participation of French forces in the War of the Two Kings in 1689–91. He also suggested that the fears generated by the failed invasion fuelled the Popish Plot and that John MacMoyer, one of Plunkett's accusers, traced Plunkett's guilt to the French plot.[148] Informer evidence given in 1680 connected O'Molony to the plot.[149] According to Hogan, O'Molony had also involved Nicholas French, Andrew Lynch the bishop of Kilfenora, and the primate Edmund O'Reilly in his plot. We have seen the evidence of O'Reilly's involvement is slight. Similarly, in the case of French and Lynch, there is little evidence to support this contention.[150] Although the evidence is tenuous, O'Molony's participation in the events of 1666–67 has not been seriously challenged, although his exact role, if any remains unclear.[151]

In 1672 he became bishop of Killaloe, and was considered 'the most dangerous (because the wisest)' member of the Irish clergy by the Lord Deputy Essex.[152] As soon as appointed, he took an active role in political matters and attempted to disrupt Essex's policy of divide and conquer by reconciling Oliver Plunkett with Peter Talbot. He tried in vain to dissuade the Dominican John Byrne from making allegations of premunire against Talbot in 1673. Throughout this period he was viewed with suspicion by the administration. Essex noted his substantial means and suspected him of being a French spy. France and England were then allied, but Essex feared that, should the alliance break down, O'Molony could be 'a most mischievous instrument'. He suggested to Arlington that, so long as the alliance held, he should take the opportunity to uncover at the French court 'what value this Molooney is there, and with whom he holds correspondences'.[153] Essex also suspected that his private secretary Sir Henry Ford was passing his correspondence to O'Molony.[154] In 1674 O'Molony was in France in response to a request to establish an Irish College in France.[155] He returned to Ireland in 1677, until evidence from informers began to implicate him in the Popish Plot and he was in France again in 1681.[156] In a long letter to Propaganda, he defended his decision to leave Ireland as a result of the turmoil caused by the Plot. He explained that he was suspected of being the leader of a conspiracy to take the life of the king, as agent of Rome and Louis XIV. Evidence had been sworn before magistrates and a reward of £150 offered for his apprehension. He was particularly suspect because of his strong connections with France, and was accused of participating in meetings with his co-conspirators at specified times in 1676, when he was not even in the country. It was only when the authorities could not capture O'Molony, and instead turned on the clergy and laity of his diocese, that he was finally forced to leave Ireland.[157]

He returned to Ireland on James II's accession in 1685 and a 1686 letter in King's *State of the Protestants* which has been attributed to him urged James II to act expeditiously and resolutely in Ireland to restore the position of Ireland's Catholics.[158] The letter anticipated many of the actions of the new administration. It urged James II to call a parliament, arguing that although there were not sufficient funds to pay an enlarged army, additional funding would flow into the Exchequer if the king were to 'take off by a Law, the Restraint that Country is under, as to Trade and Traffic'.[159] On the land settlement O'Molony warned the king that to delay was dangerous, and that he should act immediately '[n]otwithstanding the Doubts and Fears of Trimming Courtiers, and some Cow-hearted Catholics'. To effect this programme it was vitally important to ensure that Catholics were in key positions of influence: 'The Seed is sown in many parts of England, and the Harvest will without doubt be great and plentiful, but the Workmen too few, if You do not provide your self with Catholick Privy-Counsellors, Ministers, Judges, Officers Civil and Military, and Servants.' Tyrconnell had been appointed Lieutenant General of the Army in Ireland and O'Molony clearly approved: 'Men of Truth will, like Tyrconnel, serve You faithfully, without trimming, tho with never so apparent Hazard to their Fortunes and Lives.'[160] It is difficult to be sure whether he was being discerning or disingenuous when he commented: 'These Kingdoms are of Opinion, Popery will break in upon them, and it were a pity to disappoint them'.[161]

Whether James II valued his unasked-for advice is not known. In March 1686, O'Molony was one of the Catholic bishops who received a modest salary from the king.[162] But he could bite the hand that fed him, and when the king appointed him bishop of Limerick in June 1688, he opposed the appointment on the grounds that the papacy's concession to James II allowing him to appoint bishops risked the appointment of Englishmen to Irish sees. This became less of a risk when James II fled to France in December 1688.

O'Molony himself went to France early in 1689 and his activities during this period are of considerable interest in elucidating his attitudes to Stuart authority.[163] Louis XIV did not want Ireland to fall into the hands of his enemy William, and he sent James II to Ireland with 20,000 troops early in 1689. When O'Molony wrote to Patrick Tyrrell, bishop of Clogher, in March the primary purpose of his letter was to advise how James's presence should be best managed.[164] He professed himself to be zealous 'pro Fide, *Rege* & Patria', but the contents of his letter make clear that his priority was to ensure Ireland's Catholics were placed on a secure footing, and James II's restoration to the throne of England was entirely secondary.[165] The king of France should become a guarantor of Ireland's future, and should be given the promise of some of Ireland's seaports as encouragement.[166] He described the elements of his 'great and solid settlement' for Ireland. He recommended that there should be Irish members in the Privy Council, an Irish secretary of state for Irish affairs and some Irish nobles should be 'of the bedchamber'.[167] All employments, both civil and military, were to be held by 'natives of the country'. The Catholic Irish should be restored to their estates, both spiritual and temporal. Finally, Irish commerce should be conducted without reference to English interests, 'of which I would not derogate in the least'.[168] In England, 'where the number of Protestants and other sectaries is by much the greater, he can order things otherwise'.[169] In sum, he prescribed that James II should conduct Irish affairs entirely independently of England and English interests. Without specifically saying so, he in effect advocated a complete reordering of the Irish constitutional settlement.[170]

O'Molony valued loyalty to Ireland over the Stuarts and further light is thrown on his attitude in a series of letters from France written by the former secretary of state James Drummond, earl of Melfort, in October 1689.[171] Melfort wrote to the king about the disloyalty shown by O'Molony in the French court, and the independent, if not separatist line taken by him and his circle.[172] In his first report to the king Melfort said that 'one bishop Molone' claimed he was the representative of Tyrconnell, the clergy and nobility of Ireland and was the principal source of Irish slanders on James II, the essence of which was that when the king came to Ireland he undid all the good work which Tyrconnell had previously effected.[173] In a second letter, he noted that O'Molony had criticised the failure of the Patriot Parliament to ensure the repeal of Poynings's Laws.[174] He reported on the dissatisfaction of some of the Irish 'who begin to have discourses of the freedom of their nation' and who compared James II unfavourably to Tyrconnell.[175] He warned the king to 'put it out of the power of any one family [presumably the Talbots] to make Ireland change a master'.[176] Melfort reported that O'Molony was playing a central role in this movement, and there was a suggestion that he be made ambassador for the Irish faction.[177]

Melfort subsequently repeated his warning to James II about a separatist faction, 'who debated among them whether it be not their interest to join themselves to some catholic crown able to protect them, rather than be subject to the revolutions of the protestant kingdoms of Great Britain' and that most of the Irish in Paris were of this mind. For this purpose, the separatists procured letters from Ireland expressing disloyalty to the king, and these were translated by O'Molony who gave one of them to the French Queen, and proposed himself as the Irish envoy to the French court.[178] In order to undermine any such movement, Melfort urged James II to recall O'Molony to Ireland.[179] Whether recalled or otherwise, O'Molony must have returned to Ireland. After William's withdrawal at Limerick in 1690, Tyrconnell left Ireland with the French army.[180] Divisions arose among the remaining forces, many favouring giving the command to Sarsfield or a French general. O'Molony may have been part of a delegation to France, together with Henry and Simon Luttrell and Nicholas Purcell, calling for additional French forces and Tyrconnell's removal in late 1690.[181] He appeared to remain a supporter of James II, and died in France in 1702.

O'Molony's precepts for the management of James II in Ireland – almost a legislative programme for the Patriot Parliament – seemed particularly prescient. His call for complete legislative independence echoed earlier constitutional disputes and found at least partial expression in the Declaratory Act of 1689. For O'Molony, the conflict was between Jacobitism and some other form of government. He did not trust James II to act in the Catholic interest unless supervised, and he and his circle seemed to be prepared to contemplate some radical alternatives. These ranged from dependence on a foreign absolute monarch through giving France a role in Irish affairs to complete independence under an Irish-born monarch.[182]

Conclusion

Lynch and French had lived through the Confederate and Cromwellian wars; they had witnessed the destruction of the church and the dispossession of their flock. They had every reason to believe that the king's restoration would see justice restored. Instead, Charles II used legislation to copper-fasten a settlement that was unjust by any legal standard. But at no point do Lynch or French attach personal guilt to the misguided king. There is no defiance of the sovereign; loyalty to the Crown is not in question. The mark of Cain may not have been visited on the king's advisers, but in their hearts they had to recognise the extravagant injustice they had done to Ireland. Both Lynch and French believed that the only hope for restitution lay with the sovereign himself, who ought to be persuaded by the unambiguous precepts drawn from all legal authorities to restore justice to the Irish Catholics. Neither O'Reilly nor O'Molony had much loyalty to the Stuarts and both were prepared to contemplate radical measures to further their objectives. O'Reilly and O'Molony shared an outlook that maintained loyalty to the constitutional settlement represented by the Stuarts less from conviction than expedience. Given these priorities, adherence to the dictates of the system of English common law was entirely secondary.

The response of all these clerics to the law was not uniform and defies neat or ready classification. Nevertheless there are some commonalities. There is little evidence to show that they rejected the common law as a legal system. In this respect, there is hardly anything that separates the attitudes of Plunkett and Brenan. Plunkett was from an elite Old English background, and Brenan of more modest Gaelic descent, but is probable that their formation in Rome ensured a similarity of approach. Lynch and French were also from Old English families, and shared an intellectual approach, which most probably derived from their positions as exiles, well removed from day-to-day exigencies, and with the leisure to take a more principled and long-term view. They too accepted the general scheme of the common law, even as they disputed elements of its application. Like Lynch and French, O'Reilly and O'Molony were educated in France; in fact Lynch and O'Reilly were in Douai together. But in their cases, similarity of formation did not guarantee identity of thought. It is tempting to ascribe O'Reilly and O'Molony's more radical views to their Gaelic backgrounds, but there is little evidence in their admittedly meagre writings to sustain this. In principle Brenan was also from a Gaelic background, and his approach was very different from that of O'Reilly or O'Molony. Therefore neither ethnic background, nor place of formation nor political histories defined the approach of these clerics to the law.

Finally, in all of this forensic analysis, it is easy to overlook that these men were clerics, and regardless of their diverse views of the law, and the appropriateness of the constitutional settlement, they owed their first allegiance to their Catholic faith and to God. What united them, in every case, was a determination to ensure that the impact of the law's interference with the practice of their religion was mitigated insofar as possible. French wrote in defence of the Catholic religion, 'without which there is no salvation'.[183] O'Reilly argued that if the king did not love the Catholic faith, 'we must obey God rather than man'.[184] This was the driving and unifying impetus to their beliefs and actions, as it was to Plunkett and Brenan. It was their individual personalities and circumstances, and the tenor of the times, which dictated the tactics they chose to follow.

These clerics wrote in English and Latin, the languages of the subject matter and the elite audiences they addressed. But the majority of the population in the country spoke Irish, and it is to the popular culture of this important group we now turn. Alan Titley argued that Irish history is often seen as a matter of "laws and legislation" and '[w]hile "laws and legislation" always impact hugely on how a polity is ruled and how it is governed or crushed, they do not tell us what people think or feel. And what people think or feel is the single most important fact in the undercurrent of official history: it is that which is the seedbed of change and of revolutions'.[185] The poetry written by Daibhí Ó Bruadair and his near contemporaries and other literary sources in Irish are explored in the next chapter to enquire into the undercurrent of official history and attitudes to the law in the popular culture of Gaelic Catholic Ireland.

Notes

1 John Lynch, *Cambrensis Eversus*, ed. and tr. Matthew Kelly (Dublin, 1851–2), vol. 1, p. 7. All further page references are to this volume unless otherwise stated.
2 *The Historical Works of the Right Rev. Nicholas French D.D.* (2 vols, Dublin, 1846), *A narrative of the Earl of Clarendon's settlement*, vol. 1, pp. 97–8.
3 Benignus Millett, 'Archbishop Edmund O'Reilly's report on the state of the church in Ireland, 1662', *Collectanea Hibernica* 2 (1959), p. 113.
4 John O'Molony to James II, 14 Aug. 1686, appended in William King, *The State of the Protestants of Ireland* (Dublin, 1730), p. 44.
5 *Cambrensis*, p. 67.
6 *Historical Works*, vol. 1, p. 33.
7 There is quite an extensive bibliography. Éamon Ó Ciosáin, 'John Lynch' in *DIB*, vol. 5, pp. 627–9. Ó Ciosáin and René d'Ambrières, 'John Lynch of Galway (c.1599–1677): His career, exile and writing', *Journal of the Galway Archaeological and Historical Society* 55 (2003), pp. 50–63 is a biographical study, with an emphasis on Lynch's career in France. Nollaig Ó Muraíle wrote the *ODNB* entry, accessed 19 July 2023, and a study of Lynch's career, emphasising his origins and connections in Galway: 'Aspects of the intellectual life of seventeenth-century Galway' in Gerard Moran and Raymond Gillespie (eds), *Galway History and Society: Interdisciplinary Essays on the History of an Irish County* (Dublin, 1996), pp. 149–211. Ian Campbell's 'John Lynch and Renaissance humanism in Stuart Ireland: Catholic intellectuals, Protestant noblemen, and the Irish *Respublica*', *Eire-Ireland* 45 (2010), pp. 27–40, is a study of Lynch's intellectual formation and Bernadette Cunningham has examined his political thought in 'Representations of king, parliament and the Irish people in Geoffrey Keating's *Foras Feasa ar Éirinnn* and John Lynch's *Cambrensis Eversus*' in Jane Ohlmeyer (ed.), *Political Thought in Seventeenth-Century Ireland* (Cambridge, 2010), pp. 131–54.
8 *Vera Descriptio* (Cologne, 1667), *A narrative of the Earl of Clarendon's settlement and sale of Ireland* (1668), *The Bleeding Iphigenia* (1674) and *The*

Unkinde Desertor (1676). The last three can be found in French, *Historical Works*, vol. 2. French's bibliography is much less extensive than Lynch's. See P. J. Corish, 'Nicholas French' in *DIB,* vol. 3, pp. 1104–6, and the *ODNB* entry by Thompson Cooper, revised by Sean Kelsey.

9 See Raymond Murray, 'Edmond O'Reilly' in *DIB,* vol. 7. pp. 848–50. 'Archbishop Edmund O'Reilly's report on the state of the church in Ireland, 1662' is a lively account of Catholic life on the cusp of the Restoration. There are letters recorded in P. F. Moran (ed.), *Spicilegium Ossoriense* (3 vols, Dublin, 1874–84), vol. 1, pp. 446–9, 456–9 and 460–66, and vol. 3, pp. 91–2.

10 Cathaldus Giblin, 'Catalogue of material of Irish interest in the collection "*Nunziatura di Fiandra*", Vatican Archives: Part 1', *Collectanea Hibernica* 1 (1958), pp. 7–136, and 'Part 2', *Collectanea Hibernica* 3 (1960), pp. 7–136.

11 Tomás Ó Fiaich, 'Edmond O'Reilly, Archbishop of Armagh, 1657–1669' in The Franciscan Fathers (eds), *Father Luke Wadding* (Dublin, 1957), pp. 171–227, is a comprehensive and well referenced study.

12 Essex to Ormond, 14 Nov. 1673, Airy, *Essex Papers*, p. 137. See also John Cronin, 'John O'Molony' in *DIB*, vol. 7, pp. 704–5. James Hogan, 'Two Bishops of Killaloe and Irish freedom: John O'Molony II (1617–1702)', *Studies: An Irish Quarterly Review* 34 and 35 (1920), pp. 213–231 and 421–37, is an account of O'Molony's involvement in the 1667 French plot. A letter by O'Molony to John Byrne, a Dominican who was embroiled in a dispute with Peter Talbot, is in William P. Burke, *Irish Priests in Penal Times* (Waterford, 1914), p. 30 (no source indicated). There are two letters recorded in Moran, *Spicilegium Ossoriense*, vol. 1, pp. 487–8, and vol. 2, pp. 258–63. A letter he wrote on 19 Nov. 1672 concerning the resolution of the dispute between Plunkett and Talbot is recorded in Moran, *Life*, pp. 233–4.

13 Patrick Boyle, 'John O'Molony Bishop of Killaloe (1672–89) and of Limerick (1689–1702)', *Irish Ecclesiastical Record* 4th ser. 32 (1912), pp. 574–89, at pp. 579–85, a translation of the Latin recorded in *Spicilegium Ossoriense*, vol. 2, pp. 258–63.

14 The letters are in the appendix to William King's *The State of the Protestants of Ireland* (Dublin, 1730), pp. 44–9 and 80–6. Melfort's letter is included in James Macpherson, *Original Papers; Containing the Secret History of Great Britain, from the Restoration, to the Accession of the House of Hannover* (2 vols, Dublin, 1775), vol. 1, pp. 317ff.

15 Not to be confused with James Lynch (1624–1713), who was archbishop of Tuam.

16 A 3-volume edition and lively translation was published in 1851–2, which is the source of the references that follow. Many copies of the book were destroyed in the Great Fire of London in 1666; as a consequence originals are rare.

17 Cunningham, 'Representations', p. 132.

18 Michelle O Riordan, '"Political" poems in the mid-seventeenth-century crisis' in Jane H. Ohlmeyer (ed.), *Ireland from Independence to Occupation, 1641–1660* (Cambridge, 1995), p. 122.

19 *Cambrensis*, pp. 3–79.

20 *Cambrensis*, p. 9.
21 *Cambrensis*, p. 7.
22 *Cambrensis*, p. 3.
23 *Cambrensis*, vol. 2, pp. 363–87. Lynch was keenly aware of the Brehon law tracts. See Nollaig Ó Muraíle, 'Aspects of the intellectual life of seventeenth-century Galway' in Gerard Moran and Raymond Gillespie (eds), *Galway History and Society: Interdisciplinary Essays on the History of an Irish County* (Dublin, 1996), pp. 149–211.
24 See Cunningham, 'Representations', *passim*.
25 The Irish nation 'must not be stigmatised as rebellious, but as an enemy': *Cambrensis*, vol. 3, p. 83.
26 *Cambrensis*, vol. 3, pp. 53, 83.
27 *Cambrensis*, vol. 3, pp. 79–81. Lynch quotes Davies's *A Discoverie* throughout *Cambrensis*; and these sentiments align with the last page of *A Discoverie*. See Myers edition, p. 224.
28 *Cambrensis*, p. 3.
29 *Cambrensis*, p. 7.
30 James Kelly and Mary Ann Lyons (eds), *Proclamations of Ireland 1660–1820* (Dublin 2014), vol. 1, p. 5.
31 *Cambrensis*, p. 11.
32 *Cambrensis*, p. 15.
33 *Cambrensis*, p. 17.
34 *Cambrensis*, p. 11.
35 *Cambrensis*, p. 19.
36 *Cambrensis*, p. 23. Kelly, Lynch's translator, refers to correspondence between Ormond and Orrery in 1667, which of course was long after Lynch wrote the Dedicatory Epistle. More likely Lynch was referring to the proclamation of 22 Jan. 1661 forbidding public assemblies by Catholics, Presbyterians and others. See *Proclamations*, vol. 1, p. 17.
37 *Cambrensis*, pp. 25–7. Lynch was correct in this assertion. Two returns for the borough of Tuam Co. Galway had been made by the sovereign of the town, each of which named two MPs. Geoffrey Browne, a Catholic, was one of the four. On 12 June 1661, the Commons decided that no valid return had been made and ordered a fresh ballot; Browne was not elected the second time: *Commons Journal Ireland* (1796), vol. 1, p. 403. Lynch's analysis ignored that Catholic peers deemed innocent of involvement in the Irish rebellion were allowed take their seats in the House of Lords. See J. G. Simms, 'The restoration, 1660–85' in *NHI*, vol. 3, p. 423.
38 *Cambrensis*, p. 27.
39 Lynch did not side with the Nuncio and defended the 1643 cessation and the peace agreements of 1646 and 1649: *Cambrensis*, p. vii.
40 *Cambrensis*, p. 29.
41 *Cambrensis*, pp. 29/31. There was no express provision barring Catholics, and a proposal to impose the oath of supremacy, and thereby bar Catholics, was not acceptable in London.

42 *Cambrensis*, p. 31.
43 *Cambrensis*, pp. 31, 35.
44 *Cambrensis*, p. 35.
45 *Cambrensis*, p. 39.
46 *Cambrensis*, p. 43.
47 *Cambrensis*, p. 41.
48 *Cambrensis*, p. 49. Presumably a reference to the provision in the 1652 Act of Settlement which 'granted' the equivalent of one-third of their former estates to those who had fought in the Confederate war or the widows and children of officers.
49 *Cambrensis*, p. 53. Kelly explains this as a reference to the strict criteria laid down for 'innocence' in the Instructions for the implementation of the Gracious Declaration. Equally it could be seen as a more general comment on the great gulf between the expectations generated by the Declaration and the reality that finally emerged in the Act of Settlement.
50 *Cambrensis*, p. 55: a reference to the exclusion of Catholics from certain corporate towns, ordered by the Houses of Parliament to the lords justices in 1661.
51 *Cambrensis*, p. 57.
52 *Cambrensis*, pp. 69–71.
53 *Cambrensis*, p. 75.
54 *Cambrensis*, pp. 77–9. Charles had twenty-three more years to carry out this work.
55 Canice Mooney, 'The library of Archbishop Piers Creagh', *Repertorium novum: Dublin Diocesan Historical Record* 1 (1955), pp. 117–39 at p. 128.
56 See Ó Ciosáin and d'Ambrières, 'John Lynch of Galway', pp. 54–5, and Ó Ciosáin in *DIB*, vol. 5, p. 629.
57 Giblin, '"*Nunziatura di Fiandra*", part 2', pp. 15 and 30, 55, 56.
58 For a full analysis of the historical context see Jason McHugh, 'Catholic clerical responses to the Restoration: The case of Nicholas French' in Dennehy, *Restoration Ireland*, pp. 99–121.
59 McHugh, 'Catholic clerical responses', p. 109.
60 McHugh, 'Catholic clerical responses', p. 112.
61 McHugh, 'Catholic clerical responses', p. 113. In fact, there does not appear to be any such Irish decree(s); see *Proclamations*, vol. 1. French may have been referring to an Apr. 1663 proposal in the English House of Commons to extend the English penal code to Ireland; the proposal was rejected: Burke, *Irish Priests*, p. 2.
62 McHugh, 'Catholic clerical responses', p. 114.
63 Some doubts have been raised about French's authorship, but it is generally credited to him: Micheál Ó Siochrú, 'Nicholas Plunkett and Nicholas French' in *Confederate Ireland 1642–1649* (Dublin, 1999), p. 271. Similarly, Deana Rankin, *Between Spencer and Swift: English Writing in Seventeenth-Century Ireland* (Cambridge, 2005), p. 238, n. 23.
64 Rankin, *Between Spencer and Swift*, p. 237.

65 According to the anonymous editor of *The Historical Works of the Right Rev. Nicholas French D.D.*, vol. 1, p. 73.
66 *Historical Works*, vol. 1, p. 81. *Proclamations*, vol. 1, p. 5.
67 French claimed that Ormond introduced a provision to that effect in the House of Lords, which was passed without notice. He claimed that Ormond had been encouraged by promises of land and money from the members of the Convention. There seems to be no other evidence for this assertion.
68 *Historical Works*, vol. 1, pp. 82–3.
69 *Historical Works*, vol. 1, p. 88. Described as 'legislative enforcement of an outrageous falsification of history' by Rankin, *Between Spencer and Swift*, p. 238.
70 *Historical Works*, vol. 1, p. 90.
71 *Historical Works*, vol. 1, p. 91.
72 *Historical Works*, vol. 1, p. 93. The anonymous author of 'The case of the Roman Catholics of Ireland' claimed that Finch had received £3,000 to support the Protestant claims: Neil Johnston, 'Charles II's legal officers and the Irish restoration land settlement' in Coleman Dennehy (ed.), *Law and Revolution in Seventeenth-Century Ireland* (Dublin, 2020), p. 338.
73 *Historical Works*, vol. 1, p. 96.
74 *Historical Works*, vol. 1, pp. 97–8.
75 *Historical Works*, vol. 1, p. 107.
76 *Historical Works*, vol. 1, p. 103. There is no record of Clarendon having said this. There is a 'Paper' written by 'T. T.' from Apr. 1665 in the Clarendon papers which references a letter written by an English friend, in which it is said 'that ruin of the Irish natives is of absolute necessity for the preservation of English interests'. The relationship, if any, between this 'Paper' and French's later claim is not apparent. F. J. Routledge (ed.), *Calendar of the Clarendon State Papers* (Oxford, 1970), vol. 5, p. 481.
77 *Historical Works*, vol. 1, p. 103.
78 *Historical Works*, vol. 1, p. 104.
79 *Historical Works*, vol. 1, p. 105.
80 Probably in reference to the High Courts of Justice of 1652–54 which had been established by the Cromwellians to try rebels accused of murder, and which condemned several hundreds to death. See Jennifer Wells (ed.), 'Proceedings at the High Court of Justice at Dublin and Cork 1652–1654', *Archivium Hibernicum* 66 (2013), pp. 63–260, and 67 (2014), pp. 76–274. In addition there were courts held in Kilkenny, Galway and Clonmel.
81 *Historical Works*, vol. 1, p. 108.
82 *Historical Works*, vol. 1, p. 113.
83 *Historical Works*, vol. 1, p. 115.
84 *Historical Works*, vol. 1, p. 115.
85 *Historical Works*, vol. 1, p. 119.
86 A similar argument was to be made by John O'Molony in 1689: King, *The State of the Protestants.*
87 When Sall defected, French wrote a book, *The Dolefull Fall of Andrew Sall.* Sall's reply prompted French to write *Bleeding Iphigenia.*

88 French to Baldeschi, secretary of Propaganda Fide, 13 Jan. 1673: Benignus Millett, 'Calendar of volume 3 of the "Scritture riferite nei congressi, Irlanda", in Propaganda Archives: Part 2, ff. 201–518', *Collectanea Hibernica* 22–23 (1979/80), pp. 7–81 at p. 44.
89 *Historical Works*, vol. 1, p. 19.
90 *Historical Works*, vol. 1, p. 35.
91 *Historical Works*, vol. 1, pp. 37–8.
92 *Historical Works*, vol. 1, p. 38. See Jane Ohlmeyer, 'Introduction; for god, king or country?' in Jane Ohlmeyer (ed.), *Political Thought in Seventeenth-Century Ireland* (Cambridge, 2008), p. 8.
93 *Historical Works*, vol. 1, p. 59.
94 *Historical Works*, vol. 2, p. 18. 'Wee have digg'd about him to longe, and spent our dunge in vain, Ormond will yield no fruicte.' The full title is: *The Unkinde Desertor of Loyall Men and True Frinds*. Clarendon is also a target; together with Ormond 'they took the opportunity like two whales and monsters of avarice and cruelty to devour his (i.e. the king's) faithful subjects'; *Historical Works*, vol 2, p. 20. Michael Perceval-Maxwell, 'The Irish Restoration land settlement and its historians' in Dennehy, *Restoration Ireland*, pp. 21–2.
95 *Historical Works*, vol. 2, p. 13.
96 *Historical Works*, vol. 2, p. 14.
97 *Historical Works*, vol. 2, p. 18, which is also quoted as the book's epigraph: Isaiah 26: 10.
98 *Unkinde Desertor* was written in 1676; Sir Robert Lynch does not appear as a claimant in the records of the Court of Claims in 1663, Geraldine Tallon (ed.), *Court of Claims, Submissions and Evidence, 1663* (Dublin, 2006).
99 *Historical Works*, vol. 2, p. 91. French's appeal to natural law was unlikely to persuade a common law jurist.
100 *Historical Works*, vol. 2, pp. 92–3.
101 *Historical Works*, vol. 2, pp. 183–4.
102 *Historical Works*, vol. 2, p. 192.
103 *Clarendon State Papers*, vol. 5, p. 657. The Clarendon Papers contain two other references to documents that bear strong similarities to *Narrative*: vol. 5, p. 481 and n. 1 and p. 728. The first is dated 1665, before *Narrative* was published in 1668. The second is tentatively dated 1652, which seems to be improbable.
104 Boyle to Ormond, 2 Dec. 1685, HMC *Ormonde*, NS 7, pp. 398–9.
105 *CSPD* Feb.–Dec. 1685, p. 404.
106 Mary Pollard, *Dictionary of Members of the Dublin Booktrade, 1550–1800* (London, 2000), p. 602.
107 *CSPD* Feb.–Dec. 1685, p. 411.
108 Cooper, 'Nicholas French', *ODNB*.
109 Thomas Carte, *An History of the Life of James Duke of Ormonde, from his Birth in 1610, to his Death in 1688* (3 vols, London, 1735–6), vol. 2, pp. 383–5.
110 16 Mar. 1686, Lord Lieutenant Clarendon to the earl of Sunderland, *CSPD 1686–87*, p. 73. He may also have been sensitive to the treatment meted out

to his father, the first earl, in the pamphlet: Toby Barnard, *Brought to Book* (Dublin, 2017), p. 24.

111 Vincent Morley, 'Peter Walsh' in *DIB*, vol. 9, p. 759.

112 Patrick J. Corish, 'Bishop Wadding's notebook', *Archivium Hibernicum* 29 (1970), pp. 89 and 62.

113 Ohlmeyer, *Political Thought*, p. 29.

114 HMC *Ormonde*, NS, vol. 7, p. 368, cited in Perceval-Maxwell, 'The Irish Restoration land settlement' at p. 22.

115 Thomas O'Connor, 'Religious change, 1550–1800' in Raymond Gillespie and Andrew Hadfield (eds), *The Oxford History of the Irish Book* (5 vols, Oxford) vol. 3. *The Irish Book in English 1550–1800*, p. 183. Daton was bishop from 1696 to 1712. A century later, *Unkinde Desertor* was described as 'one of the scarcest pieces relating to Irish affairs' in the catalogue for the sale of Denis Daly's library: see Deana Rankin, 'Historical writing, 1750–1800' in Gillespie and Hadfield, *Irish Book*, p. 289.

116 His successor in Armagh; Oliver Plunkett, *Jus Primatiale*, p, 30, quoted in Ó Fiaich, 'O'Reilly', p. 178.

117 Apr. 1626–Mar. 1628. Ó Fiaich, 'O'Reilly', p. 175.

118 Ó Fiaich, 'O'Reilly', p. 178.

119 J. Anthony Gaughan, *The Archbishops, Bishops and Priests who served in the Archdiocese of Dublin in the Seventeenth Century* (Dublin, 2010), p. 58.

120 Peter Talbot to Clarendon, 15 June 1657, *Clarendon State Papers*, vol. 5, pp. 736–7.

121 *Clarendon State Papers*, vol. 4, pp. 7, 37, 66.

122 Giblin, '"*Nunziatura di Fiandra*", part 1', pp. 103–4.

123 Raymond Murray, 'Edmund O'Reilly' in *DIB,* vol. 7, p. 849. Ó Fiaich also noted O'Reilly's meeting with Mazarin, who gave him money and letters of commendation to the Cromwellian administration: Ó Fiaich, 'O'Reilly', p. 190. There is no record of this meeting in the Thurloe State Papers.

124 Charles was proclaimed king in May 1660. Ó Fiaich, 'O'Reilly', p. 193. Rumours of O'Reilly's stance reached the Internuncio in Brussels in June and July 1660; see Giblin, '"*Nunziatura di Fiandra*", part 1', pp. 102 and 103–4.

125 1 July 1660, quoted in Ó Fiaich, 'O'Reilly', p. 193.

126 Thomas Quinn SJ to Superior General, 29 May 1660: Vera Moynes (ed.), *The Jesuit Irish Mission: A Calendar of Correspondence 1566–1752* (Rome, 2017), pp. 432–3.

127 5 May 1660, *Clarendon State Papers*, vol. 5, p. 15. There is also an obscure report of his earlier zeal for the 'Independent party' not being confirmed.

128 Giblin, '"*Nunziatura di Fiandra*", part 1', p. 108.

129 Fr Peter Walsh almost certainly had a hand in this. See Daniel McCarthy (ed.), *Collections on Irish Church History from the MMS of the Late Very Revd. Laurence F. Renehan, D.D. President of Maynooth College* (Dublin, 1861), p. 57. But it is clear that the king had a particular dislike of O'Reilly, and his Roman superiors felt he would be safer outside of Ireland. Rome was preferred on the basis that it was far enough away to prevent O'Reilly offending the king. This was a particular concern at a time when there were high expectations that

the newly restored king would exercise his benevolence towards Catholics. The lawyer Richard Bellings also seems to have been involved in O'Reilly's recall: Giblin, '"*Nunziatura di Fiandra*", part 1', pp. 104–9.

130 Ó Fiaich, 'O'Reilly', p. 199. Moran, *Spicilegium Ossoriense*, vol. 2, pp. 201–3.

131 Ó Fiaich, 'O'Reilly', p. 200.

132 Ó Fiaich, 'O'Reilly', p. 204. Millett, 'O'Reilly's report' p. 113.

133 Ó Fiaich, 'O'Reilly', p. 204. Millett, 'O'Reilly's report', p. 114. His robust approach can be contrasted with Brenan in 1675, 1680 and 1682: *Relatio*, 20 Sept. 1675, Power, *Brenen*, p. 45; Brenan to Internuncio, 30 Jun. 1680, Moran, *Life*, p. 278; Brenan to secretary of Propaganda, 1 May 1682, Power, *Brenen*, p. 72.

134 Ó Fiaich, 'O'Reilly', p. 204. Millett, 'O'Reilly's report', p. 114. There is an eerie echo of O'Reilly's stance in one of Plunkett's last letters to his confessor, Fr Maurice Corker, 24 June 1681: 'the proconsul's command is silenced in the face of the command from the consul': Hanly, *Plunkett*, p. 577.

135 Ó Fiaich, 'O'Reilly', p. 193.

136 Millett, 'O'Reilly's report', pp. 109–10, Ó Fiaich's translation. O'Reilly's principal anxiety was the fate of the clergy; his report does not evidence much concern for the travails of the laity. There was another uncanny echo of O'Reilly ten years later when Plunkett wrote 'I shall retire to a hut in some wood or mountain in my diocese with some candles and books': Plunkett to secretary of Propaganda, 12 Nov. 1673, Hanly, *Plunkett*, p. 386. These resonances are all the more remarkable considering Plunkett's condescension to O'Reilly: 'a man of a good mother wit, but no extraordinary learning'.

137 Millett, 'O'Reilly's report', p. 113.

138 Reilly to Ormond, 22 Oct. 1665, Burke, *Irish Priests*, pp. 14–15.

139 O'Reilly and others did sign an alternative document, which seemed to be little different. Once again, O'Reilly found himself in difficulty with Rome. This document was said to contain 'atrocious errors' and to have caused 'indescribable sorrow'. It was noted that fortunately Ormond had refused to accept it: Chigi, Prefect of the Roman Curia to Internuncio, 18 Sept. 1666, quoted in J. G. Simms, 'The restoration, 1660–85' in *NHI*, vol. 3, p. 430. There is a suggestion in Ormond's correspondence that O'Reilly might act as a spy for the administration in return for a pension: see Ó Fiaich, 'O'Reilly', pp. 213–14 (who suspended his judgement on this issue) and Burke, *Irish Priests*, p. 16 (who came to no conclusion). Murray's *DIB* entry does not mention the matter. Perhaps in O'Reilly's favour is the fact that his 'ecclesiastical ornaments' were confiscated when he arrived in Dublin: Giblin, '"*Nunziatura di Fiandra*", part 2', p. 16.

140 Giblin, '"*Nunziatura di Fiandra*", part 2', p. 23.

141 17 June 1666, Bodleian, Carte MS 34, fos. 755–8. Ó Fiaich, 'O'Reilly', p. 206.

142 Ormond to Clarendon, 9 June and 27 June 1666, Bodleian, Carte MS 48, fos. 394–6 and 398v–399. Ó Fiaich, 'O'Reilly', pp. 213–14, 8. Burke, *Irish Priests*, p. 16.

143 Ó Fiaich, 'O'Reilly', p. 218.

144 27 June 1666, Ormond to Clarendon, Bodleian, Carte MS 48, fo. 399. Ó Fiaich, 'O'Reilly', p. 193. Burke, *Irish Priests*, pp. 16–17. Hogan suggests that O'Reilly had come to Ireland as a herald of the invasion: 'John O'Molony II', p. 422. Again, this seems unlikely in the light of Ormond's careful supervision of O'Reilly.

145 Ó Fiaich, 'O'Reilly', p. 204.

146 Plunkett to Fr Maurice Corker, 24 June 1681, Hanly, *Plunkett*, p. 577.

147 Hogan, 'Two Bishops of Killaloe', p. 228.

148 Curtayne, *Trial*, p. 57. A shade of this can be found in Giblin, '"*Nunziatura di Fiandra*", part 2', pp. 68 and 79 where there is a report from 1681 to the effect that Plunkett had been in a conspiracy with O'Molony, or alternatively that he had knowledge of a plot by O'Molony and Peter Talbot to import French weapons:

149 See, e.g., the evidence of David Fitzgerald and Maurice Fitzgerald in Burke, *Irish Priests*, p. 94, and 'The Information of Maurice Fitz Gerald, *Gent.*', Jan. 1680, https://quod.lib.umich.edu/e/eebo/A59376.0001.001/1:4?rgn=div1;view=fulltext, p. 10, accessed 20 July 2023. See also Giblin, "*Nunziatura di Fiandra*", part 2', p. 68.

150 Andrew Lynch, 'one of the most daring men of his time' according to Hogan, 'was entrusted with the delicate and dangerous business of passing to and from Ireland'. Hogan, 'John O'Molony II', p. 229. Lynch was in Ireland in June 1666 to participate in a meeting to consider the Remonstrance; this may give colour to the idea that his presence was in some way connected with the plot. Hogan states that Lynch was 'dispatched to Ireland' in Nov. 1666 to herald the invasion: Hogan, 'John O'Molony II', p. 422. In fact he was in Paris by that time, having evaded capture after the failure of the June meeting, and again there seems to be no evidence to connect Lynch with the plot. See Terry Clavin, 'Andrew Lynch' in *DIB*, vol. 5, pp. 615–16.

151 Richard Hayes described O'Molony as intensely patriotic and a chief figure in the movement to establish an independent Ireland with French aid from 1662 to 1666. An expeditionary force of 20,000 was ready to start out, but the project was abandoned due to a change in international policy by the French government: R. F. Hayes, *Biographical Dictionary of Irishmen in France* (Dublin, 1949), p. 246. The Franco-Irish plot of 1667 has received relatively little attention; Silke noted in *NHI*, vol. 3, p. 599, that Hogan had discussed it 'not altogether satisfactorily'.

152 Essex to Ormond, 14 Nov. 1673, Airy, *Essex Papers*, p. 137. Essex had come to rue the assurances he had given Plunkett in 1672 that 'he takes no notice of the anger of a particular individual [Ormond] as far as excluding the king's subjects [O'Molony] from the country is concerned' and thereby facilitated O'Molony's transfer to Ireland. Plunkett to Internuncio, 20 Jan. 1672, Hanly, *Plunkett*, p. 288. Plunkett had recommended O'Molony's advancement to Killaloe in 1669 and 1670, and urged him to take possession of his diocese without delay, notwithstanding activities in Paris which may have upset Ormond:

Hanly, *Plunkett*, pp. 38, 99, 276, 288. There was already a whiff of sulphur about O'Molony.

153 Essex to Arlington, 17 Apr. 1673, Airy, *Essex Papers*, pp. 76–7.

154 Essex to Sir Henry Capel, 7 May 1673, Airy, *Essex Papers*, p. 85.

155 Early in 1674 Plunkett castigated O'Molony for leaving Ireland in response to the Oct. 1673 Proclamation, and there was further criticism in 1675: 'Bishop O'Molony of Killaloe abandoned his flock and went to France although forbidden by our superiors to do so: it is three years since he came to this country and he did not spend three months in his diocese'. He suggested that O'Molony had left Ireland in order to obtain the see of Cashel for himself: Plunkett to Internuncio, 27 Jan. 1674, 5 and 20 Aug. 1675, Hanly, *Plunkett*, pp. 398, 447 and 455. This appears to be completely without foundation and Plunkett ignored his own fulsome letter to Propaganda, 14 Mar. 1673: 'It is certain that the Bishop of Killaloe will do more good by procuring for us that College than he would did he remain in his diocese during his whole lifetime.' Quoted in Boyle, 'John O'Molony', pp. 577–8 (19 Mar. in Hanly, *Plunkett*, p. 370).

156 See Gibney, *Popish Plot*, p. 85, and in particular the evidence of David Fitzgerald in Nov. 1680 which explicitly linked O'Molony to the 1676 plot, pp. 112–13. See also Burke, *Irish Priests*, pp. 85–6 and 94. This may belie Plunkett's comments in 1675. Much of Fitzgerald's evidence is reproduced by Mac Erlean in part II of his edition of Ó Bruadair's poems, pp. xix–xxvii, because in addition to implicating O'Molony, he also accused Ó Bruadair's patron Sir John Fitzgerald of involvement.

157 Boyle, 'John O'Molony', pp. 579–85, a translation of the Latin recorded in *Spicilegium Ossoriense*, vol. 2, p. 260. This is probably a reference to the allegations of the informer Maurice Fitzgerald who implicated Bishop John Brenan and Sir John Fitzgerald, among others, in the same 1676 plot.

158 14 Aug. 1686: *The State of the Protestants*, pp. 303–10. Although King could hardly be described as a dispassionate observer, there seems to be no evidence doubting the authenticity of the letter. Philip O'Regan argued that King was careful to exclude any examples from his text which were exaggerated or unsubstantiated, and which might tend to undermine his case: *Archbishop William King of Dublin (1650–1729) and the Constitution in Church and State* (Dublin, 2000), p. 48. There are opposing views as to whether O'Molony wrote the letter. Simms attributed the letter to Bishop Tyrell, without comment, in *Jacobite Ireland* (Dublin, 2000), p. 28. Similarly Éamonn Ó Ciardha in his *DIB* entry for Tyrrell, relying on Simms, it would appear. On the other hand, in *The Diocese of Killaloe from the Reformation to the Close of the Eighteenth Century* (Dublin, 1878), p. 407, Canon Philip Dwyer recorded that the Abbé Walsh (probably Jean Baptiste Walsh, the Administrator of the Irish Foundations in France, who was born in Killaloe) attributed this letter to O'Molony. It is not clear how Dwyer became aware of Walsh's opinion and, until further evidence emerges, O'Molony's authorship must remain provisional.

159 *State of the Protestants,* p. 46.

160 *State of the Protestants* p. 48.

161 *State of the Protestants* p. 49.
162 *CSPD 1686–7*, p. 79.
163 There is no reference to O'Molony's presence in France in 1689 in John Cronin, 'John O'Molony' in *DIB*, vol. 7, pp. 704–5.
164 The letter is appended in *State of the Protestants*, pp. 80–8. Again, there seems to be nothing to doubt its authenticity. O'Molony's Paris letter is dated 8 Mar. and James landed in Kinsale on 12 Mar.
165 *State of the Protestants,* p. 80.
166 *State of the Protestants*, p. 84. The proposal that Ireland should be under the protection of the French monarch is an echo of a similar proposal made by Richard Talbot in 1686: see Pádraig Lenihan, *The Last Cavalier* (Dublin, 2014), pp. 108–9.
167 He did not specify which Privy Council; from the context it would appear to be the English Council. Similarly, he did not specify the religion of the Irish members; again, from the context it is safe to assume he intended Catholics.
168 *State of the Protestants.* p. 85.
169 *State of the Protestants,* p. 86. His battle-cry was a quotation from the Vulgate: 'Nunc tempus acceptabile; nunc dies salutis; dum ergo tempus habemus operemur bonum, maxime ad domesticos fidei.' (Now is the accepted time, now is the day of salvation; while we have time therefore let us do good unto all men, especially unto them that are of the household of faith).
170 There is more than a faint echo of O'Molony's prescriptions in Nicholas Plunkett's early eighteenth-century manuscript 'A light to the blind', part of which was edited by J. T Gilbert as *A Jacobite Narrative of the War in Ireland*, 1688–91 (Dublin, 1892). Plunkett advocated the abolition of Poynings's Law, the ending of the appellate jurisdiction of the English courts and House of Lords, and full trading freedom for Irish merchants and producers. See Patrick Kelly, '"A light to the blind": The voice of the dispossessed elite in the generation after the defeat at Limerick' in *IHS* 96 (Nov. 1985), pp. 431–62, esp. at p. 455.
171 Melfort was no friend of Tyrconnell, having disagreed with him over policy in 1689, and his general unpopularity precipitated his being sent to France. What he says about Tyrconnell, and by extension O'Molony, must be considered highly partisan.
172 Macpherson, *Original Papers,* vol. 1, pp. 317 and ff.
173 Macpherson, *Original Papers,* p. 320.
174 Simms suggests that parliamentary privilege rather than a sense of Irish nationality seems to have been the primary motive: *Jacobite Ireland* (London, 1969), pp. 79–80.
175 The proposal that Ireland should have its own king, independent of the Stuarts, is an echo of a similar proposal which may have been made by Richard Talbot in 1686: see Lenihan, *Last Cavalier*, pp. 108–9. This was prompted by the possibility that James II's very Protestant daughter Mary would ascend the English throne in the event of his premature death. Were that to happen, an independent Ireland with its own monarch, under the protection of France, would be a refuge for English Catholics, and a bastion against William of

Orange. See also Philip Sergeant, *Little Jennings and Fighting Dick Talbot* (2 vols, London, 1913), vol. 2, pp. 357–62. Sergeant dismisses this proposal as incredible; for Lenihan it was not 'as outlandish as it sounds'. The birth of an heir in 1688 stilled these ideas and precipitated very different results. A later iteration of the 'independence' model was said to be favoured by Patrick Sarsfield under which Ireland would be independent of Britain, theoretically loyal to the exiled Stuarts and enjoy the protection of France: Lenihan, *Last Cavalier*, p. 185. Power suggested that O'Molony and Sarsfield 'stood for an entirely independent Ireland': Power, *Brenan*, p. 78.

176 Macpherson, *Original Papers*, p. 338.

177 Melfort's 'Instructions for Mr. Maxwell, going into Ireland', October 1689: Macpherson, *Original Papers*, p. 339.

178 Macpherson, *Original Papers*, pp. 340–1.

179 Macpherson, *Original Papers*, p. 339.

180 It is notable how much Tyrconnell was dependent on lawyers. Nagle, the secretary of state for war, and Rice, chief baron of the Exchequer, were in Tyrconnell's retinue. Thomas Nugent, chief justice of the King's Bench, and now the secretary of state, was left in charge of the government of the country.

181 There is a division of opinion as to whether O'Molony or the bishop of Cork, Peter Creagh, went on the mission. In favour of the former see Cronin, 'John O'Molony' in *DIB*, p. 705. In favour of the latter see Lenihan, *Last Cavalier*, p. 163, and Éamonn Ó Ciardha, 'Peter Creagh' in *DIB*, vol. 2, p. 982. Both were educated in France, but O'Molony was by far the better connected in that country. Further confusion was created by John O'Callaghan in *History of the Irish Brigades in the Service of France* (Shannon, 1969), pp. 100–1 who says it was Dr John O'Molony, Catholic bishop of Cork, but this is quite likely an error.

182 This strain of thought is close to that of the radical separatist Conor O'Mahony in the 1640s. O'Mahony had argued that an Irish Catholic could not pledge allegiance to a Protestant monarch, that sovereignty derived from the people, and not from God, and that the Irish should choose an Irish-born Catholic as their king: John Minahane (ed.), *An Argument Defending the Right of the Kingdom of Ireland (1645), by Conor O'Mahony* (Millstreet, Co. Cork, 2010). It is also heard in Nicholas Plunkett's *A Jacobite Narrative*: Raymond Gillespie, *Seventeenth-Century Ireland* (Dublin, 2006), p. 279. See also O Riordan, '"Political" poems', pp. 125–6.

183 *Historical Works*, vol. 1, p. 38.

184 Ó Fiaich, 'O'Reilly', p. 204. Millett, 'O'Reilly's report', p. 114.

185 Alan Titley, 'What the people thought', *Dublin Review of Books*, July 2017, http://www.drb.ie/essays/what-the-people-thought, accessed 19 July 2023.

3

Rejecting English law: Irish poetry

This tops the trick: the law that's come overseas
To flatten and scourge the race of Eibhear the Fair[1]

By an act of vigorous law of the generous prince of the east
A kind wave of wisdom and right hath been steered o'er the ocean to us,
Wherefore I now make it known that Éibhear Scot's numerous clans
That in duty they strictly are bound to yield willing allegiance to him.[2]

The literary record in Irish for the Restoration is not as extensive as in other periods of Irish history. Raymond Gillespie has diagnosed the reason:

> From the 1660s to the 1680s almost no one in Gaelic Ireland looked to the past. Indeed, almost all the writers born in the 1640s and 1650s fell silent with the exception of the poems of Dáibhí Ó Bruadair, and a handful of works by Séafraidh Ó Donnchadha and Diarmaid mac Sheáin Bhuí Mac Cárthaigh. It is as if the generation who lived through the traumas of the 1640s and 1650s did not want to look back to the past, preferring to forget what had happened in those decades.[3]

Nevertheless, there is sufficient poetry written in Irish in this period to explore how Gaelic Ireland responded to English law. Generally, Gaelic poets were not concerned with legal niceties or fine points of constitutional analysis. They experienced the application of the law in its full immediacy, and for them submission to and observance of the law was problematic because they experienced it as alien and unfair. Dáibhí Ó Bruadair's response was more volatile and nuanced: volatile in that his support for the law rose and fell with the legal fortunes of his patrons, and nuanced in that he believed Gaelic Ireland's fate was at least in part sealed by its own disrespect for legal order.

It is impossible to understand the Restoration without reference to the period immediately preceding it, and brief consideration is given to three 'political' works, from 1640 to 1659. Ó Bruadair is an outstanding figure in Irish literary history, the major poet of the second half of the seventeenth century. His long life coincided with this period, and his large output is well preserved and recognised for its quality and insight. Kiberd described him as the truest chronicler of his age.[4] He lived through all the major events of the period, the Confederate wars, Cromwell, the Restoration, the Popish Plot, James II, the 1688 revolution, the Boyne and the penal laws, to which he not only gave witness, but transformed into narratives of his own life. As in no other poet, the national and personal catastrophes of the era coincide.[5] Séafraidh Ó Donnchadha an Ghleanna participated in the 1641 rising; despite this he managed to retain his Kerry estates during the Cromwellian period until he was dispossessed in 1665. His poetry reflects his anger under the repression of the Interregnum and against Charles II's confirmation of the Cromwellian land settlement. Diarmaid mac Sheáin Bhuí Mac Cárthaigh and Seamus Dall Mac Cuarta wrote towards the end of the period. Mac Cárthaigh condemned the injustice of the English legal system at the time of the Popish Plot and celebrated the accession of James II and the changes Tyrconnell had wrought in Ireland. Finally, reference is made to the work of Seán Ó Gadhra, and Aogán Ó Rathaille, most of whose work dates from the eighteenth century.

Prelude to the Restoration

Michelle O Riordan has argued that the poets writing in Irish in the period immediately prior to the Restoration 'present an almost documentary account of the disintegration of Ireland in the mid-seventeenth century'.[6] In the introduction to *Five Seventeenth-Century Political Poems,* the editor Cecile O'Rahilly said: 'To understand the contemporary Irishman's reaction to political events and to form a picture of the actual conditions in which he lived and suffered, we must turn to the Irish poets of the period.'[7] These poems were written in accentual verse, not by professional poets but by educated laymen. Three of them provide insights into the *mentalité* of Gaelic Ireland in relation to the law at this period.[8] Little is known about Donnchadh Mac an Chaoilfhiaclaigh whose poem *Do fríth, monuar, an uain si ar Éirinn* (Ireland, alas, had to labour under adversity) predates the Cromwellian period. It traces the fate of Gaelic Ireland from the accession of James I and the extension or imposition of the full apparatus of the common law from 1605.[9] Ostensibly peaceful after the Nine Years' War, in reality Ireland was experiencing a period of growing disquiet. Dunlop wrote: 'the natives looked on in impotent rage while the chicaneries of the law stripped them one by one of lands to which they believed they possessed an indefeasible right.'[10] The depredations of the legal system on the Gaelic population in the early part of the seventeenth century were echoed in *Tuireamh na hÉireann* (Ireland's lament) which, on the basis of internal evidence, was written between 1655 and 1659 on the eve of the Restoration.[11] It seems to be the only poem written by Seán Ó Conaill from Kerry, and is an abbreviated version of Keating's *Foras Feasa ar Éirinn,* 'updated' to the seventeenth century, in respect of which it provides more detail.[12] On the basis of a statistical analysis of its transmission in manuscript over 250 years, Vincent Morley argues that the poem is probably one of the most important ever written in Ireland.[13] It traces the long history of Ireland, and in particular details the reigns of Elizabeth I and James I, and the laws which oppressed Gaelic Ireland. Ó Conaill argued that at first the Normans were relatively benign but the Reformation changed everything, and the clergy were persecuted. O'Rahilly argues one section 'deals with the English laws devised for the overthrow of the Irish, with a bitter mocking passage full of the uncouth legal terms and the strange names of English officials'.[14] The Cromwellian war devastated Ireland: *an coga do chríochnaig Éire*.[15] Gaelic leaders were executed or transported:

> O'Connor's head a spike suspends on high,
> *Transplant, Transport,* to Jamaica hie.[16]

Those who remained in Ireland were forced to choose between apostasy and losing their estates:

> By dreadful oaths the rest are forced to swear,
> Or give two parts of what fell to their share[17]

Ó Conaill's distaste for English names and legal terminology was also identified by Bernadette Cunningham, who argued that the use of English legal terms is characteristic of the extreme hostility displayed by many native Irish to the colonial administration.[18] In *Tuireamh*, the legal system and its terminology is coterminous with the administration; legal institutions and processes are the tools of oppression used by the English. The most egregious policies find expression in legal form such as Surrender and Regrant and the 1652 Act of Settlement.[19] For Ó Conaill, the law was the verbal articulation of the physical violence and coercion directed over the centuries by England against Ireland.

Cunningham reiterated the point when considering Éamonn an Dúna's *Mo lá leoin go deo n-éagad* (My eternal day of sorrow), c.1658, which also uses English words to evoke the hostile language used by the administration when describing the Irish-speaking population.[20] Practically nothing seems to be known about an Dúna's background but his poem comments vividly and in detail on events in the period 1650–57.[21] He engages with various aspects of the legal system of the period and O Riordan explained how the poem shows that 'the unnecessary and overzealous application of the law, which resulted in hanging for minor offences, robbery of goods and illegal seizures, had impoverished and defeated the Irish'.[22] The poem also mentions the High Courts of Justice held in Dublin and Cork in 1652–54, the persecution of priests and schoolteachers, and the transportation of vagrants and those who failed to transplant. The poem makes startling use of French, English and Irish, particularly in a section detailing the corruption in the legal processes that attended the Cromwellian land settlement.[23] The passage immediately following is a frenzied recitation of all the hate-words in English which Ó Dúna would admit to knowing:

> *Transport transplant,* my mind on English.
> *Shoot him, kill him, strip him, tear him,*
> *A tory, hack him, hang him, a rebel,*
> *a rogue, a thief a priest, a papist*[24]

Mac Mathúna summed it well: 'it was not legal niceties, which held sway, but orders and judgments, expressed in the form of phrases, slogans and litanies, which were a travesty of justice and stratagems in a plot to seize land, to dispossess landowners and to extirpate enemies'.[25] Yet despite an Dúna's anger at the legal system and its tyrannies, and unlike Mac an Chaoilfhiaclaigh and Ó Conaill, an Dúna prayed for the restoration of Charles II.[26] Indeed O Riordan argues that his poem shows that, notwithstanding his Gaelic heritage, in politics he was an Old English royalist.

Therefore we see that in the early 1640s Mac an Chaoilfhiaclaigh, and twenty years later Ó Conaill, demonstrated an intimate knowledge of the system of courts and their processes, and expressed their hatred of the law by crashing its terminology through Irish metres. These Munster poets showed little acceptance of the common law. On the other hand an Dúna maintained loyalty to the Stuarts despite the provocations of the English legal oppression. How these contradictions played out in the Restoration is explored in the next section.

Dáibhí Ó Bruadair and the Restoration

Dáibhí Ó Bruadair (1625–98) was the most significant poet of this period. In the opinion of his editor and translator, Fr John Mac Erlean: 'His poems form a running commentary on all the principal political occurrences of the day.'[27] During his long life he experienced and recorded much of the Catholic struggle of this period. In his earlier works he followed the bardic tradition of focusing on the family connections of his patrons. Yet even in these early poems, contemporary events and personalities such as the dispossession of Catholics and the role of the duke of Ormond are noted. In his work from 1677 to 1682 he shows a significant engagement with the law and the consequences of the Popish Plot. In the poetry he wrote from 1682 to 1698 one hears a powerful, authentic voice, untrammelled by bardic convention or poetical restraint. From the mid-1680s he was fully engaged with contemporary events, from the optimism on James II's accession to the ruined state of the country after the Irish army left in 1691, culminating in *An Longbhriseadh* (The shipwreck) and his resolve to write no more poetry. Mac Erlean translated and published all of his poetry in three volumes between 1910 and 1917.[28]

The first volume contains a limited amount of material that reflects Ó Bruadair's political awareness. An early poem, *Créacht do Dháil me* (A fateful wound hath made of me), written c.1652 when the Cromwellian plantations were in progress, laments the state of the Irish who have been impoverished by confiscation and ordered to leave their country.[29] He had only contempt for the usurpers.[30] Fifteen years later, Ó Bruadair's increasing awareness of political matters is evident. Ó Bruadair blamed Ormond for the state of Ireland and in *A Shaoi Re Gliogar* (Thou sage of inanity), the final poem of the first volume, he attacked the writer of a short poem praising Ormond – probably in 1666 – at the expense of ancient Gaelic heroes.[31] He condemned the writer's 'turgid twaddle trying to delight that darling duke of his'.[32] In reality Ó Bruadair's poem is an attack on the duke himself, whom he describes as a 'braggart old noble' who had failed to protect Ireland from tyranny, quite unlike the ancient Gaelic heroes to whom he had been favourably compared. Given the likely date of composition, it is difficult to escape the conclusion that Ó Bruadair is attacking Ormond's role in the land settlement.

The land settlement was also the principal concern of Séafraidh Ó Donnchadha an Ghleanna (c.1620–78) during this period. He was chief of the O'Donoghues of Glenflesk, Co. Kerry, and his poetry has been edited by John Minahane.[33] Although he had taken a minor role in the 1641 rebellion during the siege of Tralee with his father and brothers, Eoghan Ó Raghallaigh says the family managed to retain their estate throughout the Cromwellian period.[34] More accurately, their castle at Killaha was slighted by Ludlow in 1652, and despite their lands being forfeited the family remained in the area.[35] Two of his poems are of particular note. The date of composition of *Ní fhuilngid Goill dúinn síothughadgh i nÉirinn seal* (The Gaill will not let us settle in peace in Ireland) is not settled but it clearly describes the state of legal impotence of Gaelic Ireland.[36] The poem evokes the preamble to the 1662 Act of Settlement, which justified the continuation of the Cromwellian confiscations.[37] And even though prostrate before English rule, Ó Donnchadha was not without hope.[38] He expressed Gaelic disappointment with the effect of the Act of Settlement in *Is barra ar an gcleas an reacht do théacht tar tuinn* (This tops the trick: the law that's come overseas).[39]

The innocent Irish had no sense of the dangers that lay in the laws made by a parliament controlled by foreigners, until they learned how the Cromwellians murdered Charles I.[40] In this respect, Ó Donnchadha's views are very similar to John Lynch's in the *Dedicatory Epistle* to *Cambrensis Eversus*. Like Lynch, he was unfailingly loyal to the Stuarts; Minahane records that he kept their genealogy among his papers.[41] He did not blame Charles II for the 1662 Act of Settlement. Like Nicholas French, he blamed the parliamentary descendants of the Cromwellians.[42] The poem continues to depict the impoverished state of the country, the impotence of the Irish and the power of the foreigner. But it promises that God's will should prevail and 'restore all Ireland's Gaeil to prosperity'.[43]

A Dhia na n-Uile (O God of the Universe) is the first poem of the second volume of Mac Erlean's edition of Ó Bruadair.[44] He again turned his attention to Ormond and castigated him for deliberately creating disunity among Irish Catholics.[45] Neither was he impressed by the Catholic lawyer Sir Robert Talbot, and asked rhetorically whether Talbot could get the better of God in a dispute.[46] Similarly, in *Ionnsa d'Fhéinn Éirionn* ('Tis sad for Erin's Fenian bands) he took aim at the Franciscan Peter Walsh whose campaign for the Remonstrance had caused such dissension among Catholic clerics.[47] In this poem, he prayed for unity among the Catholic clergy, and loyalty to the king and his government, whose actions he asked God to direct.[48] While his loyalty to the king is not surprising, and in this respect very similar to Lynch and French, his support for the government is remarkable, given his views on the Cromwellians then in key positions of power.

Within a decade, Ó Bruadair's personal circumstances had declined precipitately (the reasons are not clear) and in 1678, in *Muirear re mí* (For a month past a throng) he lamented the state to which he had been reduced.[49] His own penury prevented him extending hospitality to those who visited him, but nevertheless he again showed a sense of political awareness, seeking God's clemency for the members of the old Irish elite who had chosen to remain in the country, and who might help him in his financial distress.[50] Ó Bruadair's patrons included the MacCarthys and Barrys of Co. Cork, and the Bourkes and Fitzgeralds of Co. Limerick. While he admired many members of these families, Ó Bruadair could be sharp with those who did not subscribe to his ideals of political and religious loyalty. *Is Mithid Damhsa Bann* ('Tis time at length for me) is a lament on the death of the loyal James fitz Richard Barry in 1681, who was:

> Grandson of that man who once did forfeit
> His inheritance, his lands, and castle;[51]

But other members of his family were not considered loyal and there is reference to the Protestant David Barry, first earl of Barrymore, who did not join the rebels of 1641, preferring instead the esteem of the English planters from Co. Cork with their strange names Digby, Fuitminnsata, Rathsan.[52] Similarly, *A Fhir Aitheanta Léasa* (O thou who once knewest the law) is a poem of reproach to Master Richard Verling, who had conformed to the established church for financial reasons.[53] No doubt Ó Bruadair was conscious of his own penury when he urged him to

> Reflect in thy mind on thyself and observe how accursed the deed
> To yield to the heart's base desires and sell heaven for a short spell of life.[54]

In 1680 Sir John Fitzgerald of Clonlish was arrested and brought to England on a charge of treason in connection with the Popish Plot. The events that followed throw some light on how a prominent Irish Catholic could successfully navigate the English and Irish legal systems, notwithstanding the level of anti-Catholic hysteria of the period. In *Dá Bhfaice Mo Phrionnsa* (If my Prince were to cast but one glance) Ó Bruadair argued that Charles II would never agree that Fitzgerald could be guilty, once he had seen him.[55] In fact, the king did not see Fitzgerald or play any role in his trial, and the reality was more mundane. Doubts began to emerge about the reliability of some of the witnesses against Fitzgerald in October 1680.[56] Carte explained that, notwithstanding this, Fitzgerald's trial was transferred to London because his accusers did not trust an impartial Limerick jury 'who knew the circumstances of the country, and the character and conduct of the accused as well as of the accuser'. The sheriffs of London were to empanel an English jury that would believe everything put to them by the witnesses.[57] The English House of Lords ordered that Fitzgerald be sent to London on 6 November 1680, together with three others who had been similarly accused.[58] By December they were in London and in January they appeared before the Lords, who on the basis of the information supplied by the informants Maurice Fitzgerald and Murtagh Dowling decided that there was indeed a dangerous plot in Ireland.[59] Sir John acknowledged that he knew one of his co-accused but denied any knowledge of a plot. In the event, on 12 February 1681, the grand jury of Westminster brought in a verdict of *Ignoramus*, and Fitzgerald was released.[60]

The poem *Searc na Suadh* (Love of sages) is even more closely concerned with legal matters.[61] Notwithstanding that the hysteria surrounding the Plot had abated in England, in Ireland there were witnesses who were prepared to provide evidence in connection with it and unfinished legal business. In April 1682 Fitzgerald once again stood trial on charges of treason, this time in Limerick. Ó Bruadair attributed great wisdom to Charles II, who could see through the evidence of false witnesses.[62] But legal process had to be followed. The facts concerning this second case are scarce and confusing. It seems that Fitzgerald and the other defendants had first appeared before two judges of the Exchequer, on circuit.[63] Ó Bruadair believed that the judges Hen and Hartstonge were so intimidated they failed to acquit the defendants, for fear they themselves would be sucked into the Plot.[64] Their failure to deliver justice encouraged further false charges to be made.[65] Ó Bruadair himself attended the trial in Limerick in April 1682 and his account of the legal process is probably unique in Irish poetry of this period. He witnessed how it was only when Lord Chief Justice John Keating dealt with the case that justice was done.[66] Keating unveiled the false evidence given by one of the witnesses, Bernard Dennis and ensured the informers got their due.[67]

> Son of lies and poisoned rage concealed.[68]
> Murphy and Downey were sentenced as captives to punishment base[69]

Carte explained some of the legal background to this trial. In 1681 Ormond charged the judges who went on circuit to particularly enquire into any plots in Ireland.[70] After they completed the Connacht circuit, on 5 August the Lord Chief Justice Keating and Mr Justice Herbert sent a report from Galway. They explained how, in Roscommon and Leitrim, trials collapsed because the witnesses were in England. In Mayo, John Browne of Kinturk and Dermot O'Connor were brought to trial for treason before a jury of 'able and substantial Protestants'. The Crown's witnesses, 'full of oaths and execrations', did not impress and one of them confessed that he had been suborned.[71] On the other side 'a cloud of witnesses … Gentlemen of very good quality, among them three or four Ministers of the Gospel' gave evidence on behalf of the defendants. The trial took five hours under 'the greatest quiet and order', and the jury dealt with the matter expeditiously. The judges reported the jury 'sat not down, till they returned, and brought the prisoners in not guilty'.

In November 1681 Ormond noted that 'all the business here belongs to the [legal] term and the Judges'. The Privy Council was busy hearing witnesses, some returning from England and others volunteering themselves, 'all of them … forswearing themselves'.[72] Unfortunately there is no such detailed account of Fitzgerald's trial in Limerick in 1682.[73] However a small glimpse of the proceedings can be seen in a letter from the Chief Justice Sir William Davys to primate Michael Boyle. He recounted that Fitzgerald had petitioned to be brought to trial, but the witnesses who were summoned to appear did not attend and could not be 'brought in'. This was similar to the earlier Plot trials in Roscommon and Leitrim, and the court decided that it was not safe to proceed to try him.[74]

Ó Bruadair's attitude to the trial is revealing. Mr Justice Herbert, who sat with Sir John Keating, got no credit, and the roles of defence counsel and the jury are not explored. It was enough for Ó Bruadair that a judge with the name Keating played a role, so he could write a poem in joint praise of the poet Geoffrey Keating and the judge. Neatly, both Keatings had revealed the truth; Geoffrey in his *Foras Feasa ar Éirinn*, which rebutted the falsehoods of English histories of Ireland, and Sir John, who exposed the false evidence of perjurers.[75] It was the wisdom of Charles II that had brought about this happy result and consequently loyalty was now owed to the king.[76] Ó Bruadair's euphoric reaction to the outcome of the trial owes more to his poetic sensibility than any attention to the mundane facts and circumstances. It was left to John Brenan, the archbishop of Cashel, to report the effect of these acquittals more prosaically.[77]

The third volume of Ó Bruadair's poetry shows a marked change of tone.[78] Mac Erlean described the poems as numerous, very interesting and engrossed with the politics of the period. He noted: 'These poems are of extreme importance, for they are almost the only contemporary documents written in Irish which exist to enable us appreciate the sentiments of the people of Ireland at that epoch.'[79] The first, *A Scaifaire d'Aoibh gCearbhuill* (Gallant scion of the race of Cearbhall) is dated 1682.[80] It is an admonition to a soldier to attend to his religious duties, a task made more difficult by proclamations issued at the time of the Oates plot.[81] *Suim Purgadóra Bhfear nÉireann* (Summary of the purgatory of the men of Ireland 1641–84) is a catalogue of the evils that have befallen the Irish over a forty-year period during which Ó Bruadair was an adult, and describes his attitude to the Cromwellians and their unworthy Stuart successors.[82] It is written in a direct, vigorous language, quite unlike much of his earlier work. Here, for the first time, one hears a powerful, authentic voice, untrammelled by bardic convention or poetical restraint.[83] The effect of the Cromwellian regime on royalist Irishmen – dispossession, exile and transplantation – is described.[84] The expectations of the Irish were aroused on the death of Cromwell, 'the champion of murderlust', and the advent of the Restoration.[85] But the supporters of the Stuarts were to be met with bitter disappointment in the Restoration land settlement. And even though the old owners were dispossessed, and shorn of all resources, they still raised suspicions in the minds of the new proprietors. Uneasy at the thought of a possible Catholic resurgence, they concocted the Popish Plot.[86] Ó Bruadair had lost faith in the discrimination of his leaders:

> If a rewounded soldier from keen spear-pricks shrinks timidly,
> And a child when once burnt is afraid of a spark of fire,
> Are our chieftains not fools, if after such brigandage,
> They cannot discern benefactors from brewers' bees?[87]

Even the king, who had had urged the Irish to return from foreign armies, betrayed them by leaving them powerless and without status. Their only resort was to lawlessness, and they were faced with death and dishonour.[88] Ó Bruadair summed up his attitude to the law, and the Act of Settlement:

> That last stroke sufficiently sums up this document
> On the present law's judgment of me and of Erin's clans:
> A brief, bitter instance of that Act that hath broken their backs,
> And left them cloakless and shirtless in poverty.[89]

Whether *A Shíle an Tseaca* (O Síle, cold and stately) was addressed to a real person or an allegory of Ireland is disputed.[90] It does seem clear that it was written after the Restoration and shines an powerful light on Ó Bruadair's attitude to the common law and Charles II.[91] One of Ó Bruadair's more obscure poems, the exact meaning is difficult to discern. Clearly, Ó Bruadair regards the passing of Brehon law 'westward to the Siuir' with regret. He also seems to suggest that either the real Síle (or Ireland, if the poem is an allegory) was not so foolish as to give her heart to the royal cause – or at least Charles II. To have done so was to invite disappointment, since the king had betrayed his loyal Irish followers.

But the accession of James II changed everything. Loyalty to the Stuarts was restored and from 1685 a very different tenor can be detected in the poetry. Here was a king who was Irish, albeit by descent, and a Catholic to whom full-blooded loyalty could be given.[92] *A Thrúipfhir Más Múscailt* (In command of a troop) the first of his Jacobite poems, is advice to a young soldier under the command of the Lord Mac Cárthaigh.[93] He expresses the hope that the new regime following the accession of James II and Tyrconnell's catholicisation of the Irish army would signal the end of legal oppression.[94] *Caithréim an Dara Séamuis* (The triumph of James II) is a poem in praise of James II and a response to a 1590 poem by Flann mac Eoghain mhic Chraith in praise of Elizabeth I.[95] The new king would salve the trauma caused by the Popish Plot and had secured the support of all of Catholic Ireland:

> Binding herb of relief for those who were wounded
> And stricken to earth by the Plot of Oates[96]

The army had been reformed, and James was:

> The first king of England who gave rank and dignity,
> Death-dealing weapons and uniform
> To Irishmen after the risks they encountered –
> Conduct that freed them from tyranny.[97]

In addition he had reformed the officers of the law by appointing Catholics to senior positions in the judiciary, who might have the ability to understand plaintiffs who only spoke Irish, and be sympathetic to their concerns:

> To listen to the plea of the man who can't speak
> The lip-dry and simpering English.[98]

Diarmaid mac Sheáin Bhuí Mac Cárthaigh (c.1640–1705), a friend and poetical colleague of Ó Bruadair, also chronicled the changes brought about in Ireland at this time.[99] He lived for most of his life in Blarney, Co. Cork.[100] *Céad buidhe re Dia* (A hundred thanks to God) dates from 1687 and like Ó Bruadair's *Caithréim an Dara Séamuis* (The triumph of James II) celebrates Tyrconnell's catholicisation of the army.[101] The poem noted the new military regime; Diarmaid, Cian and Maolsheachlainn are now in charge.[102] Instead of being called 'You Popish rogue' by the authorities, they now call the enemy 'You Cromwellian dog'. On guard, the challenge is 'Cia siúd thall?' said 'sternly and fearlessly' and the reply they now expect is 'Mise Taidhg'.[103]

Mac Cárthaigh catalogued the many injustices suffered by Gaelic Ireland; 'the transplants and deceits' and 'the transports in sailing ships overseas ... to the land of Jamaica'.[104] Those found guilty of insubordination 'had their hearts and their heads impaled on the city gates' or 'with horrible tortures already had been put to death'.[105] Judicial process was corrupt; what was not stolen in court was consumed in bribing corrupt officials, as in the cases of Lords Muskerry and Carbery.[106] Like Ó Bruadair, he paid particular attention to the Popish Plot, and was clearly familiar with the perjured evidence at the trials of Plunkett and Creagh.[107] A letter from the Chief Justice Sir William Davys to Archbishop Michael Boyle recounted the extraordinary events at the trial of Peter Creagh, the bishop of Cork and Cloyne. The floor of the court collapsed, several people were injured and at least one killed. Davys reported that he and Baron Worth had to escape through the windows, and 'dropped down into the people's arms who stood ready to receive us'. The trial continued, because four days later Davys wrote to Boyle to explain the witnesses had retracted their evidence and the jury found Creagh not guilty.[108]

Mac Cárthaigh also celebrated the reform of local government by the admission of Catholics as freemen of urban corporations and justices of the peace in 1686–87, and returned to the trope of Catholic names previously used with contempt:

> There is many a Diarmuid prudent in government,
> And many a Tadhg courageously jubilant[109]

This robust poem is notable for the conflation of the vulgar and sacred, and ends in a series of proposed toasts, including:

> The health of the Pope, my dear friends, do not omit
> But drink it with temperance, free from all drunkenness.

And if you should happen to meet a *Whig* anywhere,
Give him one or two *Kicks* that will make him reverberate.[110]

Mac Cárthaigh's output is relatively small, compared with Ó Bruadair.[111] There are no datable poems between 1687 and 1694, when he composed an elegy for Justin MacCarthy, Lord Mountcashel.[112] Nevertheless, he was a significant witness to the early Jacobite era, and like Ó Bruadair showed a level of awareness of Catholic resentment of abuse of legal process in the period.[113]

Like Mac Cárthaigh, Ó Bruadair celebrated the catholicisation of the army in *Caithréim Thaidhg* (The triumph of Tadhg) (1690). This poem also noted the effect of the passing of the Act for the repeal of the Restoration land settlement in June 1689.[114] Ó Bruadair took great satisfaction from the new confessional and legal order.[115] But all this delight was to be dispelled by the defeats of the Catholic army at the Boyne, and finally at Aughrim. This is also reflected in the work of Seamus Dall Mac Cuarta (c.1650–1733). Morley tells us that '[t]he earliest composition to which a date can be assigned is a lament ("*Is in Eachroim an áir atáid ina gcónaí*") for Sorley MacDonnell, who was killed while fighting in the Jacobite army at Aughrim.'[116] Even in this formal expression of grief, the 'crimes of parliament' in awarding the throne of England to William and Mary are not overlooked.[117]

The enormous military losses at Aughrim were augmented by the exodus of Irish officers and soldiers after the Treaty of Limerick. This sealed the defeat of the Catholic cause, and left Ó Bruadair to reflect on the reasons for Ireland's demise, following the optimism of the all-too-brief Jacobite revanche. Ó Bruadair wrote *A Chaithbhile Dár Thairgeas* (Battleoak for whom I always) as a lament on the departure of his patron Sir John Fitzgerald into French exile after the treaty.[118] He criticised the behaviour of the Irish troops for whom favourable terms had been obtained so that they could continue in Ireland without penalty. These terms were being abused by their loutish and thieving behaviour that could only have negative consequences for the implementation of the treaty.[119] John Bull would not scruple if the treaty were not applied, justified in part by the insubordinate and illegal behaviour of the Irish troops.

A Chaithbhile Dár Thairgeas (Battleoak for whom I always) anticipated the principal theme of *An Longbhriseadh* (The shipwreck) which is perhaps Ó Bruadair's best known work.[120] In this poem, he described the ruined state of the country after the Irish army had left in 1691, and allocated blame to the lack of unity among the leadership of the army, and especially to the lawlessness and insubordination among the lower classes. This abuse of the law echoes O'Bruadair's stance in *Suim Purgadóra Bhfear nÉireann* (Summary of the purgatory of the men of Ireland 1641–84) where he blamed the defeat by Cromwell on the lack of discipline among the Irish troops which led to plundering and murder. Several times he returns to the lack of respect shown for legal rights, and compares the Irish underclass (*caitcheann* or cathead is a favoured term of execration) to their English enemies. James II had issued proclamations reining in the excesses of his supporters in order to maintain the high moral ground.[121] But this was to no effect and the outcome was predictable.[122] Even though the result was 'gallows like shop-signs up in every place', James II's followers could not understand his disapproval.[123] Ó Bruadair blamed the irregular Irish troops for the failure to implement the Articles, and he blamed himself for not having predicted this earlier.[124] He also blamed James II for not being resolute in maintaining order, and warned others not to disobey the king's law.[125]

Ó Bruadair was not alone in diagnosing national decline as a consequence of the degeneration of the Irish underclass, and his stance reflects two earlier authors, one writing in Irish and the other in English. Part 2 of the satirical text *Pairlement Chloinne Tomáis* was written c.1660 and targets the minor tradespeople who had not only survived Cromwell, but profited during his regime when the established order was being upset.[126] In the anonymous author's view, this group was entirely self-serving, and had little regard for civil society or its institutions. They condemned the legal system and only used it cynically in their quest for land.

The character of the nobleman, not a member of Clann Tomáis, was inserted into the narrative to provide a contrasting commentary. He may have been the authentic voice of the author and made clear his aristocratic disdain for the newly emancipated lower orders. This nobleman's hauteur finds a more articulate and compelling expression in the work of Richard Bellings (c.1603–77). Bellings was a lawyer who for seven years played a key role in the Confederate administration in Kilkenny. In the 1670s he wrote what was ostensibly a history of the events of the 1640s.[127] Gillespie has argued that the parallels between the events of the 1640s and the 1670s mark Belling's *History* as a reliable guide to post-Restoration political thought.[128] Bellings believed that the exclusion of the Catholic nobility from political life in the 1630s created a moral vacuum where there was no natural leadership of the Catholic lower orders. In his view, the Ulster insurrection was not a war but the world turned upside down, and the disarray in Catholic affairs in the 1670s was not dissimilar.[129] Bellings echoes the narrative of part 2 of *Pairlement Chloinne Tomáis*. For example, he argued that in 1641 'the people assumed the right to discourse', a phrase which could describe the entire narrative of part 2. He noted that the common people were 'seldom restrained by the ties of conscience or justice' and this reflects Clann Tomáis's avid self-interest and rejection of legal order. During the 1640s, 'the will of the strongest was the rule of men's actions and sufferings', a phrase which uncannily echoes the last lines of part 2 'whoever might be the stronger, should have the upper hand'.[130] Bellings was not the author of part 2, but the similarity of thought is compelling, and he articulated the viewpoint of an experienced administrator and lawyer. He carefully analysed the causes and described the consequences in the breakdown in order when a noble elite is deprived of its natural role in enforcing social cohesion and adherence to the rule of law. There is more than an echo of both writers in Ó Bruadair's denunciation of the lawless lower orders in his post-Limerick poems. In his view, it was they who were the authors of Ireland's disastrous state in the 1690s.[131]

Ó Bruadair had hoped to end his life in a comfortable sinecure. In despair he famously resolved to write no more for the people who did not value his poetry and whom he now despised: 'so much for my writing for the men of Ireland'.[132] In fact, he continued to write until 1694. *Geadh Ainbhfiosach Feannaire* (An ignoramus of a flayer) was a continuation of the themes of *An Longbhriseadh* (The shipwreck) and repeated his attack on the miscreants who brought about the ruin of the Irish cause.[133] He castigated the raparees, who had taken to the hills and were involved in continuous law-breaking.[134] Now discharged from military duty, they are having the last laugh, as they abused the law.[135]

For the most part his last poems are a catalogue of his great poverty, and in *Is Fada Liom go Dearbhtha* (Weary is my mind for certain) (1693) he lamented that he no longer had the protection of his patrons and feared the enforcement of the hearth-tax.[136] His remaining poems are largely non-political and devoid of legal reference. He died in 1698.

After the Restoration

In 1911, Patrick Dinneen and Tadhg O'Donoghue edited the first scholarly edition of the poems of Aogán Ó Rathaille (c.1670–1729) for the Irish Texts Society.[137] Although they state that 'it is certain that he had reached the fullness of his powers before the close of the seventeenth century' they continued that 'most of his works that have reached us were written between the years 1700 and 1726'. The first poem in their edition is dated 1700 in some manuscript copies.[138] Breandán Ó Buachalla added to (and removed from) the 1911 corpus of Ó Rathaille's work in 2004, and included a lament for Justin McCarthy who died in 1694.[139] It is clear therefore that Aogán Ó Rathaille substantially belongs to the eighteenth century. Nevertheless, it would be impossible for his oeuvre to escape the political ferment of late seventeenth-century Ireland through which he himself had lived, and whose effects continued to resonate with him. Ó Buachalla identified Ó

Rathaille as a key transitional figure. The royalism of the late seventeenth century, which had underpinned the work of Nicholas French, John Lynch and Ó Bruadair, had been transformed into Jacobitism, and Ó Rathaille was the first major poet to embrace and enunciate its rhetoric.[140] Thus in his *Marbhna Sheagháin Bhrúin* (Elegy on John Brown), who died in 1706, he mourns the brother of Valentine Browne, first Viscount Kenmare, just as he laments the deposition of the king.[141] And in 1708, in *Don Taoiseach Eoghan Mac Chormaic Riabhaigh Mhic Cárrthaigh* (To the Chieftain Eoghan, son of Cormac Riabhach Mac Carthy) the banished king is accompanied in exile by religious of every rank, scholars and nobles.[142] Seven years later, in *Tarngaireacht Dhuinn Fhírinne* (The prophecy of Donn Firinne), he laments his own fate and James II's death.[143] Ó Rathaille poured scorn on the members of his own race who had become middlemen and agents of the oppressors.[144] There are echoes here of the contempt for the members of Clann Tomáis in *Pairlement Chloinne Tomáis*, Belling's concern for the absence of leadership of the Catholic lower orders and Ó Bruadair's haughty disdain for the underclass which had wreaked havoc in Ireland.

Seán Ó Gadhra (1648–c.1720), a minor figure from Sligo, is of interest for the poems from his slim oeuvre that are dedicated to lawyers.[145] *Truagh Ceas na gCarad* (Pitiful is the sorrow of the kinsmen) is an elegy on the death in 1715 of the Sligo lawyer Brian Ó hUiginn, described as Clerk of the Crown.[146] Ó Gadhra acclaimed Toirdhealbhach Óg Mac Donnchadh (c.1640–1713) as Ó hUiginn's successor. Mac Donnchadh was:

> protector of justice and religion,
> it was he alone who replaced Brian,
> who neglected neither prince nor pauper.[147]

Mac Donnchadh, was known locally as 'The Counsellor' and had petitioned to continue to practise under Article 2 of the Treaty of Limerick.[148] He was said to be the only Catholic admitted to the Irish bar at the time and Ó Gadhra offered him words of poetic advice to retire on his return from the Williamite wars.[149] The Counsellor was a poet himself and his response may be a reflection of the limits placed on Catholics practising the law after the Treaty of Limerick:

> That advice which Seán Óg kindly gave me
> I doubt he would have given it but that he felt
> The English demanded treacherously
> That my sort should not contend with the law.[150]

In fact, The Counsellor did continue to practise after Limerick, saving his own estate which was protected by the treaty and 700 acres for the O'Connors of Ballinagare, Co. Roscommon. There are many references to his saving the Ballinagare estate, despite the intervention of a Protestant Bill of Discovery filed by one French from Frenchpark. He was supported by Lords Taaffe and Kingsland, but exactly how he did so remains obscure.[151] Ó Gadhra composed an elegy on Mac Donnchadha's death, *Tá Fohla go Brónach* (Fohla is sorrowful).[152] Ó Gadhra lived on, and in a poem, *Staid nua na hÉireann* (Ireland's new condition 1697) he lashed out at fiscal tyranny:

> King's tax, land tax and clerical tax
> a nose tax, an arse tax and a heating tax,
> a poll tax at the end of each gale,
> hearth money and money for repairing roads.[153]

Although Ó Gadhra's catalogue of taxes was written entirely in Irish it continued the execration of English legal terminology used by Mac an Chaoilfhiaclaigh *and an Dúna* almost a century earlier.

Ceangal/Conclusion

Some degree of caution is required in drawing general conclusions from the heterogeneous and relatively small cohort of writers in Irish. The poetry of this period was profoundly influenced by political and legal developments. It is also clear that the common law had deeply penetrated Gaelic consciousness and all these writers show a high degree of awareness of the law, and how it was reflected in the religious and political developments throughout the period. Ó Donnchadha maintained loyalty to the Stuarts despite the provocations of English legal oppression. Twenty year later, Mac Cárthaigh celebrated the Catholic counter-revolution brought about by the accession of James II, a victory made all the sweeter when contrasted with the legal ignominy heaped on Bishops Plunkett and Creagh during the Popish Plot. Throughout this period there is a duality in the response of Catholics to the legal system: a keen awareness of its great dangers, but acceptance of its titular head and the rule of English common law. There were no advocates for a return of the Brehons.

Ó Bruadair towers over all these like a biblical prophet. His early work is not notably political, but even so it demonstrates a visceral distaste for planters and the consequences of plantation. In his later work, the intersection of law and politics becomes more pronounced, particularly after the accession of James II, when he recognised the significance of the catholicisation of the judiciary and the repeal of the Acts of the Restoration land settlement. After James II's eclipse, he cast about for culprits, and did not blame the English, but repeatedly chose to blame Irish troops who had scandalously flouted the law. Even in his last days he never lost his loyalty to the king.

Loyalty to the Stuarts, which had been articulated in Latin by Lynch, in English by French and in Irish by Ó Bruadair, was to be transformed into Jacobitism, whose rhetoric was announced by Ó Rathaille in the aisling, a new literary form which expressed Gaelic hopes for a more enduring Catholic counter-revolution.

Ó Bruadair memorably described how Charles II's loyal followers were bitterly disappointed by the Restoration land settlement:

> Yet when home they returned they got nought of their old demesnes,
> But to gaze at their lands like a dog at a lump of beef.[154]

In 1662–63 a short and limited opportunity arose to recover old demesnes through the Court of Claims. How effective that opportunity was is examined in the next chapter.

Notes

1 *Is barra ar an gcleas an reacht do théacht tar tuinn* (This tops the trick: the law that's come overseas), verse I, *The Poems of Geoffrey O'Donoghue, Dánta Shéafraidh Uí Dhonnchadha an Ghleanna*, ed. and tr. John Minahane (Cork, 2008), p. 23.

2 *Searc na Suadh* (Love of Sages), verse XLVII, John C. Mac Erlean (ed.), *Duanaire Dháibhidh Uí Bhruadair: The Poems of David Ó Bruadair, Part II* (Dublin 1913), p. 283.

3 Raymond Gillespie, *Seventeenth-Century Ireland: Making Ireland Modern* (Dublin, 2006), p. 278.

4 Declan Kiberd, *Irish Classics* (Cambridge, MA, 2000), pp. 34, 33.

5 Ó Cúiv noted that some critics regard Ó Bruadair as the finest Irish poet of all time: Brian Ó Cúiv, 'The Irish language in the early modern period' in *NHI*, vol. 3, p. 542.

6 Michelle O Riordan, '"Political" poems in the mid-seventeenth-century crisis' in Jane H. Ohlmeyer (ed.), *Ireland from Independence to Occupation, 1641–1660* (Cambridge, 1995), p. 112.

7 Cecile O'Rahilly (ed.), *Five Seventeenth-Century Political Poems* (Dublin, 1977), p. vii.

8 O'Rahilly did not specify how she had selected the poems, other than their high political content. She did not suggest that they were in any way representative; in fact, she believed that four of the five poems were the only works of the poets selected: Foreword, *Five Poems*, p. viii.

9 He may have been from Cork; O'Rahilly, *Five Poems*, p. 2.

10 Robert Dunlop, 'Ireland from the plantation of Ulster to the Cromwellian settlement' in *The Cambridge Modern History* (14 vols, Cambridge, 1906), vol. 4, p. 513.

11 Lesa Ní Mhungaile, 'Seán Ó Conaill' in *DIB*, vol. 7, pp. 188–9. Vincent Morley says it was written around 1657: *Ó Chéitinn go Raiftearaí: Mar a cumadh stair*

na hÉireann (Dublin, 2011), p. 63. Darcy also noted its popularity and has suggested a later date – 'late 1670s or early 1680s': Eamon Darcy, 'The social memory of Oliver Cromwell in Ireland' in Martyn Bennet, Ray Gillespie and R. Scott Spurlock (eds), *Cromwell and Ireland New Perspectives* (Liverpool, 2021), p. 242. Morley prepared an edition of the poem for his book (pp. 69–83), from which the line references here are drawn. A translation was first published in 1827 by Michael Clarke: *Ireland's Dirge: An Historical Poem Written in Irish by the Right Rev. John O'Connell, Bishop of Kerry, Translated into English Verse* (Dublin, 1827). Clarke was the pseudonym of James Martin, a hedge schoolmaster from Oldcastle, Co. Meath. The author of the poem was not the bishop of Kerry. Translation of title from Michael Cronin's review of Morley, *Ó Chéitinn* in 'Half the picture', *Dublin Review of Books*, 11 Mar. 2013.

12 Alan Titley, 'The hidden of Irish Ireland; An stair nach n-instear', *American Journal of Irish Studies* 10 (2013), pp. 75–91, at p. 86. O'Rahilly, *Five Poems*, p. 59. Morley, *Ó Chéitinn*, p. 66.

13 Morley, *Ó Chéitinn*, pp. 68 and 102–38. O'Rahilly notes its 'extraordinary popularity', *Five Poems*, p. 50.

14 O'Rahilly, *Five Poems*, pp. 59, 73–4.

15 The war that finished Ireland – O'Rahilly, *Five Poems*, p. 75.

16 The text is primarily in Irish; text in italics is English. O'Rahilly, *Five Poems*, p. 79. Adaptation of Clarke's translation. John O'Connor was half-hanged and then beheaded in Tralee in 1652. Morley, *Ó Chéitinn*, p. 97. 'Transplant' clearly refers to the order to transplant to Connacht and Clare before 1 May 1654, issued to Catholic landowners. 'Transport' refers to a 1655 proposal to send 2,000 Irish children to Jamaica: 'it may be taken as certain that they were not in fact transported', Corish, 'The Cromwellian regime, 1650–60' in *NHI*, vol. 3, p. 363. Mac Erlean quoted 60,000 Irish 'slaves' being sent to America, and vast numbers to the West Indies; these were inflated estimates: Mac Erlean, *Duanaire*, part 1, p. 35, n. 2.

17 See O'Rahilly's notes, *Five Poems*, p. 158. The oaths refer to the 1657 Act for convicting, discovering and repressing of Popish Recusants: C. H. Firth and R. S. Rait (eds), *Acts and Ordinances of the Interregnum, 1642–1660* (3 vols, Abingdon, 1978), vol. 2, pp. 1170–80. '[T]wo parts' is probably a reference to the loss of two-thirds of their estates by the leaders of the Irish army under the 1652 Act of Settlement.

18 Bernadette Cunningham, 'Loss and gain: Attitudes towards the English language in early modern Ireland' in Brian Mac Cuarta (ed.), *Reshaping Ireland, 1550–1700: Colonization and its Consequences; Essays Presented to Nicholas Canny* (Dublin, 2011), p. 181. See Liam Mac Mathúna, 'Growth of Irish (L1)/English (L2) literary code-mixing', in Hildegard L. C. Tristram (ed.), *The Celtic Languages in Contact: Papers from the Workshop within the Framework of the XIII International Congress of Celtic Studies, Bonn, 26–27 July 2007* (Potsdam, 2007) for a detailed consideration of code-switching,

19 'In Stuart Ireland, surrender and regrant continued to be an essential instrument of government.': Mary O'Dowd, 'Gaelic economy and society' in Ciaran Brady

and Raymond Gillespie, *Natives and Newcomers* (Dublin, 1986), p. 132. Lawyers sometimes advised the Gaelic lords in their negotiations with the English administration: O'Dowd, 'Gaelic economy', p. 135.

20 Translation of title from Joep Leerssen, *Mere Irish and Fíor-Ghael* (Cork, 1996), p. 212.

21 Like Mac an Chaoilfhiaclaigh, he may have been from Cork; O'Rahilly, *Five Poems*, p, 84. There does not appear to be a published translation.

22 O'Rahilly, *Five Poems*, p. 88. O Riordan, '"Political" poems', pp. 121–2.

23 Presumably the commissioners who sat at Loughrea and Athlone, under the 1652 Act of Settlement.

24 O'Rahilly, *Five Poems*, p. 90. Translation Mac Mathúna, 'Code-mixing', p. 223. The original text is primarily in Irish; text in italics is either French or English. Mac Mathúna described the 'fierce, rhetorical invective' of these political poems, p. 223.

25 Liam Mac Mathúna, 'Verisimilitude or subversion? Probing the interaction of English and Irish in selected warrants and macaronic verse in the eighteenth century' in James Kelly and Ciarán Mac Murchaidh, *Irish and English: Essays on the Irish Linguistic and Cultural Frontier, 1600–1900* (Dublin, 2012), p. 119.

26 O'Rahilly, *Five Poems*, p. 100.

27 Mac Erlean, *Duanaire,* part 1 (Dublin, 1910), p. xlviii. Part 1 covers the period c.1640 to 1666.

28 All translations of titles and text are from Mac Erlean unless otherwise stated. Michael Hartnett prepared English editions of some of Ó Bruadair's poems: *O Bruadair* (Dublin, 1985).

29 No. V, verses XXI–XXII, p. 35: a reference to the Cromwellian practice of dispersing Irish rebels by allowing them freely to go to Spain.

30 Verses XXIII–XXIV, p. 37.

31 No. XVI, p. 195.

32 Verse XI, p. 203.

33 See n. 1 above.

34 Eoghan Ó Raghallaigh, 'Séafraidh Ó Donnchadha an Ghleanna' in *DIB,* vol. 7, p. 362. They are not named in John Caball, 'The siege of Tralee, 1642', *The Irish Sword: The Journal of the Military History Society of Ireland* 2 (1954–56), pp. 315–17.

35 O'Donoghue, *Poems*, pp. 212 and 226.

36 O'Donoghue, *Poems*, p. 21. Probably c.1670, but Minahane notes other authority for an earlier date, 1658–60, p. 258.

37 Verse 2, p. 21.

38 Verse 3, p. 23.

39 Verse 1, p. 23.

40 Verse 2, p. 23.

41 O'Donoghue, *Poems*, p. 238.

42 In contrast, Eoghan Ó Raghallaigh argued in his *DIB* entry that this poem 'powerfully criticised' the king. Minahane's reading seems closer to the text.

43 Verse 5, p. 25.
44 Mac Erlean, *Duanaire* (Dublin, 1913), part 2 covers the period 1667–82.
45 No. I, p. 3. See Éamonn Ó Ciardha, '"The unkinde deserter" and "the bright duke": Contrasting views of the Dukes of Ormonde in the Irish Royalist tradition' in Toby Barnard and Jane Fenlon (eds), *The Dukes of Ormonde, 1610–1745* (Woodbridge, 2000), pp. 177–93, for a more detailed consideration of contemporary anti-Ormond narratives.
46 Verse IV, p. 5. See Pádraig Lenihan, *The Last Cavalier* (Dublin, 2014), p. 53.
47 No. II, p. 9.
48 Verse IV, p. 11. Mac Erlean cites other examples of Catholic prayers for the monarch during this period at *Duanaire,* pp. 8–9.
49 No. XXV, p. 169, 23 Sept 1678.
50 Verse X, p. 173.
51 No. XXXIV, p. 241. Verse XVII, p. 247. This was in the 1620s.
52 Verse XLII, p. 257. *Créacht do Dháil me* (A faithful wound hath made of me), written c.1652, also mocks the strange names of Cromwellians in verses XXV, XXVI, part 1, p. 37. Similarly, in verse IV of *A Shíle an Tseaca* (O Síle, cold and stately), written in the 1680s: part 3, p. 27.
53 No. XXXV, p. 263. No date is given for this poem, but Mac Erlean includes it in the sequence 1681–82.
54 Verse I, p. 263.
55 No. XXX, p. 219.
56 HMC, *Ormonde MS*, NS. vol. 5, p. 463. See also Ormond to Arran, 18 Dec. 1680, HMC, *Ormonde MS*, NS. vol. 5, p. 533.
57 Thomas Carte, *An History of the Life of James Duke of Ormonde, from his birth in 1610, to his death in 1688* (3 vols, London, 1735–6), vol. 2, p. 516.
58 Lord Brittas, Col. Lacy and Lt. Bradley. HMC, *Ormonde MS*, NS, vol. 5, pp. 476 and 478.
59 HMC, *Ormonde MS*, NS, vol. 5, pp. 533 and 544.
60 HMC, *Ormonde MS*, NS, vol. 5, p. 580. See also J. G. Simms, 'The restoration, 1660–85' in *NHI*, vol. 3, p. 433. A similar verdict was recorded in respect of Oliver Plunkett on the same day, but he was not released.
61 No. XXXVI, p. 265, 16 May 1682.
62 Verse XX, p. 273.
63 Mac Erlean, *Duanaire,* p. xxxviii. Verse XXI, p. 273.
64 Verse XXIII, p. 275.
65 Verse XXII, p. 273.
66 Verse XXXV, p. 279. Verses XXXVI to XL continue in praise of Judge Keating.
67 Mac Erlean says that Dennis gave evidence against Oliver Plunkett in June 1681: *Duanaire,* p. 279, n. 5. This is not supported by, e.g., Alice Curtayne, *The Trial of Oliver Plunkett* (Dublin 1975) which shows Dennis's involvement to be peripheral, pp. 131, 229.
68 Verse XXXIX, p. 279.
69 Verse XLIX, p. 285. Mac Erlean suggests that Murphy was Owen Murphy who had authority from the government to search for witnesses against Plunkett;

Duanaire, n. 1, p. 284. See Curtayne, *Trial*, p. 98. Mortagh Downey was one of these witnesses; n. 2, and was the Murtagh Dowling who gave evidence against Fitzgerald in London in 1680.

70 Carte, *Life of Ormonde*, vol. 2, p. 515.

71 The identity of this John Browne is not clear. There is no reference to this trial in the accounts of the life of Col. John Browne of Westport. Browne went to live at Kinturk in 1678 and is frequently referred to as John Browne of Kinturk in the Westport papers. See, e.g., NLI Westport Papers MS 40,889/12(11), 15(4), 40,884/5(1) and many other references. The coincidence of names and location is remarkable.

72 Ormond to Arran, 17. Nov. 1681, Carte, *Life of Ormonde*, vol. 2, app, pp. 109–10. In this letter he famously described the Plot witnesses 'that went out of Ireland with bad English and worse clothes, are returned well-bred Gentlemen, well caronated, periwigg'd and clothed'.

73 It is not noted in Paul O'Higgins, *A Bibliography of Irish Trials and Other Legal Proceedings* (Abingdon, 1986), nor in T. B. and T. J. Howell, *Collection of State Trials* (33 vols, London, 1809–26).

74 25 Aug. 1682, HMC, *Ormonde MS*, NS. vol. 6, p. 428. In the same letter, Davys gave an account of the execution of Teigene Mart, who declared on the scaffold that all his evidence in relation to the Popish Plot was false and given in order to prevent his being brought to trial for the offence for which he was about to be executed.

75 In 1690 Keating was indicted for treason having served as a judge under James II, which may have precipitated his suicide: see John Cronin and Patrick A. Walsh, 'John Keating' in *DIB*, vol. 5, pp. 45–7.

76 Verse XXVI, p. 275. Verse XLVII, p. 283. This may be the epitome in Irish of the numerous encomiums addressed to Charles II towards the end of his reign, particularly after the failure of the Rye House Plot in 1683; see Gillespie, *Seventeenth-Century Ireland*, p. 270.

77 Brenan to secretary of Propaganda, 1 May 1682, Moran, *Life*, pp. 313–14.

78 Mac Erlean, *Duanaire*, part 3 (Dublin 1917) covers the period 1682–98.

79 Mac Erlean, *Duanaire*, part 1, p. xxxv.

80 No. I, p. 3.

81 In Nov. 1678 a proclamation offered rewards for the discovery of Catholic converts in the army: James Kelly and Mary Ann Lyons (eds), *Proclamations of Ireland 1660–1820* (5 vols, Dublin 2014), vol. 1, p. 401. In Nov. 1680 licences to Catholics to bear arms were revoked and searches and seizure were ordered for unlicensed arms held by Catholics: *Proclamations*, vol. 1, pp. 424–8. In Nov. 1681 and Apr. 1682 proclamations required army officers and JPs to take the sacrament according to the rites of the Church of Ireland: *Proclamations*, vol. 1, pp. 430–1.

82 No. VI, p. 13.

83 Another example is *I n-áit an Mhagaidh* (Instead of mocking), No. XVII, Mac Erlean, *Duanaire*, part 3, p. 117.

84 Verse III, p. 15.

85 Verse VI, p. 15. The laconic marginal comment here is: Yet are excluded from the benefit of his Grace.
86 Verses VII, VII and XI, p. 17.
87 Verse XIX, p. 21. Notoriously, Cromwell's great-grandfather was a brewer.
88 Verses XXI, XXII, p. 21.
89 Verse XXIII, p. 23. Cunningham and Gillespie propose a more benign interpretation of this poem in which they suggest Ó Bruadair optimistically expected the old order to be re-established. See Bernadette Cunningham and Raymond Gillespie, 'Lost worlds: History and religion in the poetry of Dáibhí Ó Bruadair' in Pádraigín Riggs, Dáibhí *Ó Bruadair: His Historical and Literary Context* (London, 2001), p. 38.
90 No. VII, p. 24. See also Mac Erlean, *Duanaire,* part 1, p. xxxviii.
91 Verses VII and VIII, p. 27.
92 The Stuarts were said to be descended from Fergus Mór who founded the Scottish colony of Dal Riada in the sixth century.
93 No. IX, p. 39, 13 Oct. 1686. It is not clear who Lord Mac Cárthaigh was. Mac Erlean suggests either Donagh MacCarthy, the 4th earl of Clancarty or less probably Justin MacCarthy, later Viscount Mountcashel.
94 Verse IX, p. 43.
95 No. XIII, pp. 77, 79: Oct. 1687.
96 Verse V, p. 81, and Verse XII, p. 85.
97 Verse XIV, p. 87.
98 Verse XIX, p. 89. Denis Daly was appointed a Justice of the Common Pleas on 24 Apr. 1686. Sir Stephen Rice became a Baron of the Exchequer on 1 June 1686. Sir Richard Nagle was appointed Attorney General on 15 Feb. 1687. All three were of Old English descent; Daly's mother was a niece of Patrick D'Darcy. Ó Bruadair did not dwell on the likelihood they spoke little or no Irish.
99 Mac Erlean, *Duanaire,* part 1, p. xxxvii.
100 Vincent Morley, 'Diarmaid mac Sheáin Bhuí Mac Cárthaigh' in *DIB*, vol. 5, pp. 780–1. Tadhg Ó Donnchadha edited *Amhráin Dhiarmada mac Seáin Bhuidhe Mac Cárrthaigh* (Dublin, 1916).
101 Translated by Mac Erlean, *Duanaire,* part 3, pp. 95–111; the source of the line-references below. The title of the poem refers to Mac Cárthaigh giving thanks to God because James II had openly attended Mass in Whitehall in 1685, 'surrounded by priests as a bodyguard': Verse I, line 4, p. 95.
102 Verse VI, p. 99.
103 Verse V, p. 97.
104 Verse XI, p. 101.
105 Verse XVI, p. 103.
106 Verse XXII, p. 105. It is not clear what this refers to; possibly a controversy in 1687 involving a butcher from Mallow who was killed accidentally by members of MacCarthy's regiment. See Éamonn Ó Ciardha, 'Donogh MacCarthy' in *DIB,* vol. 5, pp. 796–7.
107 Verses XVII to XIX, p. 103.

108 25 and 29 Aug. 1682, HMC, *Ormonde MS*, NS. Vol. VI, pp. 429, 432–3.
109 Verses XX–XXI, pp. 103–5.
110 Verse XXXVII, p. 111. Mac Erlean omitted to translate 'iona thóin', perhaps for reasons of delicacy. See also Verse X, p. 99.
111 Ó Donnchadha collected seventeen poems. Eighty poems are attributed to Ó Bruadair.
112 Morley, 'Mac Cárthaigh', *DIB,* v, p. 781.
113 See Éamonn Ó Ciardha, *Ireland and the Jacobite Cause, 1685–1766: A Fatal Attachment* (Dublin, 2002), which situates Mac Cárthaigh in the Jacobite period more generally, esp. pp. 78–80.
114 No. XX, p. 127. Verse XVII, p. 135.
115 Verse XXXI, p. 139.
116 Vincent Morley, 'Seamus "Dall" Mac Cuarta' in *DIB,* vol. 5, pp. 889–90.
117 From a translation by Vincent Morley in *The Popular Mind in Eighteenth-Century Ireland* (Cork, 2017), p. 27. At p. 15 Morley calls the poem *'Tuireamh Shomhairle Mhic Dónaill* (Sorley MacDonnell's elegy).
118 No. XXIV, p. 161.
119 Verse V, p. 163. Mac Erlean noted that the English parliament violated the treaty three weeks after it was signed: n. 2.
120 No. XXV, p. 165.
121 In Mar. 1689, a proclamation commanded Catholics not to disturb Protestants 'under pain of our displeasure': 25 Mar. 1689, *Proclamations*, vol. 2, p. 86. James Nihell issued the first proclamation by a Court Martial General indicating that martial law would deal with any outrages caused by officers and soldiers; 14 Aug. 1689, *Proclamations*, vol. 2, p. 117.
122 Verses XXVII and XXVIII, p. 175.
123 Verses XXIX and XXX, p. 177.
124 The missing clause of the Treaty had many causes, but irregular behaviour by Jacobite troops does not seem to be amongst them. See J. G. Simms, *The Williamite Confiscation of Ireland* (London, 1956), ch. 5. The failure to legally implement the articles lay well into the future; the bill to ratify the articles was not passed until Oct. 1697.
125 Verse XXXVI, p. 179.
126 N. J. A. Williams, *Pairlement Chloinne Tomáis* (Dublin, 1981). *Párliament na mBan* bears some comparison with *Pairlement Chloinne Tomáis* since it too parodies parliamentary debate and the enactment of law. It is a didactic text written by a Catholic priest, Domhnall Ó Colmáin (c.1645–c.1704): Brian Ó Cuív (ed.), *Párliament na mBan* (Dublin, 1970). Apart from showing how far the tropes of parliamentary procedure and the passing of 'legislation' had penetrated popular consciousness, there is little in the work that reveals Catholic attitudes to law in this period. Micheál Mac Craith cited Breandán Ó Buachalla's argument that 'the anodyne prose work *Parliament na mBan* is best understood as a Jacobite text': Mícheál Mac Craith '*Aisling ghéar: Na Stíobhartaigh agus an t-aos léinn 1603–1788* by Breandán Ó Buachalla' *Eighteenth-Century Ireland / Iris an Dá Chultúr* 13 (1998), pp. 166–71, at p. 166. *Aisling Ghéar*, pp. 222–8.

127 'History of the late war in Ireland', first published in J. T. Gilbert, *History of the Irish Confederation and the War in Ireland 1641–9* (7 vols, Dublin, 1882–91).

128 Raymond Gillespie, 'The social thought of Richard Bellings' in Micheál Ó Siochrú (ed.), *Kingdoms in Crisis: Ireland in the 1640s* (Dublin, 2001), pp. 212–28.

129 Gillespie, 'Bellings', p. 221.

130 *Pairlement Chloinne Tomáis*, p. 116, lines 1961–2.

131 Bellings and O'Bruadair shared a similarly low opinion of the Cromwellian under-class: Gillespie, *Seventeenth-Century Ireland*, p. 230. Ó Bruadair's sentiments can also be heard in Charles O'Kelly's *Macariae Excidium* which described the 'revels, gaming and other debauches' of the army which contributed to Ireland's downfall: Éamonn Ó Ciardha, 'Charles O'Kelly' in *DIB*, vol. 7, p. 595. See also Darcy, 'Social memory', p. 239.

132 Verse XLI, Hartnett, *O Bruadair*, p. 41.

133 No. XXVI, p. 181, Oct. 1692.

134 Verse VI, p. 183. Ó Ciardha argues that Ó Bruadair did not understand that raparee activity was a manifestation of popular Jacobite sentiment: Ó Ciardha, *Ireland and the Jacobite Cause*, p. 93.

135 Verse VIII, p. 185.

136 No. XXXIII, p. 221.

137 The translations of the poems and their titles are taken from Patrick S. Dinneen and Tadhg O'Donoghue (eds), *Dánta Aodháign Uí Rathaille, The Poems of Egan O'Rahilly* (London, 1911), unless otherwise stated.

138 Dinneen and O'Donoghue, *Dánta*, p. xiv.

139 Breandán Ó Buachalla, *Dánta Aodhagáin Uí Rathaille: Reassessments* (London, 2004), pp. 45–7.

140 Ó Buachalla, *Reassessments*, p. 33.

141 Dinneen and O'Donoghue, *Dánta*, p. 57, lines 93–6.

142 Dinneen and O'Donoghue, *Dánta*, p. 227, lines 205–8.

143 Dinneen and O'Donoghue, *Dánta*, p. 167, lines 3–4.

144 *Marbhna Sheagháin Bhrúin* (Elegy on John Brown), Dinneen and O'Donoghue, *Dánta Aodháign,* p. 57, lines 85–8.

145 His poetry was collected by Fr Mac Domhnaill in *Dánta is Amhráin Sheáin Uí Ghadhra* (Dublin, 1955). See Diarmuid Breathnach and Máire Ní Mhurchú, 'Seán Ó Gadhra', at https://www.ainm.ie/Bio.aspx?ID=1442, accessed 20 July 2023. There is no *DIB* entry.

146 Mac Domhnaill, *Dánta*, p. 29. Translation of title and text by Deirdre Nic Chárthaigh, TCD. 'Cléirigh na coróna'; possibly in Chancery or King's Bench. O'Carolan also commemorated his death. Mac Domhnaill, *Dánta,* p. 79.

147 Mac Domhnaill, *Dánta,* p. 32.

148 Petitions of 3 and 11 Dec. 1694; Eoin Kinsella, *Catholic Survival in Protestant Ireland, 1660–1711* (Woodbridge, 2018), p. 272.

149 See Patrick A. Walsh and Éamonn Ó Ciardha, 'Terence MacDonagh' in *DIB*, vol. 5, pp. 923–5, and http://www.ainm.ie/Bio.aspx?ID=1356, accessed 22 July 2023.

150 Seán Ó Gadhra, File – XX, RIA Corpas Stairiúil na Gaeilge 1600–1926, accessed 20 July 2023.
151 See Walsh and Ó Ciardha, 'Terence MacDonagh', and J. C. MacDonagh, 'Counsellor Terence MacDonagh: A great Catholic lawyer', *Studies* 36 (1947), pp. 306–18, at pp. 308 and 314.
152 Mac Domhnaill, *Dánta,* p. 38.
153 Vincent Morley's translation from *The Popular Mind,* p. 63.
154 *Suim Purgadóra Bhfear nÉireann* (Summary of the Purgatory of the Men of Ireland, 1641–84). Mac Erlean, *Duanaire,* part 3, verse VII, p. 17.

4

Using the law: Catholics and the Court of Claims

Sirs, if you judge this man innocent, we must believe the English cut one another's throats and that there was no Irish rebellion or rebels.[1]

Are they to judge all Irish nocent? And none innocent?[2]

The next complaint is of the shortness of time the commissioners had. For they began in February 1662 and ended in July 1663. In that time 800 were declared innocent; and 8000 more claimed, but were unheard for want of time; and no further time could be allowed, because it tended to the prejudice of the members. This article hath many mistake.[3]

Whatever misgivings Catholics may have had in relation to the court system, landowners were left with little choice but to litigate in order to protect or vindicate their rights. Toby Barnard has argued that, given the centrality of the law to government and landownership, how it actually functioned is a key issue for this period, and the destruction of the records of court proceedings in 1922 was particularly damaging.[4] Nevertheless, there are alternatives to those records, and the Court of Claims of 1662–63, which was the most important site of Catholic litigation in the period between 1660 and 1690, is well documented. The short-lived first court made some of the most important decisions favouring Catholics litigants in this period, and is the primary focus of this chapter.[5]

The first section examines the constitution and operation of the court, and in particular the impartiality of its members. The particular circumstances attending Catholic participation in the court are then considered. The following three sections consider individual cases; each narrative has been assembled from the records of the court, state papers and other manuscript and calendared sources. A number of smaller cases are examined in detail. But many of the claims were much more substantial; a dozen cases involved estates of more than 10,000 acres; many of these are examined in some detail in the next section. The focus of this chapter is largely on Catholic litigants, but for some landowners in this period confessional affiliation could be fluid, responding to the political climate; the Powers of Curraghmore are a case in point. Finally some of the factors involved in securing a decree and the expense incurred are examined. The surviving records are statistically examined to identify the principal characteristics of the claimants.

The formation and operation of the first Court of Claims

The Gracious Declaration of November 1660 represented a political compromise by the recently restored Charles II, anxious to secure the Stuart monarchy by satisfying the interests of the greatest number of his Irish subjects, both Protestant and Catholic. The Cromwellian land settlement was essentially preserved, thus satisfying the most urgent claims of the Protestant interest. On the other hand the king sought to cultivate Catholic interests and the Declaration provided that 'innocent papist' landowners who could prove their loyalty and who had been dispossessed merely for being papists, would be restored by 1 May 1661, regardless of whether they had taken up their rights under the Cromwellian settlement in Connacht and Clare. A proclamation required them to submit claims within a month.[6]

Thirty-six commissioners were appointed to administer the Declaration, but they did not proceed because, after a challenge by Patrick Darcy, a judicial opinion stated that it would be unsafe to act until the Declaration had been given the force of law through legislation. There followed a period of intense lobbying as both sides attempted to influence the shape of what all understood to be the most important Irish legislation in Charles II's early reign. Protestants argued that any concessions to Catholics would be a betrayal of their evident guilt for the 1641 rising and an accommodation to popery. Catholics were a threat to government security and false rumours of another 1641 were circulated.[7] Catholics protested their unswerving loyalty to the Stuarts and the injustice of the penalty imposed on their community by the killers of the king's father. Behind these arguments lurked the unspoken threat of violent reaction by either side. In all of this the priority of the king and his advisers was to ensure the stability of the recently restored monarchy.

A parliament was called and the Act of Settlement passed in July 1662 gave legal effect to the Declaration. The outcome was another compromise reflecting the intensive lobbying by interested parties, but clearly favouring the Protestant interest. The government's fear of a dissident Protestant rising was too great to allow a substantial restoration of Catholics.[8] The seven commissioners appointed to implement the Act were all English Protestants, none of them judges and none seems to have had any previous connection with Ireland or an interest in Irish land.[9] They assumed office on 20 September 1662 and constituted the Court of Claims. A series of proclamations began to give effect to the legislation and dates were set for the submission of claims.[10] A proclamation in early October 1662 set out how claims were to be submitted and appointed a panel of lawyers who had the sole right to act on behalf of claimants and defendants.[11] Rules governing the conduct of the court were published later in October.[12]

The commissioners began hearing claims in January 1663, but in February Henry Coventry was recalled to London.[13] Because majority verdicts were required, this was more than an inconvenience for the commissioners, and the consequences throw some light on the operation of the court. Churchill complained to secretary of state Bennet in March 1663: 'We have frequently been three to three in our discussions; and unless Mr. Coventry comes back or Sir Richard Rainsford is given a casting vote (which is now much desired) we are likely often to be so in causes of great weight. At present almost every case is dismissed, "and the parties, though never so innocent, without any visible remedy."'[14] This must be considered an exaggeration. In the preceding month, only four cases seem to have been dismissed.[15] This equal division reflected a perceived preference of loyalty among the members of the court: 'McRainsford, O'Beverly and McChurchill' were considered 'friends of Teig' and thought to favour the Catholic interest.[16] The Jesuit provincial superior Andrew Sall particularly praised Rainsford for his impartiality in July 1664. Sall reported to his superiors that, when it was pointed out to the judge that several of the successful litigants were Catholic priests or Jesuits, he replied that the character of the litigants was irrelevant, and what mattered was 'the justice and the integrity of the case'.[17] Sir Allen Brodrick (whose personal Irish interests were reflected in two cases before the court) replaced Coventry in May.[18] The commissioners operated under the detailed instructions set out in the Act of Settlement, which required a quorum of five. The scant evidence shows that the normal *modus operandi* of the court required *all* commissioners to be involved in giving judgment and Coventry's absence could theoretically have caused a stalemate. But the commission appointing Brodrick shows that three commissioners were sufficient to form a quorum. One was to be from a group consisting of Dering, Brodrick, Cooke or Churchill, another from Rainsford, Beverly or Smith, and the third from either group.[19] The even distribution of the 'friends of Teig' among the two groups may have protected the Catholic interest.

Bottigheimer argued: 'Much depended on the temper of the court, for the exercise of anything like strictly impartial justice was as unlikely in 1663 as 1653. The administration of impartial law is of course impossible when the very foundations of society are in question, as they were in Ireland in the 1660s.'[20] Andrew Sall commented on the perjured evidence adduced in the court, particularly by the Protestant interest.[21] Nevertheless the evidence suggests that the operations of court seem to have been conducted with remarkable fairness.[22] In the first month, 84 per cent of the decrees were of innocence, which caused uproar among Protestant landowners. Early in 1663, Ormond wrote to Bennet that the court was deciding two to one in favour of innocents, and 'If the lottery would hold out so to the end of their commission it would prove no ill one for the Irish.'[23]

In early February, James Allen's successful claim was highly controversial.[24] Ormond wrote to the king that the early decisions of the court were making the English uneasy; he was concerned about the loyalty of the army which was 'in a very ill state', and would not be capable of dealing with any disturbance.[25] The actions of the court generated significant opposition in the Irish House of Commons, and on 5 February the House instituted a committee to prepare suggested rules and directions to be observed by the court, which resulted in Speaker Sir Audley Mervyn's ill-considered address to Ormond on 13 February. The king deeply resented the threat to his newly established authority, and together with Ormond rejected any attempt to impose new rules of evidence. At the end of February the king assured the commissioners of his support, in the light of the 'threats and disrespects' directed against them.[26] Even Chancellor Clarendon, no friend of Ireland's Catholics, supported the decisions of the court on the grounds that there should be no exercise of arbitrary power by the king: the rule of law ought to prevail and Charles's credentials thereby confirmed.

In March Lord Kingston noted that, while the court was carrying out its role 'honestly and uprightly', the 'expectation[s] of the English and Irish are raised up by the theory but disappointed in practice'. In a memorable turn of phrase he wondered whether the administration was 'but skinning a sore which may afterwards break out when we are unable to cure it'.[27] In May he raised further alarms with Bennet.[28] Matters were not helped by the provocative actions of recently restored but overkeen Catholics who abruptly dispossessed the incumbents, denying them the opportunity to find alternative accommodation or harvest their corn. Edward Vernon, a royalist officer who had been granted the manor of Clontarf, wrote to the under-secretary of state Joseph Williamson in May: 'I believe the old proprietors here being generally imprudent in those cases; for they have almost exasperated the whole English nation against them.'[29]

The court sat for little more than seven months until 21 August, and its short duration was controversial. The Act of Settlement provided that the court should last for 12 months from its first sitting. The commissioners took up office on the 20 September 1662, so in principle the court could have operated until 19 September 1663. But opponents of the court argued that the Act did not specify calendar months, that the common law definition of a lunar month of 28 days must be applied, and so the earlier termination date of 21 August was settled. They argued further that the Instructions in the Act of Settlement specified that no claims of innocence could be heard after 1 August 1662, and that the 1662 Act for the Enlargement of Periods of Time stipulated that no period could be extended for more than 12 (lunar) months from the date originally stipulated in the Act of Settlement, which would have brought the court to an end on 2 July.[30] In late June Lye wrote to Williamson noting that the commissioners had a short time left; some were saying to the end of July only. The commissioners decided to do the best they could and 'therefore they have added seven hundred more claims to their list, which is all they can determine in that time. If more time be not given by an Act of Parliament, Ireland will be at a loss.'[31] Initially, Ormond argued that he should be given the power to grant additional decrees and effectively extend the life of the court. In March 1663, even Orrery argued that all cases should be heard: 'God forbid that any innocent should be precluded for want of time to hear him. If any Englishman, were he my brother or my son, desired one foot of an Irishman's land that should be found innocent, I wish he might be buried in it.'[32] But the decisions of the court in favour of Catholics quickly changed Protestant sentiment and in June Ormond and the Irish Privy Council wrote to the secretary of state: 'We think the limitation of the period for restoring innocents should be strictly observed. If this is not done, the people will be in a perpetual state of uncertainty about their estates.'[33] All proposals to extend the life of the court were rejected by the English Privy Council, after overwhelming pressure from the Irish Protestant interest that urged this was the only way to contain the Catholic interest, and forestall a Protestant revolt.[34] Similarly, the English Privy Council rejected Ormond's proposal that he and six Irish Privy Councillors be given discretionary authority to provide certificates of innocence to persons of whose constant loyalty they had sufficient knowledge.[35] After the scare of Blood's Plot, the king could not risk provoking further disturbance and threaten the security of the throne. Nevertheless, right up to the last moment, he characteristically intervened on behalf of Catholic families who for a variety of reasons had not been capable of getting their papers in order.[36]

After the court had finished its formal proceedings, a great deal of consequential matters remained. Lord Masserene and others had attempted to prevent the execution of any judgments of the court given after 2 July on the grounds that its time period had elapsed. The court stopped for a few days but then resumed. Lye wrote to Williamson that he 'will hear more of the matter yet, for the Commissioners are loyal and honest men'.[37] Disagreements about the validity of decrees between 2 July and 21 August were not settled until the Act of Explanation in 1665.[38] Estimates of the number of cases which had not been heard vary; Richard Talbot, the advocate for the Catholic interest, thought it might be eight thousand, Russell and

Prendergast estimated seven thousand, but even the English Attorney General put the number at around five thousand.[39] Whatever the exact number, the unheard cases were a source of Catholic rancour for generations.

The most important remaining record of the court is the manuscript in the Armagh Public Library that provides details of the arguments and evidence in many of the cases, including descriptions of the lands in dispute and the history of family ownership. There are more than 900 cases in this record, but detailed judgments are recorded for about 100 only. The manuscript has been meticulously edited by Geraldine Tallon and published by the Irish Manuscripts Commission, with an introduction by J. G. Simms. This publication also includes copies of notes made by Sir Edward Dering, one of the commissioners.[40] Clearly the Armagh MS is not complete, in that it lacks the judgments in the majority of cases. It also lacks the earliest sittings of the court, from 13 to 27 January, and the rush of cases on the last day of hearings, 21 August.[41] Egerton MS 789 in the British Library is a record of the decrees of the court for the entire period of the court sittings, and gives details of the judgments, the fact that the claimant was Protestant whenever relevant, and the extent of the land in dispute. The manuscript was published in 1887 and complements the Armagh MS; it is referred to here as the Abstract.[42] Finally, mention should also be made of the thousands of petitions made to Ormond between 1662 and 1664. Many of these related to *custodiams* of estates, that is, temporary grants from the Crown, after the passing of the Act of Settlement or decrees in the Court of Claims. A record of the petitions, and Ormond's decisions, was maintained in a register calendared by John Gilbert.[43]

Catholics and the Court

For Catholics, a decree of innocence enabled immediate recovery of estates, without the Cromwellian holders being first given compensating land as a reprisal. In this respect it was superior to being a nominee under the Act of Settlement who had to wait until reprisal land had been found for displaced Cromwellians before obtaining possession. It is therefore not surprising to find that 23 of the 38 nominees pursued cases in the court, and the vast majority of these were successful and a decree of innocence obtained.[44]

In principle, the criteria for innocence were such that it was difficult for any adult Catholic male living during the period of the Confederation to qualify. The Clerk of the Crown of the King's Bench provided evidence of outlawry proceedings arising from the 1641 rebellion.[45] Evidence relating to participation in the Confederation was recorded in the Black Books held in the Discrimination Office.[46] Not every act of participation denoted guilt;

Thomas Coppinger voted to elect a member of the Confederate Association between the peace of 1646 and 1648; the Lord Lieutenant and council ruled this was not a bar to innocence.[47] The expectation was that not more than a half-dozen owners would prove innocent. But this was to ignore the burden of proof. Orrery complained to Clarendon that 'the commissioners were divided on the point that the English must prove the guilt of the Irish'.[48] A second important factor facilitated recoveries, to which Russell and Prendergast drew attention. This was the critical difference between the 1662 Act and 1652 Acts of Settlement. The latter was directed not only at the forfeiting proprietor, but also his wife, children, remaindermen and next heirs; all lost their rights.[49] In contrast, in 1663 more than 500 Catholics secured decrees; 'principally widows who claimed their jointures, remainder men their estates and younger children their portions'.[50] Neil Johnston argues that this was unintentional and that the terms of reference under which the commissioners operated were poorly drafted. But experience of the point had been established in England since the 1650s, the legislation was highly detailed, took months to draft and had the input of experienced lawyers and law-makers.[51]

The total number of decrees was 829; 566 were innocent papists, 141 innocent Protestants and 'at least 130' were *nocent*.[52] Catholics recovered approximately 930,000 acres, either as freeholds, or as remainders, life interests or incumbrances.

Smaller estates

The case of Richard Brice, a Protestant, is explored because, although most of the decrees of the court were lost in 1922, a full transcript of his decree has been recorded.[53] The three claims relating to Edmund Meara (c.1614–81), a Catholic, are useful examples of the evidence adduced and the process followed by the court.[54] Brice's decree shows the limitations and unreliability of some of the evidence but the Meara case shows how the remaining records can be combined to provide useful insights into the processes of the court. Both of these cases are of particular interest in that the economic circumstances of the claimants were relatively modest.

Richard Brice

Richard Brice inherited an estate from his father John in 1650. John had been mayor of Dublin, and the transcript of the decree from the court shows that he owned ten parcels of land, varying in size from 1 to 60 acres throughout Dublin and Co. Meath. He also owned five houses in the Liberties of Dublin, two gardens in Kilmainham and a tavern at the corner of Cornmarket and High Street. He had interests in lands in Wicklow, Louth and Monaghan on foot of mortgages, and 'several other mortgages, leases and recognizances'. He 'enjoyed the same until he was expulsed by the late usurped powers'.

The Brices, father and son, were devoted royalists. John Brice provided over £2,800 in supplies to Ormond in 1641. In 1644 he was a captain of 'trained bands' in Dublin and loaned over £2,000 to Ormond. When Ormond was camped at Rathmines, he kept him advised of the activities of Michael Jones, the governor of Dublin. For his loyalty to Ormond, the Cromwellians sequestered his property and he was imprisoned until he died in 1650.[55] His son Richard was a member of the 1634 and 1639 parliaments, representing Drogheda.[56] Not long after the king's restoration, in December 1660, he petitioned the king to have the family lands restored.[57] Lord Chancellor Eustace supported the petition and ten days later an order to restore Brice was made in London.[58] This petition and order fell into the lacuna between the Declaration and the Act of Settlement, for in 1662 Richard sought a decree from the Court of Claims, one of the earliest heard by the court. It is not recorded in the Armagh MS nor in Dering's notes. But the Abstract records that on foot of a hearing on 13 January 1663, Richard Price (sic) an innocent papist, received a decree for 249 acres of lands in Meath and Dublin.[59] Apart from the error in his name, several points of detail arise. First, contrary to the Abstract, the full transcript of the decree states that Richard was an innocent *Protestant*, and his father an innocent *papist*. Second, the Abstract records the decree was in respect of 249 acres; this is difficult to reconcile with the acreage stated in the claim submitted to the court. Third, one of the properties which Richard had claimed was excluded from the decree; presumably Richard was not able to show John's good title, and so was 'left to take such due remedy for recovery thereof either in law or equity as he shall think fitting'.[60] All the other lands included in the decree were 'put out of charge of the Court of Exchequer' and the sheriffs of the various counties were ordered to give possession forthwith to Richard.

The transcript is an example of the full text of a decree, but it also illustrates how the designation of confessional identity in the Abstract may not always be reliable. It also paints a picture of the widespread landholdings of merchants in the 1640s, and their extensive commercial transactions. Although the transcript is silent on the point, the fluid confessional identity of a Dublin family, originally Catholic, is clear even if the reasons for the change of religion are not. Finally, the decree of the court was not the last of the Brices' dealings with confiscated property; John Brice, son and heir of Richard, made a claim in respect of the houses in James's St. and Thomas St. with the Chichester House Trustees in 1700.[61]

Edmund Meara

Meara (c.1614–c.1681) was a medical doctor, the son of another doctor, Dermot (fl. 1610–46). Dermot claimed to be educated in Oxford, wrote the first medical textbook to be published in Ireland and poetry in honour of the Butler family.[62] He was indicted and outlawed in 1642 because he 'associated with and was constant with the rebels'.[63] Edmund was educated in Oxford and Rheims, and also wrote about medical matters.[64] In November 1660 he petitioned the king for restoration of his estate in Wicklow, explaining that he was the royalist Clanricarde's physician during the rebellion, and that his lands had not been allocated to soldiers or adventurers.[65] Clanricarde's widow confirmed his service and his loyalty, and the petition was endorsed by Lord Chancellor Eustace. The king ordered the lords justices to restore Meara to the land to which he could show good title and which was not in the possession of soldiers or adventurers; any other land was to be dealt with according to the rules of the Declaration.[66] But this seems to have had no practical effect and therefore Meara submitted a succession of claims to the court.

The first, in January 1663, one of the earliest recorded, was dismissed on the grounds that Meara had not made out good title to the lands but a special order from the king allowed the claim to be reheard in May.[67] Dering's notes cast some light on the nature of the evidence adduced in relation to Meara's behaviour during the rebellion.[68] They showed that he lived in Dublin, and initially attended Clanricarde in February 1641; that he was in Limerick in October and then returned to Dublin. He returned to Clanricarde at Portumna 'the first summer of the war' and was physician to the family until the war ended, 'and after till Kilcolgan'.[69] The O'Mearas had very strong connections with Tipperary but Edmund's claim related to 1,456 profitable acres in Wicklow.[70] The Armagh MS does not show how the claim was disposed of, but the Abstract shows that, on 6 June 1663, Edmund was awarded a decree of innocence in respect of 1,456 profitable acres in Wicklow.[71] Arnold states that Meara was the only Old Irish Catholic landlord to recover his estates in Wicklow, and speculates that this was due to Clanricarde's influence, but since Clanricarde died in 1658 this seems unlikely.[72] In fact there must be some doubt as to the efficacy of the award because, in 1664, 'Thomas Meara, and Dr. Dermot Meara his father' were included in a list of dispossessed landowners who had not been restored.[73]

Dering's notes also cast some light on how Meara struggled to manage his estate in Wicklow during the rebellion.[74] We know from his 1660 petition that the land had not been allocated to soldiers or adventurers. Evidence given at the court showed that Meara's tenants kept the land stocked but did not pay him rent and that, in December 1642, Meara got an order from the Council in Kilkenny against two named individuals that they should allow Meara to 'enjoy quietly his estate'. In the Court of Claims, this evidence was *Contra querentent*, that is, against Meara's interest, presumably on the grounds that it showed Meara actively participating in the Confederate's legal processes. On the other hand, the evidence showed that Redmond O'Byrne took over the estate for 18 months after the rebellion began. O'Byrne may have been the son, or a descendant, of Fiach MacHugh O'Byrne. Meara had a small part of his Wicklow estate at Ballinacor which was the ancestral home of the O'Byrnes, where Fiach was born.[75] Soldiers (presumably O'Byrne's) 'perpetually burdened and oppressed' Meara's tenants who sent a delegation to Kilkenny. They secured an order 'but never had any fruit or benefit of it'. In the Court of Claims, this evidence was *Pro querente*, presumably on the grounds that it did not show any participation in Kilkenny by Meara himself, as distinct from his tenants, but showed that he owned the property and let it to tenants.

The third claim related to Edmund's sister Cicely.[76] When Christopher Russell married Cicely some time before August 1641, the marriage settlement provided that her father Dermot would pay £500 to the groom's father. The Armagh MS does not show the outcome of the claim but the Abstract shows that claim was determined in favour of the *son* of the groom, who was decreed innocent, and awarded his remainder of 485 acres.[77]

The Mearas were prominent physicians, and this may have helped them obtain the petition to the king in 1660, and again in 1663 to secure a rehearing of their claim. The estate was modest, but the evidence adduced at the court casts light on how difficult it was to defend property interests during the rebellion.

Larger estates

According to the Abstract, the largest decrees awarded to innocent Catholics were:

Earl of Carlingford	87,954 + 15,664 by a proviso in the Act of Settlement
Sir Valentine Browne	51,521
Thomas Browne	19,603
James Coppinger	18,100

Earl of Fingal	17,334
Lord Gallmoy	16,865
Nicholas White	16,666
George Fitzgerald	14,141
Lord Slane	13,666
Lord Barnewall	11,472
James Allen	11,146
Lord Antrim	10,625

The cases relating to Carlingford, Fingal and Antrim have been explored fully elsewhere.[78] This section examines the other nine recoveries and the facts and circumstances show a wide variety of practice. The youngest plaintiff was 25 years of age and claimed the largest estate; the eldest was 71 and claimed 11,472 acres. Some of the largest recoveries were in Munster, but the majority in Leinster.

James Allen

James Allen's recovery was not the largest, but it was one of the earliest and generated considerable controversy. In October 1661 the Allen estate, St Wolstan's in Co. Kildare had been granted to the Protestant earl of Mount Alexander on the basis that James's uncle and cousin had been attainted, and the king directed that a special provision should be included in the Act of Settlement to effect Mount Alexander's grant.[79] Clearly James had been alerted to what was happening, and barely a month later he petitioned the king, correcting the record and pointing out that his title did not derive from his attainted uncle or cousin, but from his father. His father had died long before the war and James himself was 'of tender age' in 1641; neither could be considered guilty of any crime and so their interest should not have been forfeit.[80] James noted that he had earlier filed a claim in court, but before it could be heard Mount Alexander had pre-emptively obtained the October grant.[81] James secured an order that, should he prove his innocence with the commissioners, he would be restored. In March 1662, he improved his hold over the estate when he secured a further order directing that he should be restored to the tenancy of the estate, insofar as it was not in the possession of persons who were entitled to be reprised.[82] Mount Alexander was as tenacious as he was influential; provision was actually made in the Act of Settlement that he was to have the estate if it was found to be forfeit and in April the king ordered that he should be given reprisals of equal value if he failed to secure it.[83] But Mount Alexander also suffered setbacks; in January 1663 the October 1661 grant was stopped 'until further order'.[84] More ominously for Mount Alexander, Richard Talbot and Charles Berkeley had bought an interest in the estate. As always, Talbot's motive was material gain, and political leverage (see further below).[85] Berkeley's motives are not entirely clear, and Lenihan notes he claimed his intentions were altruistic; otherwise 'the poor Irish would be destroyed by the number and malice of those that sought their ruin'.[86] Arnold and Lenihan have explored the complex battle between them and Mount Alexander.[87]

When the case finally came to court, the facts were hotly disputed and at least some of the evidence seems to have been fabricated. In a letter, Mount Alexander recited the extensive and detailed evidence showing that Allen was a rebel, and claimed he was certain of success: '100 to 1 was offered on my side'.[88] Mount Alexander's evidence is not recorded in the Armagh MS and to his enormous surprise, he lost.[89] He quoted his counsel's speech to the court that 'if you judge this man innocent, we must believe the English cut one another's throats and that there was no Irish rebellion or rebels'.[90] According to the Abstract, James Allen was declared innocent on 3 February 1663 and received a decree in respect of more than 11,000 acres in Meath, Dublin, Kildare and Wicklow.[91]

The decision caused consternation in Dublin and a few days later Ormond wrote to Lord Chancellor Clarendon: 'judgment has been given in favour of one Allen; the English now conclude themselves utterly lost. ... The Parliament is so inflamed that they have cast out the Explanatory Bill without commitment.'[92] There were further political consequences when the Irish House of Commons suggested that the court should follow revised rules and Mervyn led a delegation to Ormond. Arnold suggests that this was merely in response to a change of rules by the court in relation to the scheduling of cases.[93] In fact the Allen case had precipitated a demand for a more restrictive interpretation of 'innocence' and greater latitude in relation to the admission of evidence. Mervyn declaimed that 'the alarm that Hannibal is at the Gates is hot throughout the Protestant plantations' but Ormond was not persuaded, and his immediate reaction was to dissolve parliament, or at least suspend it until the court closed.[94] On 28 February, the king wrote to Ormond, noting that the commissioners had been threatened 'merely for doing their duty', and he wanted Ormond to let the Commons know 'we can be as just as kind, and punish the insolent as well as cherish the penitent'.[95] Clarendon wrote to Mervyn that he had never seen the king so offended because of the intervention of the Commons in the working of the court. The court carried on with its work, and the Commons retreated.[96]

The verdict in favour of Allen has been attributed to a number of factors, not all of them benign. It may have been of some importance that the case was based on the claim by Allen's Aunt Mary for her jointure, and she was clearly innocent.[97] Talbot's role is less clear, but there are suggestions that he procured secretary of state Bennet to use his influence with the court, in consideration of Talbot assisting Bennet to obtain the Clonmalier estate for his own benefit.[98] The suggestion of a 'private direction' from the king is not supported by any evidence, and Ormond's reference to this in his letter to Clarendon seems to be the gossip of Dublin Protestants, shocked at the outcome of the case.[99] The court had decided in Allen's favour and Ormond seemed convinced of his innocence. Several months later he reminded his correspondent of the English membership of the court and asked rhetorically 'Are they to judge all Irish nocent? And none innocent?'[100]

Mount Alexander died in 1663; Arnold suggests that the shock of losing the estate may have hastened his death. Provision was made for his widow and children later that year.[101] In 1665, Mount Alexander's heir unsuccessfully attempted to have the case reopened, on the grounds of Talbot's fraudulent involvement.[102] The matter was effectively settled in the Act of Explanation which recorded Allen's success in the court, the appeal to the king by the heir, Talbot's part-ownership and his successful defence to the heir's appeal. Mount Alexander's heir was to have reprisals of two-thirds of the acreage of the estate.[103] Talbot had to wait until 1671 to have the patent for his quit rents granted; by then James Allen was dead.[104] Talbot and Berkeley's involvement ensured that the stakes were high in the Allen case. On the opposing side, Mount Alexander believed that his evidence would prevail. But because this was one of the earliest cases and the Allens were wealthy, it was inevitable that the judgment of the Court would be closely scrutinised for signs of leniency or rigour.

Sir Valentine Browne

Browne, the third baronet (1638–94), inherited the estate when his father died in 1640. As Browne was only 2 years of age, he became a ward of court, and the estate was in the possession of the earl of Ormond when 'the usurpers' took it. The king ordered Ormond's restoration to the Browne estates on 29 January 1661.[105] In July 1661, Lord Shannon complained to the lords justices that he had bought the land from two officers to whom it had been awarded for arrears in respect of their services in Ireland.[106] Shannon argued that, although Browne was named as restorable under the Declaration, this could only be effected after the officers had been reprised. Shannon based his claim on the rights he derived from the officers, and he sought to be reprised in their stead.[107]

In the context of these disputes, it is clear that Browne needed a decree of innocence to secure his estate without prior reprisal to the occupants, and his claim details the extensive lands held by the Brownes in Kerry and

Cork. It also lists lands mortgaged to Browne, and lands not in his actual possession.[108] The claim shows that Browne had a decree for land in Connacht, but he does not seem to have taken it up – he would have been about 14 years old at the time.[109] Although the matter is not detailed, it is clear that his minority would have ensured a decree of innocence and the award of 51,521 acres was the second biggest successful claim by a Catholic.[110]

Browne endorsed a separate claim by his uncle Thomas, because he claimed to be entitled to the reversion to his uncle's estate.[111] Thomas was the second son of the first baronet, by his second wife. The claim set out that the first baronet made a settlement probably in 1629 of certain land, separate from those in Sir Valentine's claim, in which he reserved a life interest, the remainder to his son Thomas. The first baronet died in 1632 when Thomas was only 3 years old. In 1644, aged 15, Thomas went to France to be educated and returned in 1648 to fight the Cromwellians on behalf of the king. In January 1661, he applied to the king for an order to be restored to his estate, and in April the sheriff of Cork gave him possession. But his right was disputed by the earl of Anglesey, who claimed he had bought the estate in November 1660 from Major George Walters who was then in possession. Accordingly, Thomas petitioned the king again, on the basis that his title was incontestable, whereas Anglesey's was derived from Walters, who merely had a grant from Henry Cromwell.[112] The outcome is not noted, but in May 1663 Thomas claimed extensive estates in Kerry and Cork amounting to approximately 53 ploughlands. Anglesey's claim was not mentioned. There was some slight evidence connecting him to the Confederation, but his minority and foreign education during the rebellion must have ensured he would be treated as an innocent, and his decree awarded him almost 20,000 acres in Kerry and Cork.

The third baronet's claim included two ploughlands in Tomies, near Beaufort in Co. Kerry, which were not in his possession. A report of June 1707 from the commissioners of the Revenue to the lords justices concerning land at Tomies relates that two ploughlands, returned by the Down Survey to contain 2,865 acres, were restored to Browne by the commissioners for Executing the Act of Settlement as an innocent papist. The quit rent was reserved at £60. The estate was settled on Browne's son Nicholas in 1684, at the time of his marriage, but it was forfeit due to his participation in the Jacobite rebellion. The Act of Resumption vested the Tomies lands in the trustees and a life interest was sold to John Asgill who was charged with the quit rent.[113] But the trustees allowed a claim by Nicholas's son Valentine, a child at the time of the rebellion, and thus his remainder was saved from confiscation.

Taken together the Brownes recovered more than 70,000 acres in Kerry and Cork from the Court of Claims and again at the end of the century. In all three cases, the minority of the claimant was the foundation for the case and the ultimate retention of the estate over five generations.

James Coppinger

The Abstract records that on 27 March 1663, Coppinger was found an innocent papist and given a decree for 18,100 acres in Cork.[114] The Armagh MS shows that his father Dominic held land in Cork in 1641 and died in 1642. Dominic left two-thirds of his estate to his son James, and one-third to his wife Mary in lieu of her dower. James and Mary held these lands until 1654 and both were claimants before the court.[115] They were 'always active and instrumental' in supporting the king and did not take land in Connacht and Clare. Being innocent, they were 'restored according to proof'.[116] Dering's notes provide a little more information, confirming that of the 38 owners named in the Declaration, Coppinger, together with the Lord of Strabane and Sir Valentine Browne, were 'restored upon innocence'.[117]

The fact that provision was made for Coppinger in the Declaration, and his decree for 18,000 acres, points to a figure of greater substance than the rather short description of his estate in the claim. The TCD Down Survey shows extensive holdings in over 50 townlands, mostly in West Cork. More information on the Coppinger estate is provided by the family history compiled by Walter Coppinger in 1884, largely from original documents.[118] James seems to have had long experience in protecting the family interests. During the Protectorate, it appears he made a plea to Oliver Cromwell who wrote to his son Henry in 1655 that Coppinger should be exempted from transplantation.[119] From this plea it seems that James's mother was Protestant and his father supported the English parliament and supplied the army. There are further entries in the same series, which are undated but presumably later.[120] From these somewhat cryptic entries it would appear that James sought protection from forfeiture on the basis of his father's loyalty to the English during the 1640s, and his mother and wife being Protestants. But this seems to have been of no avail, since the decree showed that they had been 'expelled by the Usurped Power in 1654'. Cromwell's 1655 letter does not appear to have saved James from confiscation, but it may have saved him from being forced to go to Connacht; there is no record of his transplantation.[121]

Shortly after his restoration, the king ordered that the 'Ancient Natives and Inhabitants of the City of Cork' were to be restored to their lands and ancient corporate privileges.[122] Coppinger made no great progress, and six months later the 'Ancient Inhabitant' sought confirmation of the earlier order. On 11 March 1661, the king confirmed his earlier order, and told the new inhabitants to appoint someone to represent their interests before the lords justices, to show cause why the order should not be executed in full. It was a mark of James Coppinger's status that he was appointed the king's agent in the matter, and the lords justices were to report through Coppinger how they had acted as a result of the king's order.[123] Clearly Coppinger's dealings with Cromwell and support for the parliamentary forces did not cause any long-term damage to his reputation in royalist circles. Coppinger tried to recover the estate under the Declaration and on 25 May 1661 he complained that the sheriffs of Cork refused to restore him.[124]

In the absence of any progress, Coppinger applied to the Court of Claims. Walter Coppinger had a copy of the 1663 decree, which he summarised.[125] The Coppingers were to be restored to all their property, which amounted to 27,338 acres English measure,[126] except the lands and houses in the City and Liberties of Cork,[127] and for these they were to be reprised in the Baronies of Barrymore and Muskerry.[128] The soldiers and adventurers displaced by the decree were also to receive reprisals, which did not give them any cause for comfort.[129] And thus Coppinger was restored, notwithstanding the plight of the displaced soldiers and adventurers.

James Coppinger made a detailed will in 1665 which sets out his very considerable property holdings.[130] There is a reference to part of his lands which came to him originally from his grandfather, but through the estate of an uncle who had died without male heirs. James's will provided that in the event he died without a male heir (as turned out to be the case), those lands were to go to his brother, but only after his brother had paid the costs of recovering that part of the estate from the Court of Claims.

The Coppinger case shows how a wealthy Catholic merchant, whose mother and wife were Protestant, could engage with the Cromwellian regime. But it must have been his wealth and social position that secured his proviso as a nominee in the Declaration, and appointment as the king's agent. Ultimately, the family did not involve themselves in the rebellion and this paved the way for their restoration.

Lord Galmoy

In November 1661, Edward Butler, Lord Galmoy, petitioned the king for the restoration of his estate on the grounds that his grandfather and father had served the king faithfully. He claimed to be restored to the entail of his grandfather's estate,[131] having been turned out of it 'by the oppression of the late power … though he was an infant and living in France during the rebellion. He had a small pittance set forth to him in Connacht of no great value.'[132] The petition was endorsed by Lord Chancellor Eustace, but like so many others, it seems to have been ineffective, and Galmoy had to approach the Court of Claims. According to the Abstract Lord and Lady

Galmoy were decreed innocent papists on 13 July 1663 in respect of 16,865 acres in Carlow, Kilkenny and Wexford.[133] The Armagh MS details the descent of the estate from Edward's grandfather.[134] Lord Galmoy claimed as an innocent, and reinforced his claim by noting that he was due to be restored without any further proof, because of special provision in the Act of Settlement, being a 'person in a special manner meriting his majesty's grace and favour'.

The relatively easy passage of his claim may have been facilitated by Galmoy's age at the time of the rebellion and the support of his relative, the duke of Ormond.[135] The Connacht lands, of which Butler spoke so disparagingly, were originally part of the estate of Thomas, Viscount Dillon, and were of sufficient value that in August 1663 Galmoy was forced to surrender them having received his decree of innocence. Frances, Viscountess Dillon, petitioned Ormond on behalf of her husband, who was named both in the Declaration and the Act of Settlement so that a *custodiam* of the lands be given to Dillon, and that no *custodiam* be granted to any other party, until Dillon was fully restored.[136]

Nicholas White

White (before 1620–64) was the great grandson of Sir Nicholas White, politician and Elizabeth I's Master of the Rolls, who was granted the Castle and St Catherine's Priory at Leixlip in 1569.[137] He was the eldest son of Sir Nicholas White, who died in 1654 and from whom he inherited a considerable estate, much of which had been confiscated.[138] After the Restoration, Nicholas set about restoring the family fortune and estates. He may have been aware of the intense political activity by Catholic and Protestant interests in relation to the land settlement, and made a pre-emptive claim in relation to his own case. In October 1660, he petitioned the king that his affairs be referred to the commissioners appointed by the Protestant General Convention in Dublin. Whether this was an act of sublime self-confidence or desperation it is difficult to tell; the commissioners were not in favour of Catholic restorations. To support the petition, Ormond and Eustace reported that both Nicholas and his father had always been loyal, and 'There is nothing against the petitioner "except that he is a recusant" which by no law can extend to the forfeiting of his estate'.[139] There seems to have been no further action taken. This is hardly surprising; White was not to know that the question of the restoration of the estates of innocent Catholics would be part of the King's Gracious Declaration a month later. In November 1660, he again petitioned the king, this time in relation to judgments given against him and his late father in favour of Sir Gerald Lowther, which the king referred to the Court of Chancery.[140] Arnold argues that Ormond 'sought the restoration, as far as practicable, of the old proprietary order as represented by the Old English Catholic gentry' and provided a certificate of recommendation for White, citing the honourable activities of his father in the royalist cause.[141] Perhaps he held this in reserve when the next day he submitted one of the earliest claims to the court.[142]

The Abstract shows that on 27 February 1663 White was declared an innocent papist and awarded a decree for 16,666 acres in counties Kildare, Dublin, Kilkenny, Offaly and Tipperary.[143] The Armagh MS shows the plentiful evidence concerning White's father but strangely, considering he was of age at the time of the rebellion, none against the son; both were declared innocent. There is some evidence that White may have even helped the royalists; he may have been the Nicholas White who made a deposition that Captain (John) Allen, together with an armed group attempted to take Leixlip in 1641.[144] In another claim it was reported that Nicholas White swore that Christopher Sherlocke had promised £500 to support the rebels.[145] Although this cooperation with the authorities is not cited in the evidence concerning his own case, Nicholas White's status as a royalist sympathiser must have been evident.

In some cases the commissioners allowed defendants time to contest the order of the court, and they did not give possession to White immediately. After declaring White innocent, the court allotted 'three weeks' time … to show cause why he should not be restored'.[146] Notwithstanding the short delay, White must have established possession in March 1663, but subsequently met with resistance from the incumbent, Sir Theophilus Jones, whose soldiers turned him out.[147] White applied to the court in October 1663, but it refrained from acting further, on the basis that it had done all it was required to do, and merely reiterated its order to the sheriff to put White in possession.[148] Jones must have conceded, because in July 1664, when resisting his eviction from Patrick Sarsfield's estate in Lucan, White's restoration was one of the grounds for his case.[149] White may have regained possession, but did not enjoy his estate for very long; he died in 1664 and was succeeded by his brother Charles, who sold part of the estate to Sir William Davis in 1666.[150] He seems to have been of the same mettle as his brother; in March 1669 he successfully petitioned the king for a special grant of his lands 'to protect him against any right or interest we [i.e. the king] may have in the same by virtue of the Act of Settlement and Explanation'.[151] The petition was endorsed by Williamson to the effect that it had come from the earl of Carlingford, an indication of the network of patronage on which the Whites were dependent. Later that year he successfully petitioned for the quit rents on the estate to be reduced to their pre-1641 level, and the arrears remitted.[152]

It is possible that the provision of information by White to the authorities in relation to the activities of the rebels and his influential friends in Court were in his favour in securing a decree, but the absence of any evidence to connect him with the rebellion seems to have been decisive.

George Fitzgerald

The Abstract shows that Fitzgerald was declared innocent in June 1663.[153] He was the son of Sir Luke Fitzgerald of Fegheroghan (*recte* Tircroghan), Co. Meath, who made a marriage settlement in 1636 with provision for his wife, reserving a life interest for himself and the remainder to his son. His father sat on the Supreme Council at Kilkenny in 1642 and was forced to surrender Tircroghan to English parliamentary forces in 1650.[154] In May 1656 Luke was awarded 1,506 acres in Galway – a fraction of the estate he had held in Meath.[155] His date of death is not recorded but seems to have been prior to 1660.[156] In August 1659, George was included in a list of suspects to be rounded up for disturbing 'the public peace of this Commonwealth'.[157] He was mentioned in the Declaration of November 1660.[158] As a result of a petition, the king ordered restoration of the parts of his estate that were not occupied by adventurers or soldiers in November 1660.[159] In December 1660, Thomas Gifford petitioned the king for the Tircroghan estate, on the grounds that Charles I had granted it to his family, in compensation for Sir Luke burning Gifford's father's house.[160] This seems to have had little impact on Charles II, who had more pressing claims to deal with, and having been mentioned in the Declaration, Fitzgerald clearly had considerable influence with the king.

The Armagh MS details the claim, which included numerous mortgages and leaseholds, and the Black Anchor public house in Dublin.[161] Because he was among the 38 nominees in the Declaration who were to be restored without any proof, he claimed the right to immediate restoration. He also relied on his youth and his being educated out of the country at the time of the rebellion. Although his father was declared *nocent*, George was restored to his remainder of 14,141 acres in Offaly, Meath, Kildare, Westmeath and the city of Dublin. The Fitzgeralds owed their recovery to Sir Luke's 1636 settlement and Ormond's influence with the king.

Lord Slane

The Abstract records that on 30 April 1663 Randall Fleming, baron of Slane, was restored to 13,665 acres in Co. Meath.[162] Like so many others, his path to restoration was not straightforward. In early 1661 the king had ordered his restoration on the strength of the service of his elder brother Charles in the French army, Charles's offer to bring his regiment 'away in the king's [i.e., Charles II] interest' and his service with Ormond in Ireland.[163] The king ordered the lords justices to treat him 'as his loyalty and good service deserve'.[164] But Fleming's path to restoration could have been blocked when he was involved in a potentially serious legal case in November 1662. He complained that he had never seen a decree of outlawry against him, and he sought a copy from the King's Bench, in order to have it set aside under a writ of error. A procedural, but extremely serious, point was at issue; whether a writ of error could be used to reverse a decree of outlawry for treason.[165] Lord Chancellor Eustace (considered sympathetic to the Catholic cause) wrote: 'If such a writ does not lie in this case, thousands of innocents will be destroyed upon this very point, and if it do, many soldiers and adventurers will lose their lands, which in my opinion is the least evil.'[166] The outcome of the case does not appear to be recorded, but it is seems likely the outlawry decree was reversed, which allowed Randall to apply to the Court of Claims for a decree of innocence.

The Armagh MS recorded details of his claim.[167] Randall was the second son of William Fleming, who had settled a jointure on his wife in 1638. William and Randall's elder brother Charles were dead, and Randall claimed the entire estate, subject to his mother's jointure. Evidence was given that William was indicted and outlawed, but Randall was declared innocent. Randall also claimed the Galway estate of his uncle James, 'murdered by the tyrant Oliver Cromwell at Drogheda'. The record showed that James had also been indicted and outlawed, but Randall claimed his uncle's estates 'by articles'.[168] An unusual aspect of the Flemings' case was the claim by Randall's son to entitlement to the entail of the estate, which was confirmed in July 1663.[169] Further, Randall's mother successfully claimed not only the life interest in the Slane lands the subject of her jointure from William, but also claimed a similar jointure from her previous marriage to Christopher Nugent, Lord Delvin.[170] It is not clear in the Armagh MS why Randall was adjudged innocent. His date of birth is not recorded and he died in 1676; it is possible he was of full age in 1641. There seems to have been no evidence produced linking him with the rebellion, despite his father's active role as a Confederate.

Lord Barnewall

Nicholas Barnewall inherited substantial property in Dublin from his father, Sir Patrick Barnewall, in 1623, and extended his holdings in the 1620s and 1630s. In addition he held over 2,000 acres in Roscommon before 1641.[171] He seems to have carefully adhered to the royalist cause and never sided with the 1641 rebels. During the Commonwealth, he was to refine his allegiance from royalist to 'English'. In 1654 he petitioned Cromwell against transplantation; he explained that, although a Catholic, he had always been loyal to the English interest. He had gone to Wales with his family shortly after the outbreak of the rebellion, and when he returned he 'served the English interest in every way he could'. He cited his great age and quoted appropriately from scripture in support of his claim to continue in his estate.[172] The petition seems to have moved very slowly; in April 1656 Barnewall sought copies of any documents that might have incriminated him, and in July a report on his case purported to show varied aspects of Barnewall's engagement with the royalist cause and was referred to the Treasury for their opinion.[173] While all this was going on, Barnewall seems to have retained ownership of his estate. In 1655 he renewed the lease of the manor of Kilmainham Beg in Co. Meath, and some additional towns, for 99 years to the notorious Jerome Alexander, agent for the adventurers.[174] He seems to have maintained good relations with the Protectorate and in 1657 secured a proviso in the Act of Attainder to the effect that, if he showed his 'constant good affection to the Interest of the Parliament of Ireland' then he would not be attainted by the Act, and neither would his estate be forfeit.[175] But all this effort seems to have been in vain, for a petition to the king in October 1660 for restoration of his estate showed that his lands had been taken over 'by the late usurper'.[176] In his favour was the fact that the lands had not been allocated on a permanent basis; instead they were leased out from year to year. A report on his case by Lord Chancellor Eustace and others confirmed his adherence to the English and Protestant cause and recommended his restoration to the part of his estate not in the hands of soldiers. This seems to have come to nothing for he was obliged to have his case heard in the court on 16 January 1663, and was awarded a decree for 11,474 acres in Meath, Dublin, Roscommon and Longford as an innocent papist.[177] His claim was too early to be included in the Armagh MS and there is no reference to him in Dering's notes.

Barnewall was a careful lawyer who assiduously sought to maintain a low-profile royalist, and later loyalist, stance. He seems to have been as confident petitioning the Protector in 1654 as the king in 1660. All the while, he conducted business with Jerome Alexander, a lawyer as difficult as he was avaricious. Yet even Barnewall had lost his estates and had to rely on the Court of Claims. Notwithstanding all that had happened, the records show that his holding was remarkably little disturbed between 1641 and 1670.[178]

Protestants and the Court – The Powers of Curraghmore: Catholic and Protestant

Under the 1652 Act for the Settlement of Ireland, royalist Protestants who had participated in, or been an accessory to, the rebellion were as exposed as Catholics to confiscation and transplantation. But an Ordinance of September 1654 allowed them to compound for their estates by paying a fine of twice the annual value of the land (which for the most part they never managed, or were required, to pay). Nevertheless there were Protestant claimants in the court. Approximately 20 per cent of the decrees were in favour of Protestants which accounted for 19 per cent of the total land dealt with by the court. The reasons for Protestant claims were various; to recover land that had actually been confiscated, or to secure a debt on Catholic land or the title to land that had been bought from Catholics. Clearly the outcome of these cases could have a direct bearing on any Catholic occupants. Arnold argues that, in some cases, the decree was taken out as a form of insurance.[179] In contrast to Catholics, there were no Protestant decrees in respect of remainders, and Protestants received proportionately fewer decrees involving life interests. Occasionally the court was the forum for disputes between Protestants, the most notorious of which was between Sir Audley Mervyn and primate Bramhall. Bramhall was intent on recovering church lands but suffered a fatal stroke while attending the court on 23 June 1663.[180] Less fatal was the case concerning the attempt by Bishop Griffith Williams of Ossory to recover lands belonging to his diocese in the early 1660s from Captain Thomas Evans.[181]

It is salutary to examine the surnames of the Innocent *Protestants* in the Abstract. Among them are many Old English and Gaelic names (Barnwall, Dillon, Dowdall, Fitzgerald, Devereux; Byrne, Farrell, O'Neill, Donovan, Murphy). Without the evidence from the court records, it would be all too easy to assume that these were Catholic claimants. We have seen from the Brice case that religious affiliation could be very fluid, and the Powers of Curraghmore provides one of the most striking examples.

The Armagh MS records a claim by the earl of Anglesey, on behalf of a person whose surname was Power, on 4 July 1663.[182] No further details are provided. The Abstract records a decree in favour of Arthur, earl of Anglesey, Guardian of Lord Power, on the same day for 4,711 profitable acres in Waterford.[183] Presumably adequate title could not be shown to a further 2,967 acres that were 'dismissed to law'. The Abstract states that the earl of Anglesey was an innocent Protestant and Power an innocent papist. This requires some comment in the light of the Powers' tangled family history and the 6th baron's subsequent career. Richard Power's father John, the 5th baron, was a Catholic who became of unsound mind around the time of Richard's birth in 1629. His mother, a Protestant, died of shock when rebels invested Curraghmore in 1641. The Powers were ostensibly Catholic, but his grandmother, a devout Protestant, was responsible for Richard's upbringing. Furthermore he married a Protestant, Dorothy Annesley, the daughter of the future earl of Anglesey in 1654. Because John was of unsound mind and Richard a child at the time of the rebellion, the estate was protected from confiscation.[184] Nevertheless the Powers took out a decree in 1663.[185]

Secondly, the legal role of the earl of Anglesey should be noted. Richard was 33 or 34 in 1663, and it seems highly unlikely that Anglesey was *his* guardian. John was still alive, but incapable of managing his affairs and would have needed a legal guardian. John had been incapable since the 1630s, and Anglesey only became involved with the family in the mid-1650s, when Dorothy married Richard. All this suggests that Anglesey was appointed John's guardian sometime after 1654 and acted on his behalf at the court. The prestige of one of the most powerful Protestant figures in the country could not have done any harm to the claim. It would seem that John was the innocent papist of the decree recorded in the Abstract.

This complicated process in relation to the parties had an unintended consequence. Because the plaintiff was identified as an innocent papist, and not a Protestant, the quit rents on the estate, some £120 p.a., were not struck out of charge by the Court of Exchequer. Richard petitioned the king and council in late 1670 that he was the true plaintiff in the Court of Claims, and being a good Protestant (unlike his insane father), should not be burdened with the quit rents. The order from the king related that Richard was the plaintiff and had claimed under his father's name through Anglesey as guardian.[186] The king ordered that the rents be remitted because Richard had been adjudged an innocent Protestant. The king also noted that his 'ancestors from their first planting ... for above 400 years have entirely preserved their faith and loyalty to the Crown of England'. In this context, 'faith and loyalty' must refer to political rather than religious allegiance, and these credentials, the fiction that Richard was the true plaintiff and Anglesey's influence must have secured the success of the petition.

After the Restoration, Richard was pardoned in April 1661.[187] The next phase of his career suggests he passed as a Protestant. He was governor of Waterford in 1661, which he represented in the Commons until his father died in 1666, when he took the family seat in the Lords.[188] There is evidence from 1666 that Richard was 'upon making his house English'.[189] In 1667, he was appointed Privy Councillor.[190] He was colonel of a regiment of Irish soldiers recruited to fight in the Anglo Dutch wars in 1672. He forced his 8 years old son John to submit to be married by the archbishop of Canterbury in 1673. Yet he fell victim to the Popish Plot and spent over four years in prison in Dublin and London. Following the accession of James II, he professed to be Catholic, accepted various public roles and a pension, and sat in the Lords in James II's short parliament. He fought at the Boyne and the sieges of Cork and Waterford. At the latter his son John, now 25, changed sides, claimed he had been 'extreamly Opprest by his father On account of his Religion' and had always been a Protestant, and obtained a certificate to that effect from William.[191]

Julian Walton noted that Richard 'appears to have taken his religious loyalties as lightly as his political ones'.[192] Brought up a Catholic, he married the daughter of a staunch Protestant in 1654. After the Restoration he presented himself as Protestant: in 1670 he claimed to be the Protestant plaintiff in the Court of Claims. He fell victim to the Popish Plot and his imprisonment should have qualified him for preferment as a Catholic during James II's reign. His Catholic credentials were enhanced at the Boyne, and the sieges of Waterford and Cork. He died in the Tower of London in 1690 and, ironically, was buried in Annesley's Protestant vault. The final irony was that his son John's Protestant opportunism saved the estate from Williamite confiscation.

Analysis

Given the limited number of cases examined in detail, there is a risk they are not representative of the universal experience. But they represent approximately 20 per cent of the total land restored to Catholics and it is clear that some conclusions can be drawn from them.[193] All of these cases were litigated in the Court of Claims, but their histories show that a wide variety of other factors, other than pure legal considerations, was involved in securing a successful outcome. Some owners had recourse to extra-legal means to secure estates before and in some cases after the decree. Power, Coppinger and Barnewall appealed to the Cromwellian regime to avoid seizure of their estates at the very earliest stage. In 1660, some such as Browne and Coppinger took the law into their own hands and took possession on the strength of the Declaration of November 1660. Even before there was an opportunity to go to court, owners sought recovery through petitions. The king's intervention was sought in many cases, and even modest families such as the Mearas and Brices, presumably through their agents, had access to the royal court.[194] Nicholas White petitioned the king so that 'his affairs may be referred to the Commissioners now waiting on His majesty', notwithstanding that Mountrath and Orrery were unlikely to look favourably on a Catholic.[195] What is most notable is that, although successful petitions may have resulted in an order from the king directing recovery, in all cases these were ineffective and recourse to the court was required. Even when court proceedings had started, petitions to the king were sought for readmission or late admission of claims.

It is interesting to explore some of the reasons why a decree of innocence was obtained. Clearly age was a factor in some cases. Of the larger cases, the average age of the claimants in 1663 was around 45, but there were significant variations between the youngest, Browne (25) and oldest Barnewall (71). Browne could clearly claim his minority at the time of the rebellion, and Galmoy, Allen, FitzGerald and Power could all claim they were too young to have participated. Non-alignment with the Catholic rebels was clearly important and Barnewall adhered to the royalist cause and never sided with the 1641 insurgents. The Coppingers claimed loyalty to the king, while giving information about rebel activities to the authorities may have influenced the court in White's case. It is more difficult to explain Randall Fleming's decree; he was simply declared innocent, without any cause being shown.

The exact legal arrangements whereby the family estates were held were certainly a factor in other cases. Russell and Prendergast claimed that those who secured decrees were 'principally widows who claimed their jointures, remainder men who claimed their estates in remainder and younger children their portions'.[196] Lords Galmoy and Slane and George Fitzgerald were able to claim interests in estates that would have otherwise been confiscated due to the activities of their fathers as Confederates.[197] White did inherit a life interest, but neither he nor his father were guilty of anything other than being Catholic.[198] But many others did not derive their interests through trusts. James Allen seems to have inherited a full interest from his uncle. Barnewall, Brice, Browne, Coppinger, Meara and Power inherited directly from their fathers. This gives the lie to Russell and Prendergast's assertion, and it is clear that many significant claimants were able to establish their innocence. This is corroborated by a statistical analysis of the records in the Abstract, which shows that 65 per cent of the Catholic recoveries were in fee, that is, not remainders or life interests (and incidentally, this is not greatly different from the 76 per cent of Protestant recoveries that were freeholds). Only 7 per cent of Catholic recoveries were remaindermen and 8 per cent life interests. The remaining 20 per cent were either incumbrances (12 per cent) or sent to law (8 per cent).[199]

In his PhD thesis, Joseph Byrne argued for the distinctiveness of the experience of the elite Old English Catholics of Fingal.[200] They were a cohesive group, united by religion, family ties, a strong sense of duty and deep loyalty to the English Crown. In the 1650s, various strategies had been used to avoid or at least defer transplantation – claiming to be Protestant, flooding the administration with petitions, delaying or simply refusing to transplant. The legal strategies they adopted to protect their estates bore considerable fruit in their remarkable success in the Court of Claims. This survival was not a function of the size of the estates involved; in other words economic power had not preserved them. In contrast to the general experience discussed above, this was in large part due to their tenurial profile. The most important asset of an innocent Fingal claimant was valid title to an estate that derived in tail from a grantor who had no role in the 1641 rebellion. Out of over 100 claims, only 17 of the Fingal claims were found nocent and nine of these were effectively voided since the successor in title gained a decree. '[H]ad the court continued after August 1663 to churn out decrees at that rate to claimants elsewhere in the country, the settlement would have been dead in the water.'[201] In 1641, Fingal Catholics owned 66 per cent of surface area, when the national average was 61 per cent. In 1688, they owned 32.7 per cent when the national average was 22 per cent. Putting it another way, the Fingal Catholics had lost about half of their estates, whereas across the island as whole the decline was two-thirds. 'The wonder is not that so many lost, but rather that so many managed to survive.'[202]

The number of female claimants in the court is striking, and may go some way to explain Russell and Prendergast's remark. An analysis of the 820 cases recorded in the abstract shows that more than 30 per cent involved women as litigants.[203] Of these, 16 per cent were claimants in their own right, and another 15 per cent through family relationship, usually as wife of a claimant, but also as daughter, sister or mother. The majority of claimants in their own right were widows. In some cases it is clear that the woman owned the estate and her husband was joined as a claimant merely in his role as spouse. In other cases the nature of the woman's relationship to the estate is not clear. Of the claimants in their own right 92 per cent were Catholic, as were 80 per cent of the women who were joint claimants. There were prominent Protestant women claimants such as the duchess of Ormonde or the marchioness of Antrim, but there were also three 'nunns'.[204]

The cost of litigation was a considerable burden, not least because the preceding 20 years had caused enormous financial loss to landowners, through disruption of economic life, loss of rents on confiscated estates, the costs associated with military service and exile. As early as 1655, the Whites petitioned Cromwell for permission to sell part of their lands to meet the debts that had accumulated 'in consequence of the late disturbances'.[205] A modest family such as the Brices must have been put to considerable expense and presumably legal fees to submit a petition in December 1660.[206] Even a relatively straightforward case in the court itself, such as the Flemings of Slane, involved Randall's appeal against his decree of outlawry and three separate claims by members of the family. In February 1663, when Richard Talbot and Garret Moore petitioned the king for an extension of time to file claims, one of the grounds was the time required to raise funds to support the claims.[207] When the court was sitting, and subsequently, Ormond dealt with hundreds, if not thousands, of petitions in relation to the land settlement.[208] Some of these related directly to the court process, such as seeking approval for an extension of time to submit a claim.[209] Others dealt with the issue of costs – in July 1663, 'Several Lords and gentlemen' petitioned Ormond for relief from quit rents; they had already sought his support to be relieved of the heavy costs of having their estates restored.[210] Thomas Dillon, Viscount Costelloe and Gallen in Co. Mayo petitioned Ormond for a deferral of the quit rents on his recently restored estate, until consideration was given to a petition to the king to remit the ground rents entirely.[211] A large number of petitions were requests for *custodiams* of land or financial assistance, while the legal process was ongoing.[212] After decrees had been awarded, there were claims for *custodiams* by one Catholic against another, as in Lady Dillon on Lord Galmoy, or by Protestants on Catholic estates, such as Sir Francis Hamilton on Valentine Browne.

Richard Talbot's role in securing the interests of individual Catholics in the land settlement cannot be overestimated. He acted as a land agent for particular clients when the Act of Settlement was being drafted, and he took an active role as an intermediary or broker between parties while the court was in session. It was alleged he was paid £1,000 by Randall Fleming to ensure a favourable decree.[213] His active participation in the Allen case was widely acknowledged and Lenihan has described his involvement in many others.[214] His Old English background may have made him less inclined to take up the cases of Gaelic Irish owners; it is notable that the O's and Macs he disdained are not among the major owners restored.[215] Talbot may have been the most eminent, but there were many others whom Lenihan refers to as the 'swarm of agents and brokers [who] emerged to peddle their influence to regain estates'.[216] The earl of St Albans, Sir William Domville the Attorney General and Sir Maurice Berkeley were among the many Protestants who used their influence and connections to ensure Catholic claimants received favourable outcomes.[217] For the Protestant interest, in February 1663 Sir William Petty had to answer to the House of Commons that he had suborned witnesses; in the event he was exonerated in April.[218]

Finally, even when a claimant successfully obtained a decree, this was only the first step in the long march to full recovery. Securing possession was a challenge, and the support of officials such as the county sheriffs to enforce the decree was not always forthcoming.[219] Almost all the above who took out decrees seem to have recovered their estates.[220] This was not the universal experience. Arnold analysed the outcome in Dublin and noted that of six substantial landowners, three partially recovered, and three others did not recover at all. Those who partially recovered, Sir Richard Barnewall, John Talbot of Malahide and Lord Netterville, had submitted claims to the court. Sir Luke Bath, Sir Luke Dillon and the earl of Westmeath did not recover; of these only Westmeath had submitted a claim. A claim may not have been successful in every case, but it was almost indispensable for restoration, especially for those unable to recover by other means.

Conclusion

Approximately 930,000 acres were restored to Catholic claimants.[221] This represented 17.5 per cent of the total land confiscated under Cromwell, perhaps 5.3 million acres.[222] The estimates of unheard cases ranges from 5,000 to 8,000. If the lower number is taken, and the percentage of *nocents* (13 per cent) applied, this represents approximately 4,350 potential further successful claims. The average award from the court was 1,620 acres, but this is distorted by awards to the largest claimants. Although the court had established rules for the ordering of hearings, they were soon abandoned and it is more than likely that most powerful, biggest owners used their influence to ensure their cases would be heard. Therefore it is impossible to know what the next tier of claimants might have generated in terms of restoration, but it is tempting to speculate and may illuminate the depth of Protestant desperation to have the court shut down as quickly as possible.[223] If the average award is reduced by 70 per cent, potentially a further 2 million acres might have been restored to Catholics.[224] The lid on this Pandora's box had to be replaced firmly and permanently. In the febrile atmosphere of late 1663, there was no possibility that the English administration would risk extending the life of the court or allowing a discretionary power to Ormond to provide more decrees of innocence. A clear link had been established between the land settlement and the risk of Protestant plotting, and had provoked 'the greatest [crisis] faced by the monarchy in the early years of Charles's reign'.[225] Catholics could never be allowed to revive the Court of Claims. Any favour to selected Catholics was to be shown by nomination in the Act of Explanation, rather than by trial in court where there would always be at least one dissatisfied party who could foment mischief. Of course in Catholic Ireland there was more than one dissatisfied party, and there was enormous frustration. The court might have been perceived as impartial, applying the law in an even-handed manner. But Catholic regard for the law was poisoned by the manner in which the court was unfairly terminated by an administration fearful to threats to monarchical authority and cowed by the threat of Protestant violence. The outcome of all these legal struggles can be told in the numbers. Catholics owned about 60 per cent of the land of Ireland in 1641; by 1675 they owned less than a quarter.

Notes

1 7 Feb. 1663, Hugh Montgomery, 1st earl of Mount Alexander to an unidentified female recipient, *CSPI, 1663–65*, p. 19.

2 2 June 1663, Ormond to the bishop of Cork, Bodleian, Carte MS 49 fo. 198.

3 'The Report of Sir Heneage Finch' in Thomas Carte, *An History of the Life of James Duke of Ormonde, from his Birth in 1610, to his Death in 1688* (3 vols, London, 1735–6), appendix XCI, p. 75. Bodleian, Carte MS 147, fos. 33–4.

4 Toby Barnard, 'Conclusion' in Coleman A. Dennehy (ed.), *Restoration Ireland* (Aldershot, 2008), pp. 187–8.

5 It can be argued that the 1662–3 Court was not the 'first'. See Colum Kenny, 'Not every judge a phoenix: King's Inns under Cromwell' in Coleman Dennehy (ed.), *Law and Revolution in Seventeenth-Century Ireland* (Dublin, 2020), pp. 112–13.

6 1 Apr. 1661, James Kelly and Mary Ann Lyons (eds), *Proclamations of Ireland 1660–1820* (5 vols, Dublin 2014), vol. 1, pp. 28–9.

7 A proclamation was issued on 1 June referring to 'the natives of [Ireland] deeply guilty of that rebellion, who have of late broken out into new acts of force and violence': *Proclamations*, vol. 1, p. 5.

8 These fears were not merely rhetorical as Capt. Blood's Plot demonstrated in early 1663. Catholics had far more to lose by any rebellion.

9 J. G. Simms, 'Introduction', p. x, in Geraldine Tallon (ed.), *Court of Claims, Submissions and Evidence 1663* (Dublin, 2006), hereafter Tallon. Sir Alan Brodrick, who replaced Coventry in May 1663, owned almost 11,000 acres in Ireland in Jan. 1663. See John Gibney, 'Sir Alan Brodrick' in *DIB*, vol. 1, p. 849. Churchill sought a property worth £400 or £500 p.a. for himself from the king; 'I think I shall be able to reserve it out of the jaws of the Act of Settlement.' Churchill to secretary of state Bennet, 24 May 1663, *CSPI 1663–65*, p. 104.

10 23 Sept. 1662, *Proclamations*, vol. 1, p. 96. 17 Oct. 1662, pp. 100–1, 18 Mar. and 27 May 1663, pp. 109–10 and 116–21.

11 2 Oct. 1662, *Proclamations*, vol. 1, pp. 96–99. It appears that all were Protestant, and only three of them were members of King's Inns. See T. C. Barnard, 'Lawyers and the law in later seventeenth-century Ireland' *IHS* 111 (May 1993), p. 263. In this context, it is difficult to understand Mervyn's comment, in his address to the duke of Ormond on 13 Feb. 1663 concerning 'The checking of the English counsel at the Bar, whilst the insolencies of the Irish counsel are passed over in silence.': *Commons Journal Ireland* 1/2 (1798), pp. 617–30, at p. 621. It seems clear that Irish Catholic counsel did appear in the court. For example in Southwell's case, the Catholic Sir Nicholas Plunkett appeared for the Protestant Southwell family, and Patrick Darcy for the claimant, Philip Barry Oge. See Neil Johnston, 'Politics, parliament and the Restoration land settlement in Ireland, 1660–1665' (Ph.D. thesis, University College, Dublin 2012), p. 243.

12 22 Oct. 1662, NLI, Thorpe pamphlets, no. 593. These rules laid down the geographic sequence in which claims would be heard, namely Leinster, Munster, Ulster and Connacht. Initially, claims relating to Dublin city and county were heard, but as the court progressed these rules of sequence were not strictly obeyed and were suspended in Feb. 1663. Claimants who had received lands in Connacht were often deferred.

13 It is not clear when he ceased to hear cases; he certainly partook in the judgment in the Meara case (see below) on 28 Jan., *CSPI 1663–65*, p. 15.

14 25 Mar. 1663, *CSPI 1663–65*, p. 48; Simms, 'Introduction', pp. x–xi.

15 Nos. 80, 115, 116 and 138 in the Abstract. (The possible reasons for dismissal have not been explored.) There were no cases heard on 25 Mar. itself, being Lady Day: Tallon, p. 47.

16 C. W. Russell and J. P. Prendergast, *The Carte Manuscripts in the Bodleian Library, Oxford: A Report Presented to the Right Honourable Lord Romilly, Master of the Rolls* (London, 1871), p. 152. The Jesuits considered Rainsford especially favourable to the Catholic interest: Moynes, *Irish Jesuit Annual Letters*, p. 895.

17 Further praise came from 'A certain Catholic nobleman' who wrote a poem in Irish wondering 'whether Ireland might not properly be compared now with Rome, since Rainsford had canonized more Irishmen than the Pope': Moynes, *Jesuit Annual Letters,* p. 895. Sall was to declare himself a Protestant in 1674, and prompted French's *Bleeding Iphigenia.*

18 Tallon, no. 868, p. 339, and no. 904, p. 355.

19 11 May 1663, king to Ormond, *CSPI 1663–65*, p. 87.

20 Karl S. Bottigheimer, 'The Restoration land settlement in Ireland: A structural view', *IHS* 18 (1972), p. 9.

21 He reported that Rainsford believed that at least 300 innocent Catholic cases had been lost through Protestant perjury: Moynes, *Jesuit Annual Letters,* p. 895.

22 This is not to suggest that the operations or verdicts of the court could not be subverted and its authority undermined. The king was not above using his influence to ensure Lord Antrim was decreed innocent, and he gave Oliver Fitzwilliam, the earl of Tyrconnell, a retrospective pardon and secured the restoration of his estates by the court. Protestants suspected the king of involvement in the Allen case. Ormond had a role in the Fitzwilliam case, and there were many people's hands involved in the Protestant Robert Southwell's case. For Lord Antrim, see Jane H. Ohlmeyer, *Civil War and Restoration in the Three Stuart Kingdoms: The Career of Randal MacDonnell, Marquis of Antrim* (Cambridge, 1993). The Allen case is considered later in this chapter. For the Tyrconnell and Southwell cases, see Johnston, 'Politics, parliament and the Restoration land settlement', at pp. 238 ff. The Armagh MS records only Tyrconnell's first appearance, when he was found *nocent* and the Southwell case is not recorded at all.

23 14 Jan. 1663, *CSPI 1663–65*, p. 9. It was 2:1 on 13 Jan. and 3:1 on 14 Jan.

24 See further below.

25 7 Feb. 1663, *CSPI 1663–65*, p. 18.

26 28 Feb. 1663, *CSPI 1663–65*, p. 31. Jess Velona makes the case that Meryn's proposals were not implausible from a legal perspective. However, he also argues that political rather than legal consideration ruled the outcome: 'The speech of Sir Audley Mervyn' in Dennehy, *Law and Revolution*, pp. 302–24.

27 Kingston to Nicholas (?), 24 Mar. 1663, *CSPI 1663–65*, p. 47. This was more likely Bennet; Nicholas had been replaced by Bennet as secretary of state in Oct. 1662.

28 Kingston to Bennet, 9 May 1663, *CSPI 1663–65*, p. 86.

29 Edward Vernon to Williamson, 22 May 1663, *CSPI 1663–65*, p. 98. Arnold, *Restoration Land Settlement*, pp. 65–6.

30 14 & 15 Charles II c. 12, *Statutes II*, pp. 496–8. The Act for the Enlargement of Periods of Time was required because the commissioners did not take up office until 20 Sept., well past the 1 Aug. deadline.

31 Robert Lye (or Leigh) to Williamson, 20 Jun. 1663, *CSPI 1663–65*, p. 142. Lye was acting as agent for a number of officials of the court in London.

32 Orrery to Clarendon, 13 Mar. 1663, Russell and Prendergast, *Carte Manuscripts,* p. 154. This uncharacteristic benevolence on Orrery's part is difficult to contextualise. It is probably best understood in the light of Orrery attempting to mollify Clarendon, given his role in managing the House of Commons in the turmoil that followed Mervyn's address to Ormond in February concerning the operation of the Court, which was badly received in London.

33 Ormond to Bennet, 25 June 1663, *CSPI 1663–65*, p. 148.

34 Capt. Blood's attempt in May 1663 to usurp the government and hold Ormond for ransom supported the argument.

35 Carte, vol. 2, p. 299.

36 Viscount Netterville, Philip Hore, Luke Dowdall: 27 June and 2 July 1663, *CSPI 1663–65*, pp. 153 and 158.

37 Lye to Williamson, 5 Sept. 1663, *CSPI 1663–65*, p. 231.

38 17 & 18 Charles II c. 12, s. CLXXXVIII, *Statutes III,* p. 114; Orrery brokered a settlement which involved payment of a year's rent, by those who had received decrees after 2 July, to the 'ensign-men' who had followed the king's standards in exile and were named in the Act of Settlement.

39 See Simms, 'Introduction', p. xv, and Russell and Prendergast, *Carte Manuscripts,* p. 87. See also 'The Report of Sir Heneage Finch' in Carte, vol. 2, appendix XCI, p. 75. Finch claimed many of the 5,000 were repeat applications, rather than claims of innocence. See Anne Creighton, '"Grace and favour": The Cabal Ministry and Irish Catholic politics, 1667–73' in Dennehy, *Restoration Ireland,* p. 154.

40 6 June and 12–21 Aug. 1663, together with follow-up proceedings on 30 Aug., 7 Sept. 1663–26 Feb. 1664 and 20 Apr. 1664.

41 Recorded by Dering: Tallon, pp. 402–7.

42 Abstract of the Decrees of the Court of Claims for the Trial of Innocents, *19th Annual Report of the Deputy Keeper of the Public Records of Ireland*, 1887, app. V, pp. 41–87. A transcript of John Brice's decree and an index of

names and locations of decrees of innocence, without any further details, is published in appendix V to the *15th Annual Report of the Commissioners of the PROI*, 1825, pp. 526–75. This report also contains Abstracts of grants of land made under the Acts of Settlement and Explanation between 1666 and 1684 (essentially a summary of *all* the proceedings under the Acts), and a list of the certificates, i.e. decrees of the Court of Claims, with no details of the decrees.

43 HMC *8th Report*, app. 1, s. 2, pp. 499b to 552a.

44 This is based on an analysis of the names of the nominees in the Declaration, against the record in Tallon. In a very few cases this analysis was limited by the difficulty in identifying names with specific individuals. Two of the nominees were found *nocent* (Ikerryn and Donagh O'Callaghan). Richard Lane was judged an innocent Protestant but did not seek restitution; he seems to have been the only Protestant among the nominees. There is no record of a claim by Sir Richard Barnewall in Tallon, but his son, Patrick Barnewall referred to his father's claim in his own case which was heard on 29 July 1663: Tallon, p. 271. There are no details of any claim by Matthew/Mathias Barnewall, Lord Trimleston in the Armagh MS, but Dering listed a case for Matthew Barnewall on 15 Sept. 1663; Tallon, p. 414. Richard Bellings was restored without recourse to the Court; see Micheál Ó Siochrú, 'Sir Richard Bellings' in *DIB*, vol. 1, p. 442.

45 Referred to in the cases as *cum clero coronae*.

46 Essentially, the Rolls of Association and the books of the Supreme Council. They had been first used by the commissioners in Athlone under the 1652 Act of Settlement to 'discriminate' the conduct of transplanters seeking grants in Connacht: Simms, 'Introduction', p. xii.

47 Tallon, pp. 338–9, Abstract no. 763. Walter A. Coppinger, *History of the Copingers or Coppingers* (London, 1884), pp. 90–1.

48 8 Nov. 1662, F. J. Routledge (ed.), *Calendar of the Clarendon State Papers* (Oxford, 1970), vol. 5, p. 280, and Bottigheimer, 'Restoration land settlement', p. 10.

49 John P. Prendergast, 'The Butlers, Lords Ikerrin, before the Court of Transplantation, at Athlone, A. D. 1656, and at the first and second Court of Claims, King's Inns, Dublin, 1662–1666', *Journal of the Royal Historical and Archaeological Association of Ireland* 4th ser. 7 (London, 1887), p. 600.

50 Russell and Prendergast, *Carte Manuscripts,* p. 87, but see further below. It is interesting to compare the position in Cromwellian England, where according to Bottigheimer, 'reversions, life estates, jointures, marriage portions or the other encumbrances ... saved the wealth of so many royalists in England' in the 1650s: 'Restoration land settlement', p. 2.

51 Neil Johnston, 'Charles II's legal officers and the Irish restoration land settlement' in Dennehy, *Law and Revolution*, p. 346.

52 i.e. not innocent. Arnold, *Restoration Land Settlement*, p. 53. Simms, 'Introduction', p. xv, quoted slightly different calculations which seem to have been made by Bagwell, relying on BL Egerton MS 789, which is a summary of the

decrees of the Court from 13 Jan. to 21 Aug. 1663: R. Bagwell, *Ireland under the Stuarts*, vol. 3 (London, 1916), p. 34, n. 1. Arnold made the point that, because decrees of the Court could relate to several family members, it may be that over 1,000 individual claims were adjudicated: L. J. Arnold, 'The Irish court of claims', *IHS* 24 (1985), pp. 417–30, at p. 419.

53 Appendix V to the *15th Annual Report of the Commissioners of the PROI*, 1825, pp. 523–5. Transcripts of individual decrees are found in other records; see, e.g., Coppinger and Bellew below. There are likely to be many decrees in family and estate records; e.g., the Decree of Innocence for Mary and Anstance Gould, can be found in the Vanderplas Cork Deeds in the Cork City and County Archives, IE CCCA/U675/35, 38, 51. See Tallon, p. 274, and Abstract no. 606.

54 Nos. 2, 285 and 321. There are various spellings of the name, including Mearah, O'Meara etc. Tallon, pp. 3, 101 and 118.

55 Petition of Walter Brice, John's son, Richard's brother, to the king, 18 Jan. 1667, *CSPI, 1669–70*, p. 585.

56 John D'Alton, *The History of Drogheda* (Dublin, 1844), vol. 2, p. 221. The Brices were a newly established family in Drogheda, and even in 1641 held no land in Louth; Hugh F. Kearney, *Strafford in Ireland 1633–1641: A Study in Absolutism* (Manchester, 1959), pp. 225–6. This suggests that this entrepreneurial family was extending its operations outside Dublin in the mid-1630s.

57 Presumably relying on the Declaration. 7 Dec. 1660, *CSPI 1660–62*, pp. 121–2. This petition suggests that the family were dispossessed in 1652, and that it was Richard (not John) who warned about the activities of the spy in Ormond's camp who had informed Michael Jones about Ormond's activities in Rathmines. See also McGrath, 'A biographical dictionary', vol. 1, p. 77, which supports this version of events, and Arnold, *Restoration Land Settlement*, p. 54, which relies on the 1667 version in Walter's petition.

58 *CSPI 1660–62*, p. 138.

59 No. 2.

60 This does not help to reconcile the acreages.

61 Trustees for the Sale of the Forfeited Estates, *A List of the Claims as they are Entered with the Trustees at Chichester House* (Dublin, 1701), p. 139.

62 Helen Andrews, 'Dermot O'Meara', *DIB*, vol. 7, pp. 692–4. See also P. Logan, 'Dermot and Edmund O'Meara, father and son', *Journal of the Irish Medical Association* 43 (1958), pp. 312–17.

63 Tallon, p. 3. See also John Barry, 'Dermot O'Meara' in *ODNB*, accessed 20 July 2018. The nature of his activities with the rebels is not known.

64 See J. B. Lyons, 'Edmund O'Meara' in *ODNB*, accessed 20 July 2018.

65 17 Nov. 1660, *CSPI, 1660–62*, p. 85. Clanricarde seemed to have regarded him as something of a martinet: see John Lowe (ed.), *Letter-Book of the Earl of Clanricarde 1643–47* (Dublin 1983), p. 118.

66 Nov. 1660, *CSPI*, *1663–65*, p. 469.

67 Tallon, pp. 3 and 102. 28 Jan. 1663, *CSPI, 1663–65*, p. 15.

68 Tallon, p. 370.

69 The meaning of this is obscure. Clanricarde left Ireland in Mar. 1653 and may have departed from the harbour in Kilcolgan.
70 Detailed in Tallon, p. 101.
71 No. 331. It has not possible to reconcile this acreage with the extent of the estate shown in the May claim (541 profitable, 1189 unprofitable).
72 Arnold, *Restoration Land Settlement*, p. 145.
73 E. G. More-O'Ferrall (ed.), 'The dispossessed landowners of Ireland, 1664', *Irish Genealogist* 4 (1972), p. 432. Thomas was categorised as H, i.e. 'submitted and constantly adhered to the peace of 1648' and Dermot as D, i.e. 'from the beginning lived inoffensively'.
74 Tallon, no. 321, p. 370.
75 Emmet O'Byrne, 'Fiach McHugh O'Byrne' in *DIB*, vol. 7, pp. 122–7.
76 Tallon, p. 118.
77 1 June 1663. No. 300.
78 The history of the earl of Carlingford's recovery is detailed in the study of his lawyer and agent, John Bellew: Harold O'Sullivan, *John Bellew, A Seventeenth-Century Man of Many Parts, 1605–1679* (Dublin, 2000). On p. 106, O'Sullivan noted that Carlingford was restored to 9,839 acres in Sligo and 2,045 in Louth. It is clear that he recovered other land, but O'Sullivan offered no comment on the enormously greater acreage in the Abstract (no. 615), which made no mention of Louth. Through Carlingford's influence, Bellew partly recovered his own estate in Louth and retained the Galway property he was awarded by the Cromwellians. Arnold has explored Fingal's recovery, *Restoration Land Settlement*, *passim*. Fingal's case gave rise to a number of procedural and legal issues. The first arose when commissioner Coventry was recalled, with the result there was an even number of commissioners. They feared dealing with Fingal's claim lest there be a division among them, and the possibility that 'Lord Fingall's case remains, like Mahomet's tomb, between heaven and earth, *in equilibrio*': Churchill to Bennet, 8 Apr. 1663, *CSPI*, *1663–65*, p. 57. The second was whether the Court could hear claimants for whom provision was specifically made as nominees in the Act of Settlement; the Court decided that it could: Arnold, *Restoration Land Settlement*, p. 63. A somewhat similar, but distinct issue arose in the case of the earl of Carlingford, who had to elect whether his claim was submitted on the basis of his innocence, or the proviso in the Act of Settlement: O'Sullivan, *John Bellew*, pp. 104–5. Finally, it seems that Fingal engaged the services of two intermediaries who facilitated the passage of his claim in Court through bribery: Arnold, *Restoration Land Settlement*, p. 77. See also Simms, 'Introduction', p. xiii. Antrim's recovery is explored in Ohlmeyer, *Randal MacDonnell*, esp. pp. 261–7.
79 19 Oct. 1662, *CSPI, 1660–62*, p. 444.
80 He was born c.1625, and would have been 16 in 1641.
81 20 Nov. 1662, *CSPI, 1660–62*, p. 470.
82 3 Mar. 1662, *CSPI, 1660–62*, p. 513.
83 16 Apr. 1662, *CSPI, 1660–62*, p. 534. This refers to the *Act*, which was not passed until July. Provision was made in para. LXVII.

84 16 Jan. 1663, *CSPI, 1663–65*, p. 9. Although this specifically related to Mount Alexander, it was part of a general policy that 'all grants not yet past the Great Seal have been stopped': 14 Jan. 1663, *CSPI, 1663–65*, p. 7. This policy was presumably out of respect to the proceedings in the Court of Claims that started hearings the previous day.

85 Talbot referred to his interest on 4 Feb. 1663, when writing to Bennet: *CSPI, 1663–65*, p. 17. Talbot bought the new quit rents, worth £240 p.a., out of which he had to pay the 1641 quit rent of £26 p.a.: *CSPD, 1671*, p. 234.

86 Quoted in Pádraig Lenihan, *The Last Cavalier* (Dublin, 2014), p. 56.

87 Arnold, *Restoration Land Settlement*, pp. 77–8. Lenihan, *Last Cavalier*, pp. 56–7.

88 Neil Johnston argued that Allen's restoration was not supported by the evidence and in support cites three TCD Depositions which show Allen's rebel activities. But on closer examination, this would not appear to be the case. In fact there is no reference to James Allen in TCD MS 809, fo. 250. TCD MS 809, fo. 287 refers to a James Allen from Coolmine, Co. Dublin, not St. Wolstan's in Celbridge, Co. Kildare. In TCD MS 824, fos. 238–9, the James Allen in question was a debtor of the deponent. Neil Johnston, 'Politics, parliament and the Restoration land settlement in Ireland, 1660–1665' (Ph.D. thesis, University College Dublin, 2012), p. 227, n. 28.

89 Tallon, p. 4. The Armagh MS records a claim for a jointure in the name of Dame Mary Allen, but the text makes clear that the principal claimant was James, her nephew.

90 7 Feb. 1663, Mount Alexander to an unidentified female recipient: *CSPI, 1663–65*, p. 19. This verbatim quotation is a rare example of the incendiary arguments offered in the Court.

91 No. 28. Johnston in 'Politics, parliament and the Restoration land settlement', p. 228, suggests that the award was in Lady Allen's favour only; this is not supported by the Abstract.

92 11 Feb. 1663, *Clarendon State Papers*, vol. 5, p. 296. In fact concerns about the terms of the Bill of Explanation had been building for some time: *Commons Journal Ireland* 1/2 (1798), pp. 617–30.

93 Arnold, *Restoration Land Settlement*, p. 68.

94 *Commons Journal Ireland*, pp. 617–31, at p. 618. Ormond to Clarendon, 21 Feb. 1663, *Clarendon State Papers*, vol. 5, p. 298.

95 *CSPI 1663–65*, p. 32.

96 Clarendon to Mervyn, 7 Mar. 1663, *Clarendon State Papers*, vol. 5, p. 301.

97 She was the wife of Sir Thomas Allen, who had settled the estate on his brothers in default of any heirs of his own. His brother Robert died without issue. His next brother, William had a son John, and it was on his death that the estate passed to James who was the son of Thomas's third brother Nicholas.

98 Arnold, *Restoration Land Settlement*, p. 78.

99 Lenihan, *Last Cavalier*, p. 57. Ormond to Clarendon, 11 Feb. 1663: *Clarendon State Papers*, vol. 5, p. 296.

100 2 June 1663, Ormond to the bishop of Cork, Bodleian, Carte MS 49 fo. 198.

101 18 Dec. 1663, *CSPI, 1663–1665*, pp. 317–18.
102 Arnold, *Restoration Land Settlement*, p. 78. This 'discovery' was the catalyst for Talbot's threat to kill Ormond in 1664; Talbot spent a month in the Tower as a result.
103 Section CLXVI, *Statutes III*, p. 99.
104 12 May 1671, *CSPD, 1671*, p. 234.
105 *CSPI*, *1660–62*, p. 198.
106 Francis Boyle (1623–99), fourth son of the earl of Cork.
107 31 July 1661, *CSPI*, *1660–62*, pp. 388–9. Shannon may have understood that Browne could be restored without reprisal as an innocent, but he was not to know the relatively lenient approach taken by the Court until almost two years later.
108 Tallon, p. 108.
109 Sir Francis Hamilton sought a *custodiam* of these lands in 1663, after Brown had secured his decree from the court: HMC, *8th Report*, app.1, s. 2, p. 503b.
110 No. 262 in the Abstract.
111 Tallon, p. 110.
112 Feb. 1661, *CSPI*, *1660–1662*, p. 241. The facts in relation to his age, dates of his education in France etc. are at variance with those in the 1663 claim, but the thrust of the narrative is the same.
113 McCarthy More Papers, TCD MS 10576/1/23.
114 No. 144.
115 Coppinger, *History*, p. 107.
116 Tallon, p. 48.
117 The claim of George Hamilton, Baron of Strabane, was heard on 4 July 1663: Tallon, pp. 192–4. The Abstract, No. 471, states that he was declared an innocent Protestant, but Strabane and his siblings were converted to Catholicism by their guardian. See Michael Wasser, 'George Hamilton' in *ODNB*.
118 See n. 47. Some of these documents may no longer be extant; e.g. part of James's decree of innocence is quoted, which probably perished in 1922. Similarly, the two documents quoted below.
119 Coppinger, *History*, p. 405 citing Commonwealth Volumes in the PROI, vol. 26, A28, p. 68.
120 Coppinger, *History*, pp. 405–6, citing Commonwealth Volumes in the PROI, vol. 39, A61, p.24 and p. 35 of the same series.
121 Robert Simington, *Transplantation to Connacht, 1654–8* (Dublin, 1970).
122 12 Aug. 1660, *CSPI, 1660–62*, p. 24.
123 11 Mar. 1661, *CSPI, 1660–62*, p. 257.
124 The Declaration provided that innocent papists would be restored by 1 May 1661, regardless of whether they had taken up their rights in Connacht and Clare. It is a measure of James's concern that he only waited 25 days before lodging his complaint with the Sheriffs.
125 Coppinger, *History*, p. 107. This has presumably since been lost; Walter Coppinger did not always reference his sources. The summary makes no reference to the family's dealings with Cromwell in 1655 or their support for his forces.

126 Not vastly different from 18,100 Irish acres, or 29,322 statute acres, in the Abstract.
127 Under the provision that denied restoration to land in corporate towns: 14 & 15 Charles II c. 2, para. XVIII, and paras. XVII–XIX of the Instructions. *Statutes II*, pp. 253, 272–3. These provisions did not apply to Dublin or Drogheda; see 'The Report of Sir Heneage Finch' in Carte, *Life of Ormonde*, vol. 2, app. XCI, p. 75.
128 It is difficult to see if and how this happened from the Down Survey Project maps. James held some land in Barrymore Barony in 1670; but this was land which his father owned in that barony in 1640. Most of the land owned by the Coppingers in Barrymore in 1640 was held by the Protestant Sir George Hamilton in 1670.
129 Roger Boyle to Ormond, 29 May 1663, Coppinger, *History*, p. 108.
130 Coppinger, *History*, pp. 108–117.
131 Also Edward, whose son Piers, the claimant's father, died before the grandfather. See Robert Armstrong, 'Edward Butler' in *DIB*, vol. 2, pp. 112–13.
132 14 Nov. 1660, *CSPI, 1660–62*, p. 80. The petition incorrectly states that Galmoy's grandfather died while serving under Sir Walter Dungan; in fact, it was his father.
133 No. 502. The Abstract says Lord and Lady Galway; this is incorrect. See Tallon for 13 July, p. 211.
134 Tallon, pp. 140–1.
135 Ormond had recommended that his grandfather be created a peer in 1646, Armstrong, 'Edward Butler', p. 112.
136 HMC, *8th Report*, app. 1, s. 2, p. 542b.
137 F. Elrington Ball, *The Judges in Ireland* (2 vols, London, 1926), vol. 1, p. 214.
138 'Whyte of Loughbrickland' in Bernard Burke, *A Genealogical and Heraldic Dictionary of the Landed Gentry of Great Britain and Ireland* (London, 1868), p. 1656. There is surprisingly little biographical information about the son.
139 24 Oct. 1660, *CSPI*, *1660–62*, p. 63.
140 22 Nov. 1660, *CSPI, 1660–62*, p. 95. Lowther was '[o]ne of the chief instruments of the Cromwellian regime in Ireland': Terry Clavin, 'Sir Gerald Lowther' in *DIB*, vol. 5, p. 576.
141 26 Feb. 1663, Bodleian, Carte MS 68, fo. 590. Arnold, *Restoration Land Settlement*, p. 76.
142 Tallon, pp. 13–14. There is no reference to Ormond's certificate in the evidence to the Court.
143 No. 68.
144 Claim of Dame Mary Allen, Tallon, p. 4. It is also possible the deponent was his father, Sir Nicholas White. John Allen may have been the cousin from whom Nicholas Allen inherited St Wolstan's; see above.
145 Claim of Phillip Sherlocke, Tallon, p. 35.
146 Arnold, *Restoration Land Settlement*, p. 56.
147 Jones was a formidable opponent; brother of Col. Michael Jones who had beaten Ormond in the battle at Rathmines, and of Henry Jones, the bishop of Meath.

148 Tallon, p. 426. This was not uncommon: see Arnold, 'The Irish court of claims of 1663', pp. 426–7.
149 Jones to Sir George Lane, 9 July 1664, NLI MS 8643/7, quoted in Arnold, *Restoration Land Settlement*, p. 80. Lane was secretary to the council of war and had total control over the armed forces in Ireland: see John Cronin and Terry Clavin, 'Sir George Lane' in *DIB*, vol. 5, p. 293.
150 Arnold, *Restoration Land Settlement*, p. 136.
151 9 Mar. 1669, *CSPI, 1669–70*, p. 628.
152 15 and 22 Aug. 1669, *CSPI, 1669–70*, pp. 218, 236. He was one amongst many; a return in Sept. 1670 showed that the king had remitted quit-rents from £9,117 to £782 p.a. The majority of the beneficiaries were Catholic: 3 Sept. 1670, *CSPI, 1669–1670*, pp. 250–252.
153 No. 399.
154 See McGrath, 'A biographical dictionary', vol. 1, pp. 156–7.
155 HMC *8th Report*, app. 1 (s. 2), p. 522b. According to O'Sullivan, Sir Luke Fitzgerald of Tircroghan was allocated over 2,000 acres in 1656: O'Sullivan, *John Bellew*, p. 67, relying on Robert Simington, pp. 64, 124 and 173.
156 See McGrath, 'A biographical dictionary', vol. 1, pp. 156–7.
157 Robert Dunlop, *Ireland under the Commonwealth* (2 vols, Manchester, 1913), vol. 2, p. 702.
158 O'Sullivan contends Fitzgerald's inclusion was due to Ormond's influence: *John Bellew*, p. 80.
159 *CSPI, 1660–62*, p. 108.
160 *CSPI 1660–62*, p. 177.
161 Tallon, pp. 102–3.
162 No. 215.
163 Charles Fleming died in 1661, when Randall succeeded to the title. See Terry Trench, 'Fleming and Conyngham of Slane', *Ríocht na Midhe* 7 (1982–83), p. 70.
164 27 Feb. 1661. *CSPI, 1660–62*, p. 233. Their father William's role as a confederate seems to have been quietly ignored: see Micheál Ó Siochrú, 'William Fleming' in *DIB*, vol. 3, pp. 1018–19.
165 Presumably many decrees of outlawry, issued during the Confederate and Commonwealth periods, were still on the record and could be used as evidence in the Court of Claims to impugn the innocence of claimants.
166 22 Nov. 1662, Eustace to Bennet, *CSPI 1660–62*, p. 631.
167 Tallon, pp. 80–1.
168 Possibly a reference to the terms under which Galway surrendered to the Cromwellians in 1652.
169 Tallon, pp. 243–4. Abstract no. 548.
170 Tallon, pp. 232–3. Abstract no. 539.
171 See McGrath, 'A biographical dictionary', vol. 1, pp. 53–4. Richard Hawkins, 'Sir Nicholas Barnewall' in *DIB*, vol. 1, p. 283. Terry Clavin, 'Sir Nicholas Barnewall' in *ODNB*, accessed 4 Jan. 2018.
172 27 July 1654, *CSPI 1647–60*, p. 540.

173 *CSPI 1647–60*, pp. 609–11.
174 Alexander, who 'has suffered much', petitioned for relief in connection with this lease: 30 Dec. 1658, *CSPI 1647–60*, p. 677.
175 An Act for the Attainder of the Rebels in Ireland, 26 June 1657: C. H. Firth and R. S. Rait (eds), *Acts and Ordinances of the Interregnum, 1642–60* (3 vols, London, 1911), vol. 2, pp. 1261–2.
176 23 Oct. 1662, *CSPI, 1660–62*, p. 59. The circumstances of this confiscation are far from clear. In the *ODNB* Clavin seems to suggest that his Leinster lands were confiscated around 1654, but we know that he was dealing with Alexander a year later. In the *DIB* Hawkins states that the Leinster lands were confiscated in 1656, his lands in Roscommon were untouched and his transplantation to Connacht not enforced: p. 283. This suggests some degree of tolerance by the Protectorate.
177 Abstract no. 14.
178 See TCD Down Survey.
179 Arnold, *Restoration Land Settlement*, p. 54.
180 John McCafferty, 'John Bramhall' in *DIB*, vol. 1, p. 780, and 'John Bramhall's second Irish career, 1660–3' in Kelly et al., *People, Politics and Power*, p. 22.
181 See Walter Harris (ed.), *The Whole Works of Sir James Ware* (2 vols, Dublin, 1764), vol. 1, pp. 425–6. There is no trace of the claims of either Williams or Evans in Tallon. Evans did obtain grants of land in 1667, 1670 and 1671 or 1672, and Williams (as bishop of Ossory) obtained a decree of innocence: *15th Annual Report of the Commissioners of the PROI*, 1825, pp. 84, 199 and 229 (Evans) and 535 (Ossory).
182 No. 499. Tallon, p. 192. Anglesey is mentioned incidentally in several other claims.
183 No. 467.
184 Julian Walton, 'Richard Power' in *ODNB,* accessed 22 Mar. 2017; John Bergin, 'Richard Power' in *DIB*, vol 8, p. 265. Further, John was exempted from transplantation by order of the Lord Protector in 1654.
185 Note the TCD Down Survey shows Lord Power's holdings at 701 plantation acres in 1641 in the immediate vicinity of Curraghmore. There are also holdings for John Power, but these seem to relate to the Kilmeadan branch of the Power family.
186 16 Nov. 1670, *CSPI 1669–1670*, p. 306.
187 25 Apr. 1661, *CSPI 1660–62*, p. 316. He was among the many who received a free pardon; the 'crimes' for which he was pardoned were not enumerated.
188 He petitioned the king for the position, which had been for 'four several descents' in the family. 10 Aug. 1660, *CSPI 1660–62*, p. 23.
189 Annesley to his daughter, 1 May 1666, quoted by Walton in *ODNB*
190 At Ormond's request. It was noted he was Anglesey's son-in-law, and 'an ancient nobleman, well allied and very well affected': 27 Feb. and 27 Mar. 1667, *CSPI 1666–1669*, pp. 309, 331.
191 Walton, 'Richard Power'. John Bergin in 'Richard Power' states that John served at the siege of Derry, was attained in 1689 and in 1692 obtained the

reversal of his father's outlawry, p. 266. According to Bergin, it was John's brother James who submitted to William at Waterford. More recently Walton repeated the *ODNB* version of events: unpublished lecture 16 July 2017.

192 Walton, 'Richard Power'.

193 The nine larger cases, and Brice, Meara and Power.

194 The petitions were requests to the king to exercise his royal prerogative. Petitioners hoped for a king's letter, an instruction to the Irish administration to carry out the king's wishes. Generally, land that had already been granted to soldiers or adventurers was excluded.

195 24 Oct. 1662, *CSPI, 1660–62*, pp. 62–3.

196 Russell and Prendergast, *Carte Manuscripts,* p. 87. A similar assertion is made in Neil Johnston in 'Charles II's legal officers and the Irish restoration land settlement' in Dennehy, *Law and Revolution*, p. 346.

197 Sir Luke Fitzgerald was declared nocent.

198 24 Oct. 1660, *CSPI, 1660–62*, p. 63.

199 This analysis derives from the Abstract, which identifies Protestant claimants; other claimants are assumed to be Catholic. Percentages refer to the profitable acres decreed. Examples of incumbrances are daughters' portions (Bath's case, Tallon, p. 16 and Abstract no. 76) or the unexpired term of a lease (Lock's case, Tallon pp. 25–6 and Abstract no. 104).

200 Desmond J. Byrne, 'Land and survival in Fingal 1630–1703' (Ph.D. thesis, NUI Maynooth, 2009).

201 Byrne, 'Land and survival', p. 264.

202 Byrne, 'Land and survival', p. 364.

203 Although there is an enormous amount of information in the Abstract, in some cases educated guesses as to confessional identity or family relationship were required. It should also be noted that, in more complex cases, there were often more than two claimants. If so, the woman's role is generally clear, but the many possible relationships involved have not been disaggregated in the analysis.

204 Nos. 776, 605 and 334 respectively in the Abstract. Unfortunately, the record does not show if the nuns appeared in court, or if they were simply represented by their counsel.

205 16 May 1655, *CSPI, 1647–1660*, p. 812. The petition was made by Sir Nicholas and his son, also Nicholas.

206 *CSPI, 1660–62*, pp. 121–2.

207 21 Feb. 1663, *CSPI, 1663–65*, p. 28. See Barnard, 'Lawyers and the law', p. 270, for observations on the expense of litigation for some Protestant landowners in the 1670s.

208 HMC *8th Report*, app. 1 (s. 2), pp. 500a–552a.

209 HMC *8th Report*, pp. 513b, 516a.

210 HMC *8th Report*, p. 532b.

211 HMC *8th Report*, p. 549b.

212 HMC *8th Report*, p. 500b.

213 James McGuire, 'Richard Talbot' in *DIB*, vol. 9, pp. 248–9.

214 See Lenihan, *Last Cavalier*, pp. 55–69 *passim*.
215 Tyrconnell's disdain extended to Ulstermen generally, a sentiment reciprocated by the then primate Dominic Maguire: HMC *Stuart Papers*, vol. 6, pp. 6, 16–17.
216 Lenihan, *Last Cavalier*, p. 61. See also, e.g., Arnold, *Restoration Land Settlement*, pp. 60 and ff.
217 Arnold listed the activities of some of these agents in Dublin alone: *Restoration Land Settlement*, pp. 76–7. St Albans assisted Philip Hore, Sir Luke Bath, Patrick Sarsfield and Christopher Archbold. Domville was to get half of the estates of Robert Preston and Marcus Fitzsimons. Berkeley blocked the earl of Mount Alexander from seizing St. Wolstan's from James Allen.
218 *Commons Journal Ireland* 2 (1796), p. 613.
219 The Dublin sheriffs were suspected of a 'combination' of resistance by Ormond: Ormond to Clarendon, 8 Apr. 1663, *Clarendon Papers*, vol. 5, p. 307.
220 Carlingford, the two Brownes, Coppinger, Fingal, Galmoy, White, Fitzgerald, Slane, Barnewall, Allen, Power and Antrim. Brice and Meara are less clear.
221 Analysis of Abstract.
222 There is surprising lack of authority on the exact extent of the Cromwellian forfeitures. McKenny estimated that 4.4 million acres were forfeited in the 1650s and not restored during the Restoration. If we add the 930,000 cited above, this would give an estimate of 5.3m acres: Kevin McKenny, 'The Restoration land settlement in Ireland: A statistical interpretation' in Dennehy, *Restoration Ireland*, pp. 35–52 at p. 44. This outcome was considerably more than Fr Andrew Sall, the Jesuit provincial superior, expected. He reported it was believed the 1662 legislation might result in scarcely 10 per cent of confiscated land being recovered: Moynes, *Jesuit Annual Letters,* p. 894.
223 The complex politics that underlay the curtailment of the court are explained in Johnston: 'Charles II's legal officers and the Irish restoration land settlement', pp. 324–53.
224 There is no factual basis for the 70 per cent reduction. These calculations are crude and entirely hypothetical.
225 Danielle McCormack, *The Stuart Restoration and the English in Ireland* (Woodbridge, 2016), p. 19.

5

Working within the law: Catholics and the legal profession

For all he cared Tyrconnell might give the secretary's place to his nephew Sir William Talbot.[1]

A small composition is better parted with, than a suit of law gained.[2]

Provide against the continuance of such dangerous instruments as the popish lawyers ... Ireland is never like to be quiet if they be tolerated.[3]

This chapter explores how it was possible for a Catholic to make a career in the law during the Restoration through the careers of three lawyers who exercised their profession mainly in the provinces. They accepted the legal system with all the challenges and imperfections it posed for Catholics, and chose to exploit the opportunities which the law offered for financial gain, recovery of estates and political advancement. Each fashioned a distinctive individual career, and at various times were near the centre of power, and so their careers complement the evidence supplied by other studies.

Family background

John Walshe of Rathronan, Co. Tipperary, was born in 1613, the eldest son of David Walshe. He was a Munster lawyer whose professional life required occasional duties in Dublin. He was a member of the King's Inns, and sat in Parliament as an MP for Waterford City. He carefully represented Ormond's interests at the Court of Claims and there are brief references to his being in Dublin on other occasions, but most of his activities, both before and after 1660, took place in Munster. In 1650, during the Cromwellian wars, Sir Anthony Morgan murdered his father, David Walshe, then in his eighties, one of his sisters and a niece. A pamphlet of 1662 recorded that the motive for the murders was the defence of Clonmel against Cromwell by David's children and relatives, and John Walshe's 'attending on the Lord Lieutenant in order to his Majesty's service'.[4] His mother's name is not known and he had at least one brother, David. Walshe's wife died in the

1651 siege of Limerick but he remarried.[5] A decree of 12 March 1679 restored Walshe to his estates and he made a family settlement soon afterwards in favour of his son Patrick.[6] There are no later records of his life and the date of his death is not recorded.

More is known of the life of William Talbot who was born c.1643, some thirty years later than Walsh.[7] Talbot's family were important Catholic politicians and lawyers, who had successfully navigated the turbulent political waters of the 1640s and 1650s into the Restoration. His grandfather Sir William (d. 1643) was the first baronet and built the house at Carton, Co. Kildare, where Talbot was born. Sir William was legal adviser to the earls of Kildare and was described by Lenihan as a 'sharp lawyer' who 'must have looted Kildare's "encumbered and decayed estate" over a period'.[8] Sir William married Alison Netterville and they had 16 children, of whom the eldest, Robert, inherited the title in 1643. He followed his father's profession of estate management for noble clients.[9] Robert's brothers included Peter Talbot, archbishop of Dublin, and Richard Talbot, duke of Tyrconnell. According to Clarendon, Robert was the best of the family.[10] He was active in the Confederation during the 1640s and a tireless advocate in London for dispossessed Catholics. A suggestion of self-interest hangs over Robert's career, and in her *DIB* entry Anne Creighton refers to the commission he received on every acre of land restored to Irish Catholics by the Court of Claims. In fact this was provided in the Act of Explanation and was recompense he and three other agents were awarded for their unpaid activities over many years on behalf of Irish Catholics.[11] A further doubt arises because, with other prominent Catholic leaders, he was accused by Ormond and the Attorney General Sir Heneage Finch of protecting his own interests by restricting the number of restorations after 1665, but this accusation is probably partisan.[12] Robert is said to have acted as legal agent for the duke of York although there does not seem to be much evidence of this.[13] Robert married Grace Calvert, a member of a prominent English Catholic family with an Irish estate, and they had two daughters and one son, William, the subject of this study, who succeeded Robert in 1671. According to Elrington Ball, Talbot 'became a suitor for the hand of a niece of the Comtesse de Grammont in 1683'.[14] This was Elizabeth Hamilton, daughter of George Hamilton by his wife Frances Jennings (who later married Richard Talbot, the future duke of Tyrconnell in 1681).[15] His suit having failed, he quickly recovered from any disappointment and on 10 November 1683, aged 40, he married Anne, widow of Lucas, sixth Viscount Dillon, and daughter of Richard Nugent, second earl of Westmeath.[16] In their marriage settlement, Talbot left a life-interest in Carton to Anne.[17] They had no children.

Gerald Dillon was a contemporary of Talbot, born c.1644, and the first official record of his life occurs when he was admitted to Gray's Inn on 16

February 1669 and was described as the son and heir of Theobald Dillon of Fimore, Co. Mayo.[18] The Westport papers contain a certificate of the death of Theobald Dillon, described as the father of Gerald Dillon, in the king's service at the siege of Carrick-on-Suir in 1649.[19] His mother was Margery Browne, daughter of Sir John Browne of the Neale, and sister of Col. John Browne of Westport, who was to be an important figure in his life.[20] He had two brothers, Thomas and Christopher; the latter was prior of Ballyhaunis Abbey and provincial of the Augustinian order.[21] After Dillon's father Theobald died, his mother Margery married John Malone as his second wife.[22] Very little is known of John Malone's background except that his father was of Cartron, Co. Westmeath.[23] John Malone's son Edmond, Dillon's half-brother, was admitted to Middle Temple on 18 June 1680, and had a busy practice in Chancery.[24] Together with Col. John Browne, he was another important figure in dealing with Dillon's affairs. Dillon's first wife was Susanna Crofton, née Clifford, the widow of Sir Edward Crofton of Mote, Co. Roscommon, who died in 1675.[25] Susanna may have been a Protestant; the Croftons of Mote were staunch Protestants and royalists, and a list of books she bought in 1676 contains a text written by Jeremy Taylor, Church of Ireland bishop of Down and Connor.[26] Notwithstanding her marriage to Dillon, she continued to be referred to as Lady Crofton, and the Westport papers contain records of Dillon paying her accounts until she died in 1682.[27] Dillon's second wife was Mary, daughter of George Hamilton, fourth baron of Strabane.[28] In fact John Browne and Dillon had married sisters; Mary was the sister of Anne Hamilton, Browne's first wife.[29] In 1690, he settled his estates on his first son Theobald.[30] Having negotiated and signed the Limerick Treaty, he chose to follow and serve James II into exile in France, and never returned to Ireland. In France he had two further sons, James and Claude. He died a few years later, 'honoured for his integrity, his learning, his eloquence and his worth'.[31] Theobald survived his father and lived until 1763.[32]

Legal education

It was common for wealthy families to send their sons to the Inns of Court in London for elementary legal training to enable them deal with the legal aspects of their landholdings and commercial matters, and John Walshe was admitted to Gray's Inn on 11 March 1631.[33] It was less common for the students to actually practise law but Walshe was admitted to King's Inns on 4 December 1635 when he returned to Ireland.[34]

There are some doubts about William Talbot's formal status as lawyer and Ball does not credit him with any legal education.[35] Stephen Talbot states that Talbot was 'educated in law', without reference to any formal legal training.[36] He does not appear in the lists of admissions to the four Inns of Court in London between 1660 and 1690. In the King's Inns Admission Papers, there is an entry for his grandfather, Sir William, but none for his father Sir Robert nor for Talbot himself. No legal qualifications were attributed to Talbot when he was appointed principal secretary of the province of Maryland in 1670.[37] The instrument appointing him referred to his quasi-legal duties: 'Keeper ... of all and singular the ... Records ... within our said Province' and also 'Judge for the Probate of wills and Granting of Administrations' and it seems possible but unlikely he was given these responsibilities without some legal knowledge.[38] Talbot was 27 when he went to Maryland, so he could have acquired a legal education in the ten preceding formative years; the question remains, what was the nature of the training and where did he receive it? Notwithstanding the absence of any formal legal qualifications, Anne Creighton describes Sir Robert as a lawyer, and acting 'as legal counsel to the duke of York, particularly in respect of the restoration land settlement in Ireland'.[39] Robert (b. 1608) could have worked alongside *his* father William who was a successful lawyer and died in 1634.[40] Similarly Talbot could have worked with his father, and it seems most likely that Talbot acquired his informal but effective legal education at home, and in particular inherited from his father and grandfather their estate management skills, together with the opportunities for personal enrichment. He became a lawyer because of his background; that was what the Talbots of Carton did.

Nothing is known of Dillon's early education, but it is highly likely that he knew Latin which, despite Henry Cromwell's attempts at reform in the 1650s, remained in use in court until at least the end of the seventeenth century. He must also have known Law French for professional purposes because in 1676 he bought Rolle's *Reports* which were published in French and in 1687 he bought Saunder's *Reports* where the records are in Latin and the arguments in French. Dillon was admitted to Gray's Inn in 1669, and spent five years in London. He was only six months in London before he became involved with John Browne's financial affairs. In August, together with Lucas Dillon of Middle Temple, he was party to Browne's unusually complicated bond for £35 of in favour of James Bradshaw, a London merchant tailor.[41] By the time his term as a law-student in London was coming to an end, he was familiar with living on credit. He bought goods from James Presscott for £7 12s, and eight years later had still not paid for them.[42] He was admitted to the Irish bar in 1674 and began an extensive practice, much of it based in Connacht.[43] Land law was the staple of Irish legal practice, and it is unlikely that Dillon learned much of the practice of that subject when in London. It is possible, although there is no evidence for this, that Dillon in effect apprenticed himself to Browne after his return from London, and before he set up in individual practice. In order to furnish his library, in 1676 he spent the considerable sum of £28 13s 9d on texts bought from James Malone, a Catholic bookseller in Dublin. While it has not been possible to identify all of the books, the vast majority were law reports or procedural guides. There was also a small number of works of religion and history, and some miscellaneous items.[44]

Of the three, Talbot had the easiest access to a legal education at home, although he acquired no formal qualification. Walshe and Dillon had to study in London, which imposed a financial burden, but was practicable for a comfortable or well-connected family. Dillon had to invest a considerable sum in Dublin to furnish his library with legal and other texts. For Walshe and Dillon, access to family resources or willing creditors were essential to a legal education.

Early years

Walshe lost little time in establishing a legal practice, and in January 1636 'young Mr. Walshe of Rathronan, the lawyer' (then 23 years of age) advised his father's landlord, the staunchly Protestant Richard Boyle, earl of Cork and the largest landowner in Ireland, in relation to the redemption of a mortgage over lands near Clonmel.[45] Walshe was an active entrepreneur in Waterford, in addition to his legal practice.[46] In mid-1641, before the outbreak of the rebellion in October, he made arrangements for the transport of some 8,000 soldiers to Spain.[47] He was mayor of Waterford when Ormond knighted him in February 1649. For many years the Walshe family represented Waterford City in parliament and John Walshe's own political career began at 27 years of age, when he was elected to the 1640 Parliament where he quickly became a busy and trusted member of the Commons.[48] Like many others of his background, Walshe became involved in the 1641 rebellion and his activities during the earlier years of the revolt are recorded in the TCD Depositions and elsewhere. It is difficult to reconcile Walshe's activities as a rebel with his subsequent legal career. It could be argued that he was swept up in the rebellion like many others of his generation, such as Pierce Butler, the son and heir of Sir Richard Butler of Banshagh. Piers Butler, the eldest son of Viscount Galmoy (who also attended Gray's Inn) and yet another Piers Butler, the first Viscount Ikerrin, also joined the rebellion at an early stage in 1641, but these latter Butlers commanded troops of soldiers as distinct from operating as marauding bandits. It is possible that the depositions refer to a different person – Walshe is a common surname in

Tipperary. Having considered the evidence however, on balance it would appear that John Walshe was an active rebel in early 1642.[49]

Walshe was one of the many lawyers active in the Catholic Confederation and its General Assemblies and carried out a number of judicial functions. In 1644 he was one of the judges appointed by the General Assembly to a new central court of judicature in Kilkenny, to try civil and criminal cases.[50] In 1651 he was appointed a judge of a single judicial authority to 'have cognizance of all pleas'.[51] He frequently acted as the Confederates' agent in negotiations. There is little trace of his activities from 1650 until 1653, when he was dispensed from transplanting, on the dubious grounds of his 'many good and acceptable services to the commonwealth'.[52] There is also a curious deposition from 1654 which recounts that on 13 February Walshe was examined about Darcy's activities in Kilkenny during the Confederation.[53] Whether there is any connection is not clear, but a month later, on 13 March 1654, he was living in Amsterdam and was of sufficient note that Edward Hyde, later the earl of Clarendon, recorded Walshe's concern that the end of the First Anglo-Dutch war would force him to leave the Dutch republic for Antwerp.[54] But Walshe's career as a politician and judge were over and his movements between the end of 1654 and 1660 cannot be traced.

Talbot's mother was Grace Calvert, a daughter of George Calvert, first Lord Baltimore. Calvert had been an English lawyer and successively MP, secretary of state and Privy Councillor. He was granted 2,300 acres in Longford in 1622, and created Lord Baltimore of Longford in 1625, the year he resigned as secretary and publicly declared his Catholicism. He surrendered the Longford lands and bought an estate at Clohamon in Wexford, where he stayed in 1625–26. Calvert also had interests in the Americas, and he secured a royal charter for lands which eventually became the state of Maryland – its capital Baltimore is named after his Irish title. George Calvert died in 1632 and was succeeded by his son, Cecil, the second Lord Baltimore, and brother of Talbot's mother Grace. Although the proprietor of Maryland, Cecil never visited his colony, and appointed various governors, usually family members. Cecil's son Charles was governor in 1670 and Talbot was appointed secretary of the colony by his uncle. His duties were described in the instrument of appointment: 'Sir William Talbot Baronet Principal secretary of the province of Maryland and also Keeper of all and singular the Records within the said Province and also chief Judge for Probate of wills and Granting of Letters of Administration'.[55] In addition to his formal duties, Talbot was given detailed instructions in relation to protecting Cecil's landed interests and rents.[56]

Initial reports marked his tenure as a great success, but Talbot's stay in Maryland was cut short by his father's death in 1671. Charles Calvert took over the administration of Talbot's business in the colony, and hoped he would return.[57] But he was fearful that Richard Talbot would persuade William to stay in Ireland, notwithstanding that the post of secretary was very remunerative. Calvert was not blind to Talbot's faults, and he noted Talbot's greed for money.[58] In fact, Talbot had other sources of income and could assume his father's position as the duke of York's legal counsel with its salary and perquisites. More importantly from Calvert's point of view, he also expressed concern to his father 'that Sir William Talbot gives you cause to fear he will not be so kind to his mother as he ought'.[59] Notwithstanding these reservations, he concluded his letter fearing that Talbot would not return: 'for I should be much disheartened if it should be so, for he was a great comfort to me both in respect of his relation and parts'.[60] It is clear that the Calverts believed that Talbot had neglected his mother, whose fortune had probably declined with her husband's.[61] Barely a year later, Charles Calvert was no longer in any doubt: 'I am heartily sorry to hear that my cousin Talbot hath so behaved himself towards your Lordship and his mother, and truly I must confess in this he hath much deceived me in my thoughts of him.'[62] Talbot recognised that he could not return to Maryland without Baltimore's blessing. He owed his career as a colonist to family connections, and it was those same family connections which ensured that his brief career as a colonist was over.

After his return from Maryland in 1671, there is very little known about Talbot's career for the next ten years, until the early 1680s. There is a tantalising glimpse of his activities in August 1678, just before the eruption of the Popish Plot. Robert Southwell reported to Ormond that Talbot had secretly given the Lord Chancellor, Sir Heneage Finch, an abstract of the Bill of Confirmation. This suggests Talbot was acting at the highest levels in relation to exceptionally sensitive matters of state.[63] On the other hand, he may have been involved in more nefarious business. In November 1678, at the start of the Popish Plot hysteria, he was the recipient of what seems to be a very unwise letter from one A.W., writing from London, apparently 'flowing out of your distressed sister's heart'.[64] The letter called on him to 'act vigorously in your station while it is called today, lest we all perish in Ireland as we all do in England. Our plots are daily more and more discovered, which makes all sorts of people to rejoice in our calamities, and most people do come in duly to take the damnable Oath of Allegiance and Supremacy, so as the Pope will be cast out of his chair of State.'[65]

Talbot became deeply engaged with the Plot when, sometime in 1679, he wrote his Observations.[66] This is an exceptional document and casts Talbot is a more reflective and erudite light than any other aspect of his career. It is not clear why he wrote it, or to whom it is addressed; it is possible he may have intended to publish it as a pamphlet, but there is no evidence for this. Neither is it clear how it came to be in Bishop King's papers. His professed object was to impartially compare the actions of Catholics and Protestants since the Reformation, and in more recent times, in order to judge the accusations against Catholics made by Oates and others. He distinguished the tenor of Protestant and Catholic reaction to the plot.[67] Alarmed Protestants seemed to regard the extirpation of Catholicism as the only means to ensure their own security. Incredulous Catholics pointed to a prejudiced justice system which accepted the evidence of unreliable witnesses. This baffled Talbot, knowing how difficult it is to securely carry out a conspiracy such as the witnesses averred, even more a plot said to involve so many participants. In order to better understand the origins of the Plot, Talbot analysed the legal aspects of the many religious disputes and conflicts in England and elsewhere which had occurred since the Reformation.

He began with a very recent event in England, the execution of Edward Coleman, which Talbot considered a miscarriage of justice. Examining events in his own lifetime and prior to the Restoration, Talbot recounted what had happened in England during the Civil War, and under the Commonwealth and Protectorate, and in the Irish rebellion over the same period. Moving from the plot itself, he turned back to show how the civil order of England had been undermined by religious disputes in the less recent past, during the reigns of James I, Mary Queen of Scots, Queen Elizabeth and Queen Mary. Similarly, and in considerable detail, he showed how the Reformation destabilised France and caused religious upheavals in Germany, Switzerland, Sweden and Poland. Cities and states such as Hildesheim, Flanders, Brandenburg, Bohemia and Hungary were all convulsed by religious strife. The Spanish monarchy was so intent to ensure the Reformation would not destabilise Spain that it was prepared to tolerate the horrors of the Inquisition.

In an even-handed vein he summarised: '[W]hereas accusations are strongly laid to accuse papists of murder fagot and fire massacres conspiracies infinite villanies, the protestants are not behindhand with them in any sort of crime though not always of the same nature yet equivalent if not more outrageous'. The plot had caused him to consider the true nature and consequences of religious conflict. He concluded that to foment religious strife was to invite injustice and bloodshed and create civil and international disorder. The rights of kings to rule were sacred, and could not be overthrown by religious imperatives. No doubt his sweeping generalisations on the course of Reformation history can be challenged as religiously partial and legalistic. But his breadth of reference is remarkable, and shows engagement with lively cultural and intellectual exchange. His insistence on regal authority and the maintenance of legal order is consistent with a lawyer's approach to constitutional propriety. His even-handed approach to the iniquities committed by all denominations might be read as judicial impartiality. For a brief period in his later career he had the opportunity to bring these principles to bear in the public arena.

Talbot's interest in the Plot may have been more than academic. According to the evidence given by Maurice Fitzgerald, an important but unreliable Popish Plot witness in 1680, he attended a meeting in the winter of 1679, when among other arrangements, Col. Fitzpatrick and Sir William Talbot 'were to have some great commands'.[68] The Plot had direct repercussions for Talbot's family. He appealed for the release of his uncle Peter in vain.[69] Yet he seems to have borne no animus toward Ormond, because barely six months after his uncle's death he was facilitating important correspondence between him and the duke of York.[70] Ball tells us he was protecting recusants in Ireland as late as 1682, when the turmoil occasioned by the Plot had largely subsided.[71] Notwithstanding this, in June of that year there was a flurry of correspondence between Ormond, his son the earl of Arran and the Protestant primate, Michael Boyle, concerning a mass house which Talbot was suspected of setting up or tolerating. Ormond hesitated to act directly against Talbot, who denied all knowledge of it.[72] The Plot had run its course.

Unlike Walsh's early years as a Confederate, or Talbot's sojourn as a colonial administrator and commentator on the Popish Plot, Dillon's early career was spent more conventionally, building up an estate. The Westport Papers provide some information relating to how Dillon built and managed his estate. In 1675, he bought a quarter (of a townland) in the Mayo barony of Costello from Cun Oge Jordan for £15.[73] In 1677, Richard Talbot of Malahide sold his interest in 333 acres in Roscommon to Dillon for £50, subject to Talbot and Dillon's interests being confirmed by the commissioners for determining the claims of transplanted persons.[74] Shortly afterwards the commissioners issued the relevant certificate.[75] Dillon managed his estate by letting it to a wide range of tenants, often for relatively small amounts.[76] An undated note in the Westport Papers purports to set out Dillon's lands in Roscommon and Leinster.[77] While there are some correspondences with other records, the note is far from comprehensive and its principal value is to give some indication of the tenants to whom part of the lands were set, and the rents they paid. He engaged agents to manage many of his properties, and they prepared accounts that showed the rent received and how the money was disbursed.[78]

Most of Dillon's significant debts were incurred jointly with his uncle John Browne, to which we will turn later. But he incurred many small debts in his own right, of which the Westport Papers record probably only a very small part. Even while still a student in London, he had run up notable debts.[79] Back in Ireland, at first the amounts involved were relatively modest,[80]

But as time went by the amounts increased. For example, in 1681 he borrowed £102 10s and in 1684 £151 5s.[81] Throughout 1684–85 he continued to borrow, mostly small amounts.[82] It was not long before Dillon started to encounter legal pressure in respect of the money he owed. It was difficult to get good tenants and the local economy was poor.[83] A case in early 1685 in respect of a modest debt of £100 related to the purchase of land.[84] In 1686 he was sued, together with several co-defendants, in three cases in the King's Bench by Richard Thompson and Robert Johnson.[85] Keeping track of Dillon's finances, particularly with respect to his dealings on behalf of the Crofton family, was never going to be an easy task, and he seems to have gone through a succession of agents and scriveners who had the unenviable task of monitoring numerous transactions and dealing with requests for payment.[86] Francis Rice prepared an account showing total payments and charges in the period of three years and three months of £429 8s 8d, including interest of £76. This was partly funded by receipts from Dillon's land agent and others, but the balance of £297 15s 8d was due from Dillon.[87] The relationship seemed to sour and Rice pressed Dillon to repay him.[88] Dillon seemed to subsequently transfer his allegiance to Thomas Palmer, the scrivener, who in January 1686 accounted to Dillon for receipts and payments.[89] Dillon was appointed prime serjeant in February 1687, and in March there is a note of financial panic in his letter to Palmer, concerning the purchase of some land.[90] The responsibility for dealing with Dillon's affairs next fell to Ignatius Browne of Galway, a landowner with whom Dillon had many transactions.[91] Notwithstanding his appointment as prime serjeant, he was not immune from having to defend substantial claims for £700 and £706 in the King's Bench in 1687.[92] By 1688, even a modest debt could provoke serious difficulty. Dillon and William Jones from Dublin had jointly borrowed £100 from Samuel Hughes, who could not obtain repayment and secured a judgment against them.[93] But by April 1688 normal commerce was coming to a close.

Dillon was well capable of getting into debt in his own right, but in the late 1670s he joined his uncle in business, and became intimately involved in Browne's financial affairs. The earliest evidence in the Westport Papers is a power of attorney in April 1677, which relates to money borrowed by Dillon, Browne and George Kennedy.[94] It did not take long for them to end up in court. James Knight from Dublin had loaned Browne and Dillon £100, and not being repaid got a judgment of £200 in the Court of Exchequer in January 1678.[95] Henry Monk loaned £300 to Dillon and three others in February 1682. Five years later, in June 1687, he incurred costs of £6 18s 4d in entering judgment against them.[96] Browne, Dillon and, frequently, Kennedy continued to borrow relatively small sums throughout 1682–84.[97] A spate of borrowing at the end 1684 included some smaller amounts but also the substantial sum of £1,500 from William Caulfeild, Viscount Charlemont.[98] A list of Browne's debts drawn up by the scrivener and notary Thomas Sisson in January 1685 does not include the Charlemont debt.[99] Despite this, the total was £3,510, and Dillon was a joint party for £2,160.[100] Neither Browne nor Dillon seems to have been touched by any religious bias when borrowing money; there are few if any Catholic creditors on the list. The principal amounts outstanding continued to grow in 1685–86 and the interest on unpaid debts at 10 per cent continued to mount up.[101] For example, a bond for £300 taken out in November 1685 remained unpaid seven years later in December 1692, when an account was drawn up. The debt then stood at £448, despite £17 being paid in 1686 and the lender having given a credit for interest 'to be deducted as other creditors do being a year and a half, £45'.[102]

As was the case in relation to the debts he incurred in his own right, in 1685 legal pressure began to mount against Dillon and Browne jointly. In 1686, Richard Thompson, Thomas Bullmore and Robert Johnson took action against Browne and Dillon in the King's Bench.[103] As a precaution, and in order to secure Browne and Kennedy's interests, Dillon indemnified Browne and Kennedy in 1686 by transferring all his Irish estates to them for 99 years for one grain of wheat, unless Dillon discharged the debts by which the three of them were jointly bound.[104] The last insight we have into Dillon's financial affairs before the Jacobite War is a list of judgments against him, presumably still outstanding, obtained in the Court of Exchequer, between 1680 and 1689.[105] They amounted to £23,591 in total, and of these, the not insignificant sum of £7,755 related to judgments against Dillon in his own right. The overwhelming majority of Dillon's creditors were Protestant, the chief of whom was Elinor Warren who was owed the prodigious sum of £11,000.[106] Of his debts incurred with other parties, inevitably John Browne featured prominently.

Walsh's career as Ormond's seneschal

At the Restoration, Walshe returned to a very different country from the Ireland he had left in the 1650s. His legal career was radically transformed by his relationship with James Butler, then the marquess of Ormond. Ormond would have been aware of Walshe's public role as an MP in 1640. Certainly, he encountered Walshe as one of three representatives of the Confederate Catholics who presented a remonstrance to the king's commissioners in March 1643 and Walshe was frequently an intermediary between the Confederation and Ormond in the period 1643–50. All of this must have given Ormond an appreciation of Walshe's skills and character. Ormond's business dealings with Walshe also stretched back many years – possibly to 1641 when he arranged the transport of some 8,000 soldiers to Spain. The records of early dealings are sketchy. Perennially short of money, in March 1644 Ormond borrowed £500 from Walshe, notwithstanding Walshe's involvement in the Confederation.[107] In April 1644 Ormond expressed a preference for doing business with Walshe, and urged his agent Edward Comerford to negotiate with him.[108] Patrick Archer, the Kilkenny merchant, had extensive dealings with Walshe on behalf of Ormond, including the provision of funds for the marchioness, at a time when Ormond's future in Ireland was precarious. But all did not run smoothly, and on 22 August 1650 Archer complained to Ormond that the terms under which Thomas Preston had surrendered Waterford to Cromwellian forces ensured 'that counterfeit knave and traitor Sir John Walsh' would save his goods in the city, whereas Archer lost all his.[109]

On 24 July 1660, the English House of Lords restored Ormond's estate and his agents began to repossess his land. It was not until November however that the king signed the warrant giving effect to the Lords' resolution and immediately, in December 1660, Walshe was appointed by Ormond 'to be seneschal, steward and stewardship of all my manors, lands, tenements and hereditaments in Ireland'. Ormond made the appointment 'out of the special trust and confidence which I repose in the integrity care and circumspection of John Walshe', and allowed him to appoint a 'sufficient and able deputy or deputies'.[110] Walshe appointed his brother David as deputy seneschal. Ormond trusted Walshe implicitly and in 1661 a cypher was devised so that they could communicate securely.[111] The appointment as seneschal gives little indication of the extent of the responsibilities assumed by Walshe, which included the recovery and management of Ormond's estate, acting as legal adviser to the duchess, general political and legal counsel and advising on the political and personal aspects of the Acts of Settlement and Explanation.

In this latter capacity, Walshe was intimately involved in the discussions leading to the Gracious Declaration of November 1660, and the Acts of Settlement and Explanation, which was arguably the greatest service Walshe rendered Ormond over his entire career.[112] As early as December 1660, Ormond wrote to his long-standing physician and friend Dr Gerald Fennell to tell Fennell that he had been omitted from the Declaration for 'reasons ... you would not disapprove' and that John Walshe would 'tell all things more at large'.[113] In 1661, Walshe took a staunchly pro-Catholic position and advised Ormond that for many reasons adventurers and soldiers should be compensated with money rather than land.[114] He was particularly concerned that they would become too influential: 'In martial and civil government they will carry all before them – they will be the strongest party in parliament.'

He argued that, if they are satisfied with money, 'all of them being mechanics', they would return to their former trades in England where they were sure to be successful. Walshe believed that if the native Catholics were restored to their former estates, and were granted the estates of delinquents, for which they would pay more than the adventurers and soldiers, 'by this means [they] will make the most considerable party'. He insisted that a strong, Catholic Ireland would act as a counterweight to the other kingdoms, with whom it would not join in mischief.

The Act of Explanation was a daunting problem for Ormond. He had to devise a formula to balance Protestant and Catholic interests in order to achieve a legislative settlement to the land problem. In addition, he had to calibrate carefully how much of his own interest might be ceded to the common fund of land to facilitate passage of the Bill, while limiting the damage to his own estate. Walshe played an important role in both considerations. In contrast to the strategy in relation to the Act of Settlement, Walshe's advice in relation to the Act of Explanation was much less political and more practical. In May 1664, a series of four schedules was prepared, one for each province, 'of the Irish Claimants to Lands ... distinguishing their behaviours severally in and after the Rebellion'. The schedules listed families that lost their lands under Cromwell, were not compensated 'for the most part' with lands in Connacht or Clare, and were not restored by the 1663 Court of Claims.[115] The lists were prepared for Ormond from which he would select the nominees for restoration to their estates under the Act of Explanation. Walshe seems to have been directly involved in the preparation of the documents relating to Munster and Leinster and gave them to Ormond on 29 May.[116]

Ormond's personal position was to be set out in a proviso in the Bill and in April 1664 the king asked him to come to London to take part in the crucial discussions to finalise the text. It is noteworthy that Ormond relied on two Catholics, Sir Nicholas Plunkett in London and Sir John Walshe in Ireland, to provide the legal advice to protect his own vital interests. In turn, Walshe engaged counsel in Dublin to advise on the Irish aspects of the proviso. One of Ormond's concerns was to ensure that the new Act did not in any way endanger his grant under the Act of Settlement.[117] In July 1664, Walshe submitted to Ormond a detailed history of his estate in Tipperary, 'from the reign of King Henry II to this day'. The document is no longer extant, but it is clear that it was intended as an aid in the preparation of the proviso. Legal advice was sought on complex issues involving the precise rights of the king in what might otherwise be Ormond's estate and Walshe prepared a brief for counsel. This document is not in Walshe's hand, but the clear style of reasoning is typical of him.[118]

Ormond's intention was to preserve his rights under the Act of Settlement, but it became clear that, together with others, he would have to compromise in order to bring about a lasting solution. Ormond had to balance the importance of ensuring that the stock of land should not be insufficient 'as to disappoint the whole work', and on the other hand secure adequate provision for his own family, given his enormous debts.[119] It was natural that Ormond would turn to Walshe to advise him of the consequences of surrendering some of the forfeitures granted to him under the Act. In his *Life of Ormond*, Carte described Walshe's role: 'a good lawyer, a wise and an honest man who had the chief care of all [Ormond's] estate and affairs and managed both with great abilities and fidelity'.[120] Together with the Attorney General Sir William Domville, Walshe advised Ormond on the legal and financial consequences of the various proposals which were advanced to deal with the issue.[121] A new proposal began to emerge that Ormond should receive a lump sum of £50,000, sourced from one year's rent on the lands assigned to adventurers and soldiers. Sir Nicholas Plunkett had been in London since 1663, primarily representing Catholic interests, but clearly keeping a weather-eye on Ormond's affairs – 'a person to whom I shall owe my whole substance'.[122] In December 1664, and again in January 1665 he wrote from London in relation to Walshe's observations on the proviso.[123] In a rare departure from his focus on Ormond's affairs, and an even more rare display of Catholic partisanship, Walshe was also worried about rumours concerning lands previously held by Irish Catholics, and lands assigned to transplanters being 'brought in'. This would be against all conscience and justice, if 'honest and meriting persons and their posterity must beg' as a result.[124] Throughout 1665, Walshe continued to advise Ormond and the Act of Explanation was finally passed in December 1665.[125]

The process of recovering Ormond's land was long and complex. Ormond not only had difficulty in recovering his estate; once recovered he had difficulties in retaining it. Under the Act of Settlement, the duke of York had been granted the estates of the regicides, and if regicide land was not available, then lands of equal value were to be set out for him. This put Ormond in opposition to York in cases where ownership of the lands was unclear or contested, as in Gowran, Co. Kilkenny. This case merits no mention in Carte's *Life* or any of York's biographies, but Ormond proceeded with great care against such a powerful opponent, and Walshe was centrally involved in resolving Ormond's issues with York.[126] Walshe trod cautiously, and in April 1665 he noted Ormond's instruction not to meddle in anything touching York's estate until further instructed.[127] Under the Act of Explanation, York was exempted from the provision requiring retrenchment of one-third of his estates. But his entitlement under the Act of Settlement had been considerably whittled down by land which had been decreed under the Court of Claims, land bought *bona fide* from regicides and land granted to certain individuals, including Ormond, and in all these cases York was to be reprised. This was another recipe for conflict between Ormond and York and in November 1666 Walshe reported to Ormond on a possible dispute with York in relation to land in Carlow, which neither Ormond nor York wanted aired in the Court of Claims – there was to be 'no clashing in public' – and so agreed among themselves. It was Walshe's 'humble opinion that a small composition is better parted with, than a suit of law gained'.[128]

In 1667, Ormond faced other challenges to his ownership, some of which were supported by his political opponents, including Lords Berkeley, Robartes, Ashley and Buckingham, and he relied on Walshe's help to advance his interests.[129] In 1668, Ormond was in deep political trouble and in April of that year he was forced to go to London to defend himself. Walshe prepared some material for his defence.[130] Ormond's financial administration was under scrutiny, and he had been accused of enriching himself and his followers. Walshe supported him, showing the lands that Ormond had surrendered for the consideration of £50,000.[131] The total acreage was 319,062 acres; the yearly value, at 2 shillings per acre, was £31,906. Another challenge, and a potential source of embarrassment, arose in Kerry. Ormond was Chancellor of Trinity College Dublin, and the College had written to him that his agents in Kerry were inappropriately claiming land that Trinity considered theirs. Ormond asked Walshe to send Trinity's complaint to his agents for a report of the details of past ownership that supported his claim. Ormond thought it was as likely that Trinity was misinformed as that his agents were acting inappropriately. But Ormond insisted that he should have a prompt report 'so that the university of which I am Chancellor may receive no wrong, whilst I am Governor, much less under any pretence of my own interest'.[132] There is no record of Walshe's report.

Ormond was frequently a litigant in the second Court of Claims where he was represented by counsel, appointed or approved by Walshe. Walshe kept Ormond informed of proceedings and in at least some cases seems to have had a powerful, if not determinative, influence over how the cases would be run, even to the point of overruling Sir Nicholas Plunkett, probably the most distinguished counsel of the period.[133]

Ormond's financial situation had been precarious for decades; in the 1630s he had debts of £45,000 and the annual rents from the estate were c.£7,000.[134] Aggressive estate management was required to relieve the debt. Toby Barnard argues that in the 1630s Ormond attended to the needs of his patrimony, in much the same way as the earls of Cork in Munster or Antrim in Ulster. He 'was not only willing to experiment, but even to reconstruct the Butler interest on his lands'. But the period of the Confederation cut him off from his seat and rents, and subsequently he 'was absent from Kilkenny or pre-occupied with the affair of state'.[135] Barnard argues that Ormond was incapable of managing his estates and was ill-served by agents who defrauded him.[136] In fact, Ormond's correspondence with Walshe shows that, far from being averse to estate management, Ormond worked with his agent and seneschal to ensure his estate was maintained, enlarged and profitably managed. In 1663, Walshe reported that rents had risen by 130 per cent; whether this was due to Walshe's stewardship or the more settled times it is impossible to tell.[137] A steady rental stream was required to manage Ormond's indebtedness, which Walshe reported on in June.[138] Ormond asked for an account of all mortgages compounded a few weeks later.[139]

Ormond's lands in Kerry provide a good example of the problems he faced and his attention to the minutiae of his dealings with his tenants. He was in England in June 1664, when Walshe reported on how the duke's commissioners for Kerry sought to increase the rents of his tenants. In May 1664, the commissioners wrote to Walshe. They noted that they had sought to increase rents, but because of the duke's order of 7 May to not remove English tenants, nor increase their rents, they were unable to increase his revenue. As a consequence some of the English tenants would have 30 or 40 ploughlands, contrary to the duke's instructions that no more than 12 ploughlands should be set to any one person. The commissioners felt the tenants should have the land they occupied with their own stock, and no more. Two of Ormond's 'English' tenants were obstructive, and the commissioners sought guidance whether the two should be confined strictly to the lands they actually occupied, or be allowed retain the lands they had profitably sub-let to under-tenants in prior years.[140] The Lord Deputy did not want to give an opinion in the matter other than to warn the commissioners not to meddle in Sir William Petty's lands, and to await the duke's advice.[141] Ormond replied later that month that his priority was that his title should be acknowledged, and he did not want his possessions altered or the rents changed.[142]

George Mathew, Ormond's Catholic half-brother and agent, and Walshe were involved in supporting the duke in securing reliable tenants, at least some of whom were Catholic.[143] In addition to responding to requests for tenancies, Ormond dealt with estate employees.[144] Contrary to Barnard's assertion, in these cases Ormond was intimately involved in the management of his estate, with the assistance of Mathew his agent and Walshe his lawyer. His priorities were to deal equitably with his employees and secure prospective tenants who would be reliable and profitable.

In a dispute over succession, the Ormond patrimony had been split by James I between the earl of Ormond and Sir Richard and Elizabeth Preston in 1618. The Prestons' only surviving daughter, also Elizabeth, became a substantial landowner in her own right when her parents died in 1628. Her marriage to James Butler in 1629 reunited the Butler estate, which amounted to some 300,000 acres over seven counties. He became duke in 1661. Perceval-Maxwell described her spending lavishly on entertainment to support her husband's state, and at the same time concerned to reduce the family debts and working tirelessly to restore and improve the Ormond estates.[145] When the duke was engaged on matters of state, it would fall to the duchess to manage family affairs. Walshe frequently took his instructions from her in relation to how he and the other trustees of her estate were to deal with the family's finances.[146] He was obliged to tread a wary path depending on the facts, relying variously on the commissioners, the king or the lords justices to secure the Butler interest.[147] The duchess consulted the duke, who broadly approved Walshe's strategy in each case.

In June 1664, Ormond was once again preoccupied with affairs of state, having been summoned to England by the king to deal with the Bill of Explanation. A letter from Walshe to the duchess touched on many issues of the day. Ormond owed money to Sir John Temple, and although Ormond had doubts, Walshe advised payment of the debt.[148] He was not solely occupied with estate matters and gave thanks to the Almighty that 'my Lord of Ossory begins well, & his place becomes him, as well'.[149] He is observed 'to be vigilant, careful, and very wary'. In a very rare reference to his own family affairs, he apologised for having written to the duke concerning his father's interest, 'which is upon the list'.[150] He added that '[th]e sufferings of himself and his family are generally known'.[151] In July 1664, he provided the duchess with a summary of the effect of the Act of Settlement on the Ormond's private Deed of Settlement of 4 January 1664, which, inter alia, granted certain lands to a younger son, the earl of Arran, subject to a life interest for the duke. There was also a general account of the duke's estate, including observations on the value of the Mayo estate ('cannot be less than £700'), the setting of tithes ('the Comptroller expects will amount to £1,000') and the collection of the chief rents ('which are more considerable than six times as much of any other rent').[152] Relations between the earls of Ossory and Arran were clearly uneasy. In October 1664, Walshe wrote to Ormond about 'the loving expressions of my Lord Deputy towards Lord Arran' which Walshe hoped would lead the latter to do something 'for his encouragement'. Walshe argued that Arran 'will be found a loving brother and an obedient child, if others will leave him to himself'. Walshe also gave details to Ormond of the rentals in connection with the provision to be made for Lord John Butler, Ormond's seventh child and later earl of Gowran.[153] Family relations had clearly improved by 1665, when Walshe was involved in the disposition of family assets. He confirmed to the duchess that he had conferred with Lord Deputy Ossory to obtain his approval for a settlement in favour of the earl of Arran, his younger brother.[154]

At the Restoration, Ormond's palatine jurisdiction over Co. Tipperary was restored. In addition, as an extensive landowner, he had the rights to hold a variety of manorial courts, leet and baron and it fell to Walshe to supervise Ormond's courts and their jurisdictions, which he did with great zeal. In 1663 the mayor of Clonmel wrote to Walshe suggesting that he write to his brother, the deputy seneschal, to desist from holding a court leet for the duke in Clonmel, since there was no basis for it either by prescription or charter, and any such courts were the preserve of the Corporation.[155] Walshe refused to accede in carefully graded language that teased out the legal background, and in particular the relative rights of the Corporation and Ormond to hold courts leet.[156] Similarly, in May 1665, Walshe reported on various events concerning the management and tenure of Ormond's estates in Tipperary. He told how Sir John Cole had a 'long and hot discourse' with him concerning certain Ormond lands, the substance of which was to 'absolutely deny your Grace's tenure'.[157] Cole told Walshe he should forebear summoning the people there to the court baron in Nenagh.[158] The outcome is not recorded, but the matter illustrates the disputes that could arise when title to lands was fluid.

James Kearney, a Catholic, was Deputy Clerk of the Crown in Ormond's courts, and was Walshe's eyes and ears when the latter was in Dublin. In addition, he had a wide range of administrative functions. More importantly, Kearney was to regularly brief Walshe on legal and other matters relating to Ormond's manors and palatinate. These letters provide an insight into Walshe's control over almost every aspect of the exclusive jurisdiction of Ormond's courts, and Kearney's almost obsequious deference to Walshe. Thus, in October 1663, he reported to Walshe, who was in Dublin, on a recent session of the Liberty Court in Cashel. The fees and fines from the court were an important part of Ormond's revenues, and Walshe required meticulous accounts.[159] In January 1664 he gave Walshe a report on proceedings at Clonmel court, including the lawyers and attorneys present, the amounts of the fines, forfeits and recognisances (£356 6s 4d) and issues connected with court procedure.[160] These amounts show the economic importance of the courts to the Ormond estate. The courts were also a source of prestige and an important means of exercising social and political cohesion and control in the Palatinate. Any disruption to their effective functioning reflected badly on Ormond and thus it is not surprising that Walshe paid so much attention to them on behalf of his patron.

Walshe reported to Ormond on a variety of issues, particularly when the latter was in London on matters of state. This included potential religious disturbances by Catholics, notwithstanding Walshe being Catholic himself.

For example, in June 1664 he reported to Ormond that Denis Magee, a Franciscan, had been commissioned to hold a visitation of his order throughout Ireland and also intended to hold a general chapter. Michael Boyle, the Protestant archbishop of Dublin, had been consulted and given advice. The earl of Ossory was to issue a warrant for Magee's arrest, together with Anthony Doherty the minister provincial. But Ossory would take the advice of the Privy Council before issuing the warrants.[161] Ormond placed a high level of trust in Walshe in relation to matters of state and in July he wrote to Ossory that 'there will be both security and advantage in acquainting John Walshe and Peter Walshe that information is possessed of endeavours to raise the Irish in rebellion – which they as much detest from honesty, as from knowing it to be ruinous to *their* [emphasis added] country'.[162] This is a rare example of Ormond making reference to John Walshe's confessional loyalty. Fr Peter Walsh was Ormond's ally and the promoter of the Remonstrance, the declaration of Catholic loyalty to the king; any suggestion of Catholic disloyalty was anathema to him. Another example occurred in July 1667, when Ormond's nemesis Orrery informed him of certain gatherings which had taken place. Ormond trusted Walshe to provide him with information, particularly in relation to matters in Tipperary, and asked him to investigate. Walshe reported four days later that there had been a meeting on 24 June at the first mass of John Geough, a young priest. He listed the principal gentlemen in attendance; most of them were Butlers. Four English Protestants were in attendance, including one Jones from Tipperary. There had been an earlier gathering under the guise of a hurling-match. He listed the principal gentlemen in attendance at the match; most of them were Ryans and there were three Protestants. Walshe checked with Kearney and his own family in relation to a reputed meeting by the roadside near Fethard, and could get no report of it, other than those who went to the parish priest on Sunday and holy days. He was clearly aware of the sensitivity involved and recommended that a list should be made of those in attendance and they should be examined 'to find out the bottom of it'. If any were found guilty of illegal assembly, they deserved no mercy, 'in this county, of all the counties of Ireland'.[163] Ormond replied two days later, reflecting on Walshe's report, and said that until he had heard from Ossory, he had no more to say: 'other than this: that it had been better the young Priest had said his last mass than his first, with so much ceremony and ostentation, and that unless those of that country shall demean themselves in such things with more caution, I shall be forced to give them more trouble, than I am otherwise willing to do'.[164]

Apart from securing Ormond's estates, Walshe did not neglect his own. Notwithstanding his powerful patron it took some considerable time before he was fully restored. According to the 1654 Civil Survey, his father David owned about 1,600 acres in fee, and Walshe himself owned a further 140.[165] Walshe also had some holdings in Kilkenny, and would have inherited his father's estate in 1650. In the light of his activities as a 1641 rebel and Confederate, at least 1,750 acres were liable to confiscation under the Cromwellian forfeitures. In 1654, Walshe is described as of Lisronagh, midway between Clonmel and Fethard, but there is no indication that he held any lands there.[166] It seems clear from Simington that he did not get a decree for lands in Connacht or Clare.[167] Ó Siochrú, however, tells us that Walshe returned to Ireland after the Restoration, and recovered his lands as a reward for his loyal service to the Crown.[168] It is not clear by what means this recovery was effected, but there can be little doubt that Ormond played a key role. Clause CCXXV of the Act of Settlement 1662 provided that John Walshe, and many others 'shall be forthwith restored to their former respective estates'.[169] As discussed earlier, many of those mentioned in the Act submitted applications to the Court of Claims. But some did not, and John Walshe was among them. This may have been because his activities in the 1640s and 1650s were such that it would be impossible to establish his innocence. In these circumstances he needed to rely on the provisions in the Act of Settlement or the intervention of his highly placed patrons.

One of the earliest entries on a list of 'Dispossessed landowners of Ireland 1664' for Co. Tipperary relates to John Walshe of Ballibechane and David Walshe his father.[170] That their names should feature prominently on the list is not surprising since Walshe was involved in its preparation for Ormond. The number 400 appears against their names, possibly the extent of lands to which they might be restored. Under the Act of Explanation 1665, Walshe was one of the 54 nominees to be restored to their personal seats with 2,000 acres adjoining. But it was not until a decree of 12 March 1679 that Walshe recovered 1,793 acres, including Rathronan House; this was essentially all the land he and his father held in 1654 according to the Civil Survey.[171] Almost immediately afterwards, Walshe settled his estate on his son, and D'Alton recorded that 'in 1679 John Walshe passed patent for 1,793 acres in Tipperary, to hold to him, his heirs and assigns, and to the heirs of Patrick Walshe, who was grandson of David Walshe the proprietor in 1641'.[172] It would seem that the Walshes managed to retain their estates after the Jacobite War; in 1698, Master Walshe, heir of David Walshe of Ballybeaghan in the county of Tipperary was among the many landowners whose land titles were confirmed under the Acts of Settlement and Explanation.[173]

In 1675, Walshe was 62 and one of his last recorded letters to Ormond relates to arrangements for the transfer of responsibility for his work to Ormond's nephew Thomas.[174] It would seem that Thomas was studying law, most likely in London. The letter is not in Walshe's hand, but the signature is, and is notably frail.[175] It cannot have been easy to follow in

Walshe's footsteps. Perhaps only a relative could have navigated the relationships within the Ormond family, as Walsh had managed so adroitly with the duchess and her sons. But the sheer range of Walshe's endeavours on behalf of the duke would have been an even greater challenge, and point to the many aspects of the law with which he engaged during his career.

Talbot and Dillon's careers in the 1670s and 1680s

William Talbot had an even more prestigious client than Walshe. The duke of York had a significant presence in Irish affairs when he profited considerably from the Irish Act of Settlement of 1662. This granted him the confiscated Irish lands of the regicides; other lands were to be found for him if sufficient regicide land was not available. Initially, the duke had been slow to exert his claims in the belief that most of the land would be allocated to Catholics. But when he discovered the extent of the grants given by the king to others, he decided to pursue his rights under the legislation. The exact extent of York's entitlement is contested; and it is problematic how much of this estate was actually in his hands.[176] Regardless of its precise extent, it is clear that York needed help in securing his legal entitlements and in the administration of his estate, and a succession of agents was involved. Talbot was described as principal agent for the duke of York's estate in 1677.[177] It is not clear when exactly Talbot became the manager of James's personal estate, but Lenihan is in no doubt that he owed the position, to which he was formally appointed in 1685, to the intervention of Richard Talbot.[178] This appointment ratified Talbot's earlier activities and secured a salary for his favoured nephew.

A vivid picture of Dillon's professional activities in the 1670s and 1680s can be found in the Chancery Bill Books for this period in the National Archives, which record the plaintiffs, defendants and counsel in each case, together with the dates of procedural documents in some cases.[179] It may be a token of Dillon's own eminence that many of the Catholic counsel he worked with in cases at the Chancery bar had distinguished careers, particularly after the accession of James II. Richard Nagle, who became Attorney General in 1687, is the most frequent presence in the Chancery Bill Books, often on the same side as Dillon, but frequently not.[180] Brian O'Neill, who entered Gray's Inn five years before Dillon and became a judge in 1687, acted in several cases in which Dillon was involved, and was defended by Dillon in 1680.[181] Theobald (Toby) Butler participated in many of the cases in which Dillon acted. Together with Dillon, he was involved in the negotiation of the articles of Limerick and had a distinguished clientele until he died in 1721.[182] In 1683, Dillon was in a case with Stephen Rice, who became chief baron of the Exchequer in 1686.[183] Of course it was inevitable there were many cases where Dillon opposed Protestant counsel such as Henry Whitfield, Thomas Whitshed, Henry Langford and Robert Rochfort.[184]

Dillon acted for a number of prominent Protestants, notwithstanding that the majority of his clients were Catholic. Thus he was counsel for the Cromwellian John Eyre from Co. Galway in November 1677.[185] He acted for the first Viscount Rosse twice in 1688; the first case related to disputes within the Parsons family, and in the second the plaintiffs were both Catholic and Protestant.[186] Other Protestant clients in this period were Carey Dillon, the future fifth earl of Roscommon, and William Rothery and John Whinnery, who had lent money to Sir William Ellis, the Protestant developer of the Oxmantown area.[187] Humphrey Jervis was another Protestant who developed a significant part of the city east of Oxmantown.[188] In November 1687 he gave clear and succinct instructions requiring Dillon to act on his behalf.[189] Thus it would seem that Dillon engaged with two of the most prominent property developers in late seventeenth-century Dublin. Perhaps Dillon's Protestant clientele is not surprising in an era where most litigation concerned land and Protestants had become the majority landowners.

Dillon's clients also included prominent Catholics such as Edward Bermingham, Lord Athenry, whose second wife was Bridget Browne, daughter of Col. John Browne, and Dillon's aunt.[190] He acted for Luke Plunkett, the earl of Fingal, in 1682 and 1684, and possibly against him in 1683.[191] The Preston family of Gormanston were clients in their 1688 suit against Peter Wybrants, the lord mayor of Dublin and Henry Moore, the earl of Drogheda.[192] Later that year, Dillon represented Sir Patrick Trant, an extensive landowner in Kerry and many of the counties of Leinster.[193] A month later he was defending William Dongan, the earl of Limerick.[194] As might be expected, his kinsmen the Viscounts Dillon of Costello-Gallen and the extended Dillon family, most of whom were Catholic, were important clients.[195] His most significant client was John Browne who in 1687 transferred his estate in Mayo and Galway to Dillon as sole trustee, to pay off his debts of some £13,000 due to 40 creditors.[196] Browne's rents and the profits from his ironworks were assigned for the benefit of his creditors and Dillon had to account for how he dealt with Browne's money.[197]

Talbot and Dillon as Jacobites

Talbot's life underwent something of a sea change on James II's accession in February 1685. Four months later Talbot's uncle Richard was raised to the peerage as earl of Tyrconnell.[198] It is an indication of Tyrconnell's regard for his nephew that, in the absence of any heir, Talbot would have succeeded to the peerage.[199] Talbot seems to owe his political and legal preferment to the influence of his uncle. Tyrconnell's patronage was powerful and Talbot's ascent was meteoric.[200] In March 1685 he was appointed to recover forfeited estates belonging to the king with an annual salary of £500.[201] This was clearly a continuation of his family's professional activities; his grandfather was legal adviser, agent and trustee to the earls of Kildare and his father legal counsel to the duke of York. Talbot continued the family business of estate management and was described as principal agent for the duke of York's estate in 1677.[202] In August 1685 there were rumours he was to be appointed a revenue commissioner. A year later he was discharged from his duties as land agent of the king, but he maintained his income; the salary of £500 was converted into a pension of the same amount.[203] In early 1687 he was made a Privy Councillor, an appointment that seems to have been largely honorary.[204] He seemed to be eligible for every possible appointment. When Tyrconnell was appointed Lord Deputy, Thomas Sheridan was appointed his secretary. Clarendon did not approve of Sheridan and warned him about his conduct. Sheridan replied 'that for all he cared Tyrconnell might give the secretary's place to his nephew Sir William Talbot'.[205] In 1689 he was elected MP for Meath in the Patriot Parliament and sent by the Commons to urge the House of Lords to expedite the Bill repealing the land settlement.[206] On 22 April 1689 Talbot became Master of the Rolls; the final appointment in Tyrconnell's catholicisation of the judiciary. In May 1689, he was named one of the commissioners for Meath to collect the subsidy voted to James II to pay for the army which Tyrconnell had raised.[207]

But Talbot's greatest success came in the summer of 1689, when Tyrconnell lobbied James II to dismiss Melfort as secretary of state. Talbot's name was mentioned as a possible replacement in July.[208] By the end of August, Talbot had been appointed, notwithstanding some reservations.[209] In fact Talbot's appointment as secretary was limited to civil matters and Richard Nagle was charged with military affairs.[210] James II soon came to regret the appointment and Lenihan suggests that there may have been some element of disgrace.[211] After five months Ignatius White, the grandly entitled Marquis d'Albeville, replaced Talbot who played no further part in the momentous events of 1690–91.

After Talbot's death in 1691 and subsequent attainder, a report was prepared in 1693 to enquire into the extent of James's private estate and Talbot's discharge of his royal duties as principal agent.[212] This throws some interesting light on how James exploited his estate for private and political purposes and how Talbot may have conducted his stewardship. The report observed that Talbot managed the private estate for many years and helped himself liberally while doing so. In addition to the yearly salary of £500, Talbot claimed 'poundage' or commission of 5 per cent on rents collected from remote counties and 3.75 per cent for the others. It is not clear how remote was defined, but if an average rate of 4 per cent is applied to the annual rents, Talbot would have charged an additional £300 per annum. In the account he drew up to November 1684, he charged over £4,000, which would suggest that he had been managing the estate for 13 years; in other words from his return from Maryland. In this account he also charged £5,500 for 'expenses at law', a sum which the report observes was probably more than the lands in question were worth. It is not clear to whom the 'expenses at law' were paid, but it is possible he charged for his own legal services. In addition, his charge for 'contingencies' of over £1,400 included £900 for travel; the same report tartly observes 'for he ridd not 20 miles but reckoned 30s. per diem'. Tyrconnell was blamed for approving all of these expenses.

Talbot died in Galway on 18 May 1691. The defeat of the Jacobite forces at Aughrim in July and Tyrconnell's death in Limerick in August signalled the end of the regime that sustained Talbot. No longer were there any patrons to dispense favour, or estates to exploit. This had far-reaching consequences for Talbot's own family estate which seems to have been at best partially restored to Robert Talbot between 1669 and 1670. We know from the TCD Down Survey that in 1641 the Talbots were extensive landowners in Wicklow and Meath, and from other sources it seems clear that they owned Carton. By 1670, the Wicklow estate had effectively disappeared, with only one townland remaining in his ownership.[213] The Meath estate was considerably reduced and it seems that Robert did not recover the family home at Carton, which may have returned to the Talbots only after his death and through the influence of Richard Talbot.[214] Notwithstanding his eminence and connections, and more than one instance of royal intervention, Robert had lost almost all of his extensive patrimony, and when he died in 1671, he left a very modest estate in Wicklow and Meath to his son. Talbot was attainted in 1691, when he was described as of Liscartan, Co. Meath. The baronetcy became forfeit, and his estate sold, subject to life interests for his wife.[215] The 1693 report noted that Talbot owed almost £8,700 to James II 'of which he never paid any part'. It was suggested that, although Talbot's estate was forfeit, because part of it was settled on his wife the debt should be charged on his wife's portion. As the widow of a high-ranking official in James II's retinue, it must be doubtful she ever enjoyed her life interest and she died in 1710.

On the accession of James II in 1685 Dillon was appointed King's Counsel and Recorder of Dublin.[216] In December 1686 the Lord Lieutenant wrote to secretary of state Sunderland in relation to appointing a successor in the Court of Common Pleas. He reviewed the 'most considerable lawyers at the bar'. He doubted Dillon would accept the appointment, 'he being in very great practice; he is a very honest gentleman and it is not fit for me to omit the best men'.[217] On his appointment as prime serjeant early in 1687 Dillon turned to his usual bookseller, James Malone, to enhance his library. His account for 1687 shows far fewer legal texts than in 1676.[218] Some of the works relate to contemporary matters, such as Peter Walsh's *Letters* or history, such as Flaherty's *Ogygia*. But the majority of the works relate to religious matters, and in particular Catholic apologetics.[219] Of these, there are works reflecting on the state of the Catholic Church in England and the French Catholic Church. It has to be wondered how a busy lawyer, now dealing with the demands of the serjeancy, had time for such refined reading.[220]

The position was not overly onerous, but it did carry some responsibilities, which are well illustrated in the book of the pleas of the Crown at Longford for 23 March 1687.[221] It was prepared by the Clerk of the Crown and shows the extent of Dillon's workload and the expeditious way in which cases were dealt with. It lists the names of the 41 defendants on the day, the nature of their crimes, and the court's decisions in a form of legal shorthand. Most of the charges related to the theft of horses, cattle and sheep, but some defendants were accused of breaking and entering, and stealing money. The majority had Irish names, although there were 'English' defendants such as William Henderson, who had been bound over at a previous session, was due to appear to show he had been of good behaviour in the interim, but in addition was now charged with stealing Cormuck Farrell's yellow cow. There were also political matters reflecting the tenor of the times. John Deane and William Stewart were charged with publishing a scandalous libel against the earl of Tyrconnell. John Akins junior and Henry Lenon were charged with speaking seditious words; Lenon had said 'he did not care a fart for any justice of peace in the Kingdom, and you rogues, you begin to Insult over us, because you have a papist King and papist Judges'. Protestant disquiet with Tyrconnell's catholicisation policy had become justiciable. Further, William King reported that Dillon was not above interfering mischievously in defending a Protestant minister *gratis* against his superior in order to 'Weaken the Jurisdiction of a Protestant Bishop and do a mischief to our religion'.[222]

While serving as serjeant, Dillon continued to attend to his legal practice.[223] Maynard records him in eight cases in the year 1687/88. Although the nominal remuneration for the role was modest, the position was lucrative in itself. Hart estimates that the office of second serjeant was worth £1,000 p.a. in the 1680s, and there is no reason to think the prime serjeant was at a relative disadvantage.[224] Although many of Dillon's clients were Catholic, some were not and his correspondence with them throws some light on the nature of the remarkably polite relations between Catholics and Protestants, notwithstanding the pressure of events. For example, on Christmas Day 1688 William Blayney wrote to Dillon from London apologising for the haste in which he left 'your Kingdom' due to his wife's entreaties.[225] He said that he had drawn a bill for £30, enclosed the balance, asked that Dillon should not fail the bill and to hear from him directly, at Mr Nott's in Pell Mell. Turning to politics and making clear where his allegiance lay, he gave Dillon an update following James II's flight to France two days earlier.

Dillon became an MP in the 1689 Jacobite parliament, although his election was not without controversy. William King stated that Tyrconnell had sent letters to the mayors and sheriffs recommending individual candidates, together with the election writs.[226] In the only case where a contest arose, Dillon failed to be appointed as a burgess in Dublin because he was too closely identified with the 'New Catholic Interest'.[227] He had bought an estate under the Act of Settlement and it was believed he would not support its repeal.[228] In the event he represented Mullingar. Although there is no direct evidence, since Dillon's nomination to the Dublin seat was rejected on the grounds that he was a new interest man and would object to the repeal of the settlement, it is likely he sided with his fellow legal colleagues who formed a pressure group to stymie the proposal.[229] Neither the king nor the New Interest could resist the calls to repeal. The parliament closed on 18 July, having voted to repeal the Restoration land settlement and the Cromwellian forfeitures.

In April 1690, in order to finance the war, James II raised a land-tax of £20,000 per month, and in his capacity as recorder, Dillon was appointed one of the Dublin commissioners charged with responsibility for collecting the tax.[230] Dillon was also actively involved in military affairs and commanded a troop of horse in the regiment of his brother-in-law Claud Hamilton, the earl of Abercorn.[231] He is described as Col. Garret Dillon in the Treaty of Limerick, but it is difficult to establish his precise military role.[232] There are records in the Westport Papers that give some small insight into the cost of maintaining the army, such as the saddlers' bills for Dillon's troop of cavalry.[233] In 1690 he was quartered in Dublin and was to be repaid for his outlay on munitions.[234] Abercorn's regiment fought at Enniskillen, Newtownbutler, the Boyne and Aughrim, but there is no evidence that Dillon did so.[235] It is a measure of his status that he was one of the commissioners who signed the Articles of Limerick on 3 October 1691. On 28 September a full conference of military, religious and legal leaders took place. The latter consisted of Dillon, together with his colleagues Sir Toby Butler and Col. John Browne.[236] Kinsella suggests that Dillon was favourably disposed to the thirteenth article of the civil treaty, which charged Catholic landowners with the payment of Browne's Protestant debts.[237] Because Dillon and Browne's affairs were intertwined, Dillon would certainly have gained from this; the role of the other leaders is less clear.[238] After the conclusion of negotiations, and together with other Jacobites who wished to continue to serve James II, Dillon left Ireland, his Irish estates and his Irish debts and opted to go to France.[239]

In the normal course, Dillon would have inherited his father Theobald's estate, when the latter died in 1649. Given his father's activities, it is highly likely that he was dispossessed. In the Mayo *Books of Survey and Distribution*, Feamore, which was Dillon's home according to the King's Inns records, was a modest estate of 149 profitable and 113 unprofitable acres in the ownership of Gerrald Dillon in 1641, subsequently disposed to Gerrald Dillon, and finally to Bryan Higgins. This is consistent with the family history: Gerald Dillon of 'Femore' in Mayo was father of Theobald and grandfather of Gerald, the subject of this study.[240] It is also consistent with the devolution of the estate after 1691, when Bryan Higgins bought it.[241] But Dillon owned more than his paternal estate. In July 1677, the commissioners for determining the claims of transplanted persons in Connaught and Clare issued a certificate in Dillon's favour over 1,420 acres (including Feamore) in the baronies of Clanmorris and Costello, in Co. Mayo.[242] A year later, a further grant was made to Gerrald Dillon of 4,098 acres in Co. Roscommon, 2,018 acres in Co. Mayo and 289 acres in Co. Galway.[243] There are no records to show by what means Dillon was entitled to these grants.

When Dillon decided to withdraw from Ireland he left a trail of legal and financial chaos. He had been outlawed and his estate forfeit, and the financial consequences of his departure to France were complex and long-lasting. The rents and other income that would normally have serviced his debts and paid interest were no longer available. The 1686 transfer of Dillon's estate to Browne, whose own affairs were far from straightforward, was to plague the latter for many years. Much of Dillon's debt was secured on his estate and the task of settling his debts began in 1692, and involved not only Browne, but other members of Browne's family, including his son Peter, his son-in-law Lord Athenry, his nephew Edmond Malone and George Kennedy.

The process was inevitably complicated by the fact that much of Dillon's debt was tied up with Browne's. For example, in June 1700 Browne paid the proceeds from the sale of 7,647 acres of his own land in the barony of Erris, Co. Mayo, to Robert Johnson in partial satisfaction of a debt owed to him by Dillon.[244] In August 1700, Browne entered into an agreement with Thomas ffotrell in relation to his own debts and joint debts with Dillon, setting out a schedule of payments.[245] But Browne and George Kennedy took the most important step when they sought the cooperation of the trustees for the forfeited estates to settle Dillon's debts and reimburse Browne and Kennedy for the payments they had made on Dillon's behalf.[246] Eventually, the petition to the trustees was heard in February and March 1702, and the majority of the claim was allowed.[247] But even this did not mean the end of Browne's dealings in Dillon's estate. In May 1703 he proposed to transfer the remaining interests he held under Dillon's 1686 arrangement to John Usher, a barrister and one of the masters of the High Court of Chancery, who was to pay £2,742 to Browne's Protestant creditors, under the thirteenth article of the Treaty of Limerick. Edmond Malone became involved at this stage, and received an acknowledgement from Usher that he held the Dillon lease in trust for the benefit of Browne and Malone equally.[248] Dillon was a forfeiting owner of more than 5,000 acres in Mayo, Roscommon and Westmeath, which were mostly bought by Bryan Higgins, for £300 on 19 June 1703.[249] The consideration seems remarkably small, but undoubtedly reflects the encumbrances on the land.[250] It would appear that these lands were somehow returned to Browne's control, because in the Westport Papers there is a draft deed of release of July 1703, in which Dillon transferred all his rights and estate, except his lands in Roscommon, and in the baronies of Costello and Clanmorris in Co. Mayo to Browne. This has the appearance of Dillon retaining his family lands, but absolving himself of all other matters, whether assets and liabilities, to Browne. This is not in Dillon's hand and it is not clear that it was ever executed, but it seems to be the last evidence in the Westport Papers of Dillon taking an active part in his Irish affairs.[251] In October 1703 Malone wrote to Browne that he intended to realise parts of Dillon's estate to provide for family members. However he intended to maintain some small part of Dillon's patrimony intact and had not made a demise of Feamore and Kelnecleally 'an entire farm about the seat of the family', which he would not let on any account, and where he was likely to install one of his nephews.[252] As late as March 1707, 16 years after Dillon had left Ireland, Dillon's debts continued to haunt Browne.[253]

Conclusion

The careers of these lawyers show how it was possible for Catholics to survive, and even thrive, in Restoration Ireland, despite an environment that was ostensibly hostile. Two of the three were clearly men of ability; Carte attested to Walshe's competence, and Clarendon somewhat grudgingly acknowledged Dillon's abilities. Perhaps it is not surprising there are no such encomiums for Talbot, and notwithstanding the wide breadth of historical reference disclosed in his Observations, he relied on his family connections rather than his wits for progression. But family connections, networks, and patronage were fundamental to the success of all three.

Talbot's was the most privileged family background. His father owned a large estate and his mother was the daughter of the first Lord Baltimore. As the only son he was at the centre of Talbot and Calvert networks, and stood to inherit his family's entire estate. Walshe's father owned a substantial estate in Tipperary. In contrast Dillon's father had a more modest estate but the family was connected to Viscount Dillon. More importantly, his mother Margery was one of the many daughters of Sir John Browne of the Neale, and his uncle was John Browne, the founder of the Westport dynasty. Walshe was married twice, but nothing is known of the identity of his wives. Talbot's wife was the daughter of the earl of Westmeath and the widow of Viscount Dillon. Dillon first married Susanna Crofton, née Clifford, the widow of Sir Edward Crofton of Mote, Co. Roscommon. His second wife was one of the daughters of the Baron of Strabane, and the sister of the earl of Abercorn. Talbot and Dillon's wives, therefore, came from distinguished families that enhanced their familial networks.

It is clear that all three came from an elite, privileged background that, in the case of Walshe and Dillon, could fund an expensive legal education in English Inns of Court over five years. Their religion would have made them especially aware of the anti-Catholic bias of English law and politics. Spending five years with their fellow students, the majority of whom were Protestant and English, and observing the operation of the courts in London, must have shaped their outlook on England and the English. At the very least, it enabled them to circulate in the world of the common law, and deal confidently with Protestant English lawyers, judges and other officials. Although Talbot did not attend the London Inns, his father's role as the duke of York's agent familiarised him with professional activity for the most exalted clients.

Their family background was instrumental in each of them assuming public leadership roles. Walshe's family had long represented Waterford in parliament, and he began his public life as an MP and became a significant figure in the Catholic Confederation during the 1640s. The Talbots had long service as MPs and William represented Co. Meath, but his public offices owed a great deal to the opportunities that his uncle Tyrconnell afforded him. Dillon was an MP for Mullingar and public office holder, and owed much to Tyrconnell's policy of catholicisation of legal and public appointments. Their family relationships also gave them the confidence and ability to develop networks of professional patronage and a clientele, and all three went about earning their living in very distinctive ways.

Walshe seems to have been a confident self-starter and had a prestigious and wealthy client in the staunchly Protestant earl of Cork from the earliest years of his practice. He had an independent career before 1641 but after his return from exile he seems to have had no intention of returning to conventional practice. By then he had encountered Ormond, and it was the latter who was to be his sole client and patron. He became quickly involved in Ormond's affairs and never looked further than the briefs provided by the duke for the last 15 years of his life. It is difficult to exaggerate the centrality of Walshe's position in Ormond's economic life, and the extent of the trust that Ormond placed in him. Ormond worked with other Catholics, such as George Mathew, Sir Nicholas Plunkett and James Kearney. Mathew was in a particularly trusted position as Ormond's half-brother and agent. Plunkett played an extremely important role in relation to the drafting of Ormond's proviso in the Act of Explanation. But Walshe was above all of these.

As a Confederate, Walshe was on the opposite side to Ormond in the 1640s, yet his career after 1660 was entirely in the service of Ireland's most prominent Protestant. After he became seneschal, one could doubt whether Walshe's work for Ormond was at all defined by his being Catholic. There are instances, however, where his Catholic sensibility emerges. He could cloak his sympathy for the restoration of Catholic estates under cover of the advice he gave Ormond to exclude English adventurers and soldiers as landowners. And later, when the Act of Explanation was being prepared, he was concerned about proposals relating to some Catholic estates. Walshe made a very rare request for Ormond's support in procuring the return of his own and his Catholic neighbours' estates. But for much of his later career, Walshe's religion was invisible in his dealings with Ormond. Thus, for Walshe, the Court of Claims was a forum to protect Ormond's interests, rather than for Catholic recovery. The anti-Catholic agitation of 1673–74 seems to have had no impact on him. There are a very few passing references to Walshe's confessional identity in Ormond's extensive correspondence, but for the most part it goes unnoticed. Nevertheless, there were occasions when Walshe's Catholicism could be exploited. Thus Ormond could ask Walshe to use his personal networks to report on Catholic gatherings in 1667. And this points to the larger truth in the nature of Walshe's relationship with Ormond. Ormond was a Protestant in a sea of Catholicism. The majority of the tenants on Ormond's estate were Catholic, as were many of the neighbouring gentry. The legions of servants, agents, employees and court officials who sustained Ormond's palatinate were mainly Catholic. Walshe was the intermediary who could navigate with ease and discretion between Ormond's Protestantism and the Catholic world of his palatinate. His career as Ormond's seneschal is a remarkable example of collaboration between a Catholic lawyer and his Protestant patron.

Talbot's career was almost completely dependent on family connections. His short sojourn as a colonist was entirely due to his Calvert relations. On his return from Maryland, and under the influence of his uncle Richard, he inherited the career and clientele which his family had worked for generations, and in particular his father's practice as the duke of York's agent. It was a measure of Tyrconnell's influence that York entrusted the significant task of managing his extensive Irish estates to Talbot. Although Tyrconnell presented him with many other opportunities, Talbot did not display any great flair for public office. After a year as the king's agent he was discharged from his duties, but characteristically retained his income from the office. The position of Master of the Rolls was a sinecure. He held the office of secretary of state for a mere five months. The 1693 report casts a poor light on Talbot's retaining York's funds and exacting every possible perquisite. The opportunities provided by Talbot's family connections far outstripped his ability to exploit them.

Of the three, Dillon had the most conventional legal career, building up an extensive and varied litigation practice over 20 years. Even when appointed prime serjeant, he could continue his private practice, notwithstanding his public duties. Although Dillon had a busy practice and achieved high legal office on his own merits, it is difficult to separate his career from his involvement in the financial affairs of his uncle John Browne. This began when he was a student in London, and continued long after he left Ireland in 1691. Given his family networks, it was inevitable that many of his clients were Catholics, but Dillon's professional life was marked by a high degree of collaboration with Protestants, a characteristic he shared with Walshe. Many of his clients at the Chancery bar were Protestant, as were many of the counsel he worked with or opposed. The fact that most of the people who lent him money were Protestant, and his polite relationships with Protestant clients in 1688 and 1689 when political friction was mounting, are measures of the confidence he could cultivate in lenders and clients.

Notwithstanding their professional skills and powerful connections, it is remarkable how difficult it was for these three Catholic lawyers to recover their family estates. The Talbots had royal patronage and Walshe was indispensable to the Lord Lieutenant. Robert Talbot, William's father, had spent a decade representing his own and his client's interests, and left William with a very modest estate in 1671. Walshe was in his last years when he was finally restored in 1679. Dillon received grants of his own and family lands in Mayo and Roscommon in 1677 and 1678. The long delays reflected the vulnerability of dispossessed Catholics and the determination of Protestant incumbents to retain their holdings. Catholic lawyers were tolerated and accepted in Restoration Ireland, and Protestants gladly used the skills of the most talented. But the fissures created by the Cromwellian land settlement ran very deep and when Protestant landed estates were threatened, even the most gifted and influential Catholic lawyers struggled to recover what was legally theirs.

These fissures became even more pronounced when the Jacobite parliament threatened to reverse the land settlement. When war began, professional collaboration was at an end. With James II's defeat, no forms of Catholic patronage remained and Dillon's Protestant clients had become his enemies. The careers of Talbot and Dillon were over. After 1691, they suffered the loss of their family estates for the second time in two generations. Talbot's stewardship of James II's revenues was picked over by the Williamites. Dillon left Ireland and it remained to his uncle to deal with his debts and estate. Their careers reflect the vulnerability of the Catholic elite in late seventeenth-century Ireland. These Catholic families were excluded from Parliament, many had lost their lands and influence, and all of them had to resort to a variety of strategies to maintain their social status. Apart from their estates, these lawyers had no financial resources on which they could depend. Of the three, Walshe was the most financially conservative and relied on the patronage of his employer. Dillon freely accumulated debt and Talbot used the duke of York's rents to fund his lifestyle. Even though highly placed and well-connected, they were entirely dependent on political stability and the retention of networks of influence. The rise and fall of James II proved their undoing as it did for all of Catholic Ireland.

Notes

1 Richard Bagwell, *Ireland under the Stuarts* (3 vols, London, 1963), vol. 3 p. 167.
2 John Walshe to Ormond, 27 Nov. 1666, Bodleian, Carte MS 35, fo. 150.
3 Arthur Annesley, *A Letter from a Person of Honour in the Country* (London, 1681), p. 31.
4 Morgan's troopers refused to kill them, and Morgan is said to have murdered them himself: R.S., *A Collection of Some of the Murthers and Massacres Committed on the Irish in Ireland since the 23rd. of October 1641* (London, 1662) pp. 20–1, EEBO, accessed 23 July 2023.
5 Sir Nicholas Plunkett wished him and Mrs Walshe a 'good Christmas' on 2 Dec. 1664, HMC *Ormonde MS*, NS 3, p. 186.
6 *15th Annual Report of the Commissioners of the PROI 1825*, vol. 16, app. I, Grants under Acts of Settlement (hereafter *15th Annual Report*), p. 264. John D'Alton, *Illustrations, Historical and Genealogical, of King James's Irish Army* (2nd ed., 2 vols, Dublin, 1860), vol. 2 p. 216.
7 In this study he is called Talbot, to distinguish him from his grandfather Sir William, his father Sir Robert and various other members of the extended Talbot family.

8 Pádraig Lenihan, *The Last Cavalier Richard Talbot (1631–91)* (Dublin, 2014), p. 8.
9 To the extent that in the turbulent times after the Ormond peace was concluded in 1649, the Lord Lieutenant put him in charge of managing Strafford's estates, which Ormond had taken 'into his special care': 27 Apr. 1649, HMC *Ormonde MS*, NS 1, p. 128. Lenihan, *Last Cavalier*, pp. 8 and 64.
10 Earl of Clarendon, *The Life of the Earl of Clarendon* (3 vols, London, 1827), vol. 3 p. 117.
11 Anne Creighton, 'Sir Robert Talbot' in *DIB*, vol. 9, p. 257. *15th Report,* p. 654. 17 & 18 Charles II c. 2, *Statutes III*, s. CLXX, pp. 101–2. Lenihan, *Last Cavalier*, p. 64.
12 Creighton, 'Sir Robert Talbot', p. 257.
13 Lenihan, *Last Cavalier*, p. 64. Creighton, 'Sir Robert Talbot ', pp. 256–7. For example, there is no reference to him in Maurice Ashley, *James II* (London, 1977) or John Miller, *James II: A Study in Kingship* (Hove, 1978).
14 F. Elrington Ball, *Judges in Ireland 1221–1921* (2 vols, London, 1926), vol. 1, p. 365. Ball gives no source for this information.
15 In April 1683 Frances explained to the duke of Ormond that her daughter had declined his offer since she had 'inclinations to a court life in France': Frances Nolan, *The Jacobite Duchess, Frances Jennings, Duchess of Tyrconnell, c.1649–1731* (Woodbridge, 2021), p. 77.
16 Anne Dillon may have had independent means, having secured her jointure from her son and the estate of her late husband: see NLI Westport Papers, MS 40,896/3(21), 26 Feb. 1683.
17 Lord Walter Fitzgerald, 'Carton', *Journal of the County Kildare Archaeological Society,* 4 (1905), pp. 3–34, at p. 7.
18 *The Register of Admissions to Gray's Inn, 1521–1889* (London, 1889), p. 306. It is almost certainly Feamore in the civil parish of Annagh in the barony of Costelloe in Co. Mayo.
19 15 Mar. 1661, MS 40,893/5(9).
20 Browne was a lawyer, admitted to Gray's Inn on 17 Apr. 1662, *Register of Admissions to Gray's Inn*, p. 293, and to King's Inns 5 Feb. 1669, Edward Keane, Beryl P. Phair and Thomas U. Sadleir, *King's Inns Admission Papers, 1607–1867* (Dublin, 1982), p. 57. Although Browne was Dillon's uncle, he was only twelve years older. John Lodge and Mervyn Archdall, *The Peerage of Ireland* (7 vols, Dublin, 1789), vol. 4, p. 176, states that Dillon's mother was called Marcella; this is wrong.
21 Lodge and Archdall, *Peerage,* vol. 4, p. 176.
22 *CSPD 1693*, pp. 281–2.
23 *CSPD 1693*, pp. 281–2. John sought to have his outlawry reversed since he claimed he was merely a justice of the peace who had been plundered by some part of the Jacobite army because he had submitted to King William.
24 Hazel Maynard, 'Irish membership of the English Inns of Court, 1660–1699: Lawyers, litigation and the legal profession' (Ph.D. thesis, University College

Dublin, 2006), pp. 83, 282. Edmond was pardoned after the Jacobite war and went on to practise law for many years.

25 Dillon and Susanna had no children, but from her first marriage she was the mother of the second Sir Edward Crofton, who supported William III and was attainted by the Patriot Parliament, 7 May 1689, of which Dillon was a member. Lodge and Archdall, *Peerage,* vol. 7, pp. 252–3, nn.; John Bergin and Andrew Lyall, *The Acts of James II's Irish Parliament of 1689* (Dublin, 2016), p. 124. The second Sir Edward Crofton recovered his estates after 1689 and made no effort to help his stepfather.

26 NLI Westport Papers, MS 40,907/7/3.

27 E.g., NLI Westport Papers, MS 40,916/2. NLI Westport Papers, MS 40,896/18 provides an entertaining account of the expenses of her funeral, 14 June 1682.

28 Lodge and Archdall, *Peerage*, vol. 4, p. 176. There are few references to Mary in the Westport papers, apart from incidental reference to her as the sister of Claud Hamilton, the 4th earl of Abercorn, a Jacobite officer: NLI Westport Papers, MS 40,899/2(10), MS 40,890/1(8–9) and MS 40,893/5(8).

29 Lodge and Archdall, *Peerage*, vol. 5, p. 116.

30 D'Alton, *King James's Irish Army*, vol. 2, p. 249.

31 Oliver J. Burke, *Anecdotes of the Connaught Circuit* (Dublin, 1885), p. 59.

32 For more on Theobald's family, see D'Alton, *King James's Irish Army,* pp. 249–50.

33 *Register of Admissions to Gray's Inn,* p. 192.

34 *King's Inns Admission Papers,* p. 506. Again, Welsh, not Walshe.

35 Ball, *Judges in Ireland,* vol. 1, p. 365. Of the judicial figures appointed between 1660 and 1690, only Chancellor Michael Boyle and Master of the Rolls William Temple share this distinction.

36 Talbot, *Lion's Den*, pp. 125–6.

37 Discussed further below.

38 Archives of Maryland, vol. 5, pp. 70–2. http://aomol.msa.maryland.gov/000001/000005, accessed 23 July 2023, hereafter referred to as Maryland Archives.

39 Creighton, *DIB*, p. 257.

40 Robert was then 26.

41 NLI Westport Papers, MS 40,893/4 (13–14).

42 NLI Westport Papers, MS 40,896/4 (6), 15 Dec. 1682.

43 16 Nov. 1674, *King's Inn Admission Papers*, p. 132. Technically, Catholics were unable to practise at the bar, but the requirement to take the Oath of Supremacy was not imposed: see Colum Kenny, 'The exclusion of Catholics from the legal profession in Ireland, 1537–1829', *IHS* 100 (1987), p. 349.

44 NLI Westport Papers, MSS 40,907/7/3, 5.

45 Alexander B. Grosart, *The Lismore Papers* (1st ser., 5 vols, London, 1886), vol. 4, pp. 144, 149.

46 In the list of members of the Commons summoned for 16 Mar. 1640 he is designated as a 'Mercator': *Journal of the House of Commons* (Dublin, 1746), p. 131.

47 This may have been Walshe's first contact with Ormond. In the event, the army did not travel to Spain.
48 McGrath, 'A biographical dictionary', vol. 2, p. A 58.
49 In these depositions, he is generally described as James and not John, which points against his involvement. The exception is TCD MSS 820 fo. 147 where both names are used, but James struck-through. In TCD MSS 820, fos. 71 and 72, although named James, he is described as son and heir of David Walshe; this is particularly significant, since it is clear that John was David Walshe's heir. Aidan Clarke, *The Old English in Ireland 1625–42* (London, 1966), p. 197.
50 Micheál Ó Siochrú, *Confederate Ireland 1642–1649* (Dublin, 1999), pp. 85–6. This was to separate judicial matters from the Council, which had previously carried out these functions.
51 Bellings to Ormond, 18 Feb. 1651: John T. Gilbert, *History of the Irish Confederation* (7 vols, Dublin, 1882), vol. 7, p. 364.
52 William P. Burke, *History of Clonmel* (Waterford, 1907), p. 86. George Mathew of Rehill was similarly dispensed.
53 TCD MS 830, fo. 249 r–v.
54 13 Mar. 1654 Hyde to Nicholas: W. Dunn Macray (ed.), *Calendar of the Clarendon State Papers* (5 vols, Oxford, 1869), vol. 2, p. 323.
55 Maryland Archives, vol. 5, pp. 70–2. Calvert was gilding the lily; William did not become a baronet until his father died a year later.
56 Maryland Archives, vol. 5, pp. 72–5.
57 Charles Calvert to his father, 26 Apr. 1672: Maryland Historical Society, *The Calvert Papers* (Baltimore, MD, 1889), p. 254.
58 *Calvert Papers*, p. 265.
59 *Calvert Papers*, p. 274.
60 *Calvert Papers*, p. 276.
61 The first Sir William had left a life interest in the estate to his widow Alison Netterville in lieu of her jointure when he died in 1634. She did not die until 1672 so the estate, such as it was, was thinly spread: Talbot, *Lion's Den*, pp. 118–19.
62 Charles Calvert to his father, 2 June 1673: *Calvert Papers*, pp. 277–8.
63 27 Aug. 1678, HMC *Ormonde MS*, NS 4, p. 448. Probably the Heads of the Bill: see Bodleian, Carte MS 53, fo. 50. The Bill of Confirmation related to a proposal to secure doubtful land titles on the payment of fines to the Crown and was not enacted.
64 Talbot's sister Frances married Richard Talbot, Lord of Malahide and his sister Mary married James Nugent of Coolamber, Co. Westmeath: Talbot, *Lion's Den*, p. 125. Neither appears to be A.W. It must be doubtful the letter is from a member of Talbot's immediate family. The salutation is 'My good Friend' and sister may be generic for a female acquaintance.
65 17 Nov. 1678, HMC *Ormonde MS*, NS 4, pp. 237–8.
66 TCD MSS 1995–2008/3a from the Lyons collection of the correspondence of William King, consists of six and a half pages of closely written text, the only document in Talbot's hand of which the writer is aware. It is salutary to

recall that his uncle Peter was under arrest from Oct. 1678 in Dublin Castle and his uncle Richard went into exile in France in July 1679.

67 Catholic and Protestant reaction in *England*; he seemed to pay no regard to matters in Ireland.

68 *The Several Informations of John Mac-Namarra, Maurice Fitzgerrald and James Nash Relating to the Horrid Popish Plot in Ireland*, p. 11. https://quod.lib.umich.edu/e/eebo/A59376.0001.001, accessed 23 July 2023. See also *CSPD 1682*, p. 224.

69 Talbot, *Lion's Den*, p. 152. Sergeant, *Little Jennings*, vol. 1, p. 271. Ormond was no friend of Peter Talbot and ordered his arrest on 8 Oct. 1678. He died in Dublin Castle, 15 Nov. 1680.

70 13 July 1681, Carte, *Life of Ormonde*, vol. 2, app., p. 108. At this time York was banished to rule Scotland, and Ormond was seeking a messenger he could 'safely chose or trust' to convey sensitive correspondence to the duke.

71 Ball, *Judges in Ireland*, vol. 1, p. 365.

72 20–27 June 1682, HMC *Ormonde MS*, NS 6, pp. 386, 388 and 392–3.

73 NLI Westport MSS 40,894/2(8–9), 13–14 Apr. 1675.

74 NLI Westport MS 40,895/1(10), 6 June 1677.

75 NLI Westport MS 40,889/4(2), 28 July 1677.

76 NLI Westport MS 40,895/2(4), 25 Apr. 1678.

77 NLI Westport MS 40,916/2.

78 NLI Westport MS 40,896/8(1), Michaelmas 1681; NLI Westport MS 40,907/2(6), 27 Sept. 1685.

79 NLI Westport MS 40,916/2, 15 July 1672.

80 £21, NLI Westport MS 40,916/2, 9 July 1677. £37, MSS 40,895/6(9–13), July 1680.

81 NLI Westport MSS 40,896/2(3–10) 17 May 1681, MSS 40,897/3(8–19), 21 Oct. 1684.

82 NLI Westport MS 40,897/6(11), 18 Mar. 1684, £57.10s; MS 40,916/2, 13 Dec. 1684, £52; MS 40,907/2(9), 3 Dec. 1685, £11; MS 40,897/4(20), 11 Dec. 1685, £1.

83 Eoin Kinsella, *Catholic Survival in Protestant Ireland, 1660–1711* (Woodbridge, 2018), p. 28.

84 NLI Westport MSS 40,897/5(9A–B), 4 Feb. 1685.

85 NLI Westport MSS 40,898/3(1–4), 1686.

86 NLI Westport MSS 40,896/8(21–3) and MSS 40,907/4 (1–2).

87 NLI Westport MS 40,907/1(1), drawn up to 30 Mar. 1686.

88 NLI Westport MS 40,897/7(11), 9 Mar. 1686.

89 NLI Westport MS 40,907/4(3), Jan. 1686.

90 NLI Westport MS 40,898/5(21), 3 Mar. 1687. There are other references to Palmer at NLI Westport MSS 40,907/4(3–20).

91 NLI Westport MS 40,907/1(2) and MS 40,898/6(4).

92 NLI Westport MSS 40,898/3(11–12) and MS 40,899/1(11).

93 NLI Westport MSS 40,898/6(11–12), 26–30 Apr. 1688. Curiously, this judgment is not included in NLI Westport MS 40,899/1(11), app. 4, for which see

further below; perhaps it had not been obtained or registered in the Court of Exchequer.

94 NLI Westport MS 40,895/5(8), 7 Apr. 1677.

95 NLI Westport MS 40,895/1(13), 12 Jan. 1678.

96 NLI Westport MSS 40,896/3(20–21), 22 Jun. 1687.

97 NLI Westport MS 40,896/3(16), 17 July 1682, £50; MSS 40,897/3(1/2), 18 May 1683, £210; MS 40,897/3(10), 17 Mar. 1683, £210.

98 NLI Westport MS 40,897/3(15), 14 Nov. 1684, £1,500; MS 40,897/3(17), 1 Dec. 1684, £100; MS 40,897/3(18), 19 Dec. 1684, £50; MSS 40,907/2(10–11), 24 Dec. 1684, £250.

99 NLI Westport MS 40,897/4(1). Sisson was to lend substantial amounts to Browne over the years.

100 The Charlemont debt was not the only one excluded from the list at the end of Jan. 1685. See NLI Westport MS 40,897/4(2), 12 Jan. 1684, £100; MSS 40,897/4(5–8), 2 Mar. 1684, £100; MS 40,897/4(11), 8 Mar. 1684, £100.

101 NLI Westport MSS 40,897/4(16–17), 16 Jun. 1685, £100; MS 40,897/4(19), 20 Nov. 1686?, £300; MS 40,897/4(21), Dec. 1685, £300; MS 40,897/4(22), 5 Jan. 1686, £100.

102 NLI Westport MS 40,900/4(10), original bond 20 Sept. 1685, account drawn up to 20 Nov. 1692.

103 NLI Westport MSS 40,898/3(1–4). Thompson got a judgment for £600, Bullmore for £200 and Johnson for £441: see NLI Westport MS 40,899/1(11). Thompson and Johnson were to have extensive dealings in Browne's estates over the years; how they became embroiled in Browne's affairs defies understanding. Stephen Rice leased part of Browne's estate to Thompson in 1692: Kinsella, *Catholic Survival*, p. 154. Johnson was appointed third baron of the Exchequer in 1703: Ball, *Judges in Ireland*, vol. 2, p. 67.

104 NLI Westport MS 40,898/1(3) is a copy made on 29 Jan. 1702 of the original dated 28 July 1686.

105 NLI Westport MS 40,899/1(11).

106 This was a joint debt with Browne, and it is difficult to understand how Mrs Warren had the resources to advance credit to Dillon and Browne to this extent; there seems to be little other information about her.

107 Walshe sent Stg. £500 to Ormond, via Edward Comerford, 6 Mar. 1644 and on 13 Mar. 1644, Ormond mortgaged land to Walshe for £500: NLI MS. 2308, fo. 357 and Edward McLysaght, 'O'Grady Papers', *Analecta Hibernica* 15 (1944). p. 45. Comerford was Ormond's agent, an MP and Confederate.

108 HMC *Ormonde MS*, NS 1, p. 74.

109 7 and 22 Aug. 1650, HMC *Ormonde MS*, NS 1, pp. 156, 159.

110 NLI Ormond Family Papers, MS 11,044, fo. 121. Walshe's position should be distinguished from the appointment of Robert Butler, later earl of Arran, as seneschal of his father's restored palatine liberty of Tipperary on 22 Apr. 1662: Robert Armstrong, 'Richard Butler' in *DIB*, vol. 2, p. 173.

111 Bodleian, Carte MS 50, fos. 456–7.

112 There are two documents in the Carte collection, MS 44, fos. 131–2 and 133–6, which may relate to advice given on the Declaration. Neither appears

to be in Walshe's hand. Similarly, Bodleian, Carte MS 44, fo. 270, relating to observations on the Act of Settlement, does not appear to be in Walshe's hand.

113 HMC *Ormonde MS*, NS 3, p. 11. Ó Siochrú, *Confederate Ireland*, p. 65.

114 Undated, assumed 1661, Bodleian, Carte MS 44, fo. 238.

115 More-O'Ferrall, 'Dispossessed landowners', pp. 429 ff. The originals are in Bodleian, Carte MS 44, fos. 49–103v.

116 Bodleian, Carte MS 44, fos. 56–77 and 79–99 respectively. Lord Athenry was involved in the Connacht document and Sir Richard Bellings in Ulster: Bodleian, Carte MS fos. 44, 49–53 and 101–103v. Carte *Life of Ormonde*, vol. 2, p. 304.

117 25 June 1664, Bodleian, Carte MS 49, fo. 264.

118 July 1664, Bodleian, Carte MS 33, fo. 473.

119 8 Aug. 1664, Bodleian, Carte MS 49, fo. 274.

120 Carte, *Life of Ormonde*, vol. 2, p. 306.

121 10 Aug. 1664, Bodleian, Carte MS 33, fo. 520. 20 Aug. 1664, Bodleian, Carte MS 33, fos. 561–2. Carte, *Life of Ormonde,* vol. 2, p. 307.

122 Micheál Ó Siochrú, 'Sir Nicholas Plunkett' in *DIB*, vol. 8, p. 190. 17 Dec. 1664, HMC *Ormonde MS*, NS 3, p. 184.

123 17 and 24 Dec. 1664, 28 Jan. 1665, HMC *Ormonde MS*, NS *3*, pp. 184, 186, 187.

124 27 Jan. 1665, Bodleian, Carte MS 34, fo. 27.

125 May 1665, Bodleian, Carte MS 34, fos. 226–7. 18 June 1665, Bodleian, Carte MS 34, fo. 266. 29 June 1665, Bodleian, Carte MS 34, fo. 264. 1 July 1665, Bodleian, Carte MS 48, fo. 197. 11 July 1665, Bodleian, Carte MS 34, fos.319–20.

126 Peter Earle, *The Life and Times of James II* (London, 1972); Ashley, *James II*; Miller, *James II*; W. A. Speck, 'James II' in *ODNB*, accessed 17 Aug. 2018.

127 Walshe to Ormond, 11 Apr. 1665, Bodleian, Carte MS 34, fo. 139.

128 Walshe to Ormond, 27 Nov. 1666, Bodleian, Carte MS 35, fo. 150.

129 Carte described some of these challenges in detail, and the separate claims by other Adventurers and the Nominees under the Act of Explanation: Carte, *Life of Ormonde*, vol. 2, pp. 357–60.

130 Bodleian, Carte MS 37, fos. 385–96. There may be some doubt as to whether Walshe actually prepared this. It could be his hand, and the degradation of the script after several pages is typical.

131 Bodleian, Carte MS 37, fos. 397–418. This was endorsed by Walshe on 12 Apr. 1668.

132 19 June 1667, Bodleian, Carte MS 49, fos. 413v–414. Carte, *Life of Ormonde*, vol. 2, app. p. 34.

133 30 Oct. 1666, Bodleian, Carte MS 215, fo. 298.

134 Michael Perceval-Maxwell, 'James Butler' in *DIB*, vol. 2, p. 132.

135 Toby Barnard, 'Introduction: The Dukes of Ormonde' in Toby Barnard and Jane Fenlon (eds), *The Dukes of Ormonde, 1610–1745* (Woodbridge, 2000), pp. 24–5.

136 Barnard, 'Introduction', p. 24.

137 Late 1663, Bodleian, Carte MS 40, fo. 674.

138 7 June 1664, Bodleian, Carte MS 33, fos. 405–6.
139 25 June 1664, Bodleian, Carte MS 49, fo. 264.
140 31 May 1664, HMC *Ormonde MS*, NS 3, p. 172.
141 7 June 1664, Bodleian, Carte MS 33, fo. 405. Thomas Butler was the duke's eldest surviving son, and became Lord Deputy in May 1664, when his father was in England in connection with the land settlement.
142 25 June 1664. Bodleian, Carte MS 49, fo. 264.
143 26 July 1670, Bodleian, Carte MS 160, fo. 56. 30 June 1671, Bodleian, Carte MS 160, fo. 59.
144 24 July 1674, Bodleian, Carte MS 160, fo. 73.
145 Michael Perceval-Maxwell, 'Elizabeth Butler' in *DIB*, vol. 2, p. 120.
146 Bodleian, Carte MS 31, fos. 147–147v, 19 Apr. 1661.
147 The commissioners established to administer the Gracious Declaration of 1660.
148 It is not clear if this was the father (1600–77) or son (1632–1705): both were prominent and powerful.
149 Ormond's son Ossory had taken over as Lord Deputy in his father's absence in London.
150 This would appear to be a reference to the 'Dispossessed landowners of Ireland', 1664, which was given by Walshe to Ormond in May 1664; see More-O'Ferrall, 'Dispossessed landowners'.
151 7 June 1664, Bodleian, Carte MS 33, fos. 403–4.
152 Bodleian, Carte MS 33, fos. 498, 500–1. There are further letters from Walshe to the duchess concerning estate matters in Aug. 1664 and June 1665: Bodleian, Carte MS 33, fos. 411 and 583.
153 26 Oct. 1664, Bodleian, Carte MS 33, fo. 657.
154 Walshe had to deal not only with Ormond's affairs, but also with those of the earl of Arran. In Aug. 1666, he was asked to intercede with Arran by a Galway landowner Robert Clarke. 24 Aug. 1666, NLI Ormonde MS 11,044, fo. 172.
155 Walshe's younger brother David was the deputy seneschal.
156 14 and 26 Oct. 1663, HMC *Ormonde MS*, NS 3, pp. 92, 245.
157 Sir John Cole was the son of Sir William Cole who founded the Enniskillen dynasty. He was one of the commissioners appointed to implement the Acts of Settlement and Explanation. His sons had interests in Kilkenny and Tipperary; see Lodge and Archdall, *Peerage*, vol. 6, p. 48. It says a lot for Walshe's capacity that he should engage successfully with such a formidable opponent.
158 May 1665, Bodleian, Carte MS 34, fos. 226–7.
159 25 Oct. 1663, NLI Ormond Family Papers, MM 11,044, fo. 145.
160 17 Jan. 1664, NLI Ormond Family Papers, MS 11,044, fo. 147. Sir Thomas had been in contact with Walshe a few days earlier: MS 11,044, fo. 146.
161 7 June 1664, Bodleian, Carte MS 33, fo. 405.
162 12 July 1664, Bodleian, Carte MS 48, fo. 174.
163 17 July 1667, Bodleian, Carte MS 35, fo. 553.
164 19 July 1667, Bodleian, Carte MS 49, fos. 413–14.

165 Robert C. Simington, *The Civil Survey A.D. 1654–1656: County of Tipperary* (10 vols. Dublin, 1931), pp. 288, 291–3, 302.
166 TCD MS 830, fo. 249 r–v. Burke, *History of Clonmel*, p. 86. It is possible that these are part of the lands which Ormond mortgaged to Walsh in 1644.
167 Robert C. Simington, *Transplantation to Connacht, 1654–58* (Dublin, 1970).
168 Micheál Ó Siochrú, 'Sir John Walsh' in *DIB*, vol. 9, p. 739.
169 *Statutes II*, p. 347. It is possible that this is a reference to John Walshe of Shangangh, but many of the other names in the legislation refer to Walshe's 'peace-party' Confederate colleagues.
170 More-O'Ferrall, 'Dispossessed landowners', p. 429. The originals are in Bodleian, Carte MS 44, fos. 49–103v.
171 *15th Annual Report*, p. 264.
172 D'Alton, *King James's Irish Army*, vol. 2, p. 216. Dalton's source cannot be traced, but the coincidence of dates suggests that, once confirmed, Walshe made a disposition of his estate.
173 10 Will. III, c. 7, *Statutes III*, p. 479. This was presumably a reference to Patrick, John Walshe's son.
174 Most likely he was Thomas Butler, 'nepos' of the duke of Ormond, admitted to the Inner Temple on 23 Oct. 1669: Maynard, 'Irish membership of the English Inns of Court', p. 398. Of course, it is possible he may not have been a Butler; the Carte website does refer to Thomas *Butler* – this is not correct.
175 18 Feb. 1675, Bodleian, Carte MS 38, fos. 262–262v. Not in Walshe's hand.
176 Arnold, *Restoration Land Settlement*, p. 137. To complicate matters further, James sold or gave away parts of his estate, notably to Tyrconnell.
177 Charles McNeill, 'Report on the Rawlinson MS', *Analecta Hibernica* 1 (Mar. 1930), p. 114. Examples of Talbot acting on behalf of the duke (and later king) can be found in *CSPD 1677–1678*, p. 187, *CSPD 1678*, p. 57, *CSPD October1, 1683–April 30, 1684*, p. 346, and *CSPD February–December 1685*, vol. 1, p. 324.
178 Lenihan, *Last Cavalier*, p. 69.
179 The analysis which follows is based on samples of the Bill Books in the National Archives of Ireland for 1677–8 and 1687–8 taken by Hazel Maynard for her Ph.D. thesis, 'Irish membership of the English Inns of Court' which she generously made available to me, and for which I am extremely grateful. This material is very useful in painting a picture of the activities of barristers in this period, but it is subject to some important limitations. First, it is not always possible to identify for which party counsel was acting; in some cases an educated guess is required. Secondly, it does not identify the nature of the cause in action. Thirdly, the religious affiliation of the parties can generally be identified, particularly for more prominent litigants, but this is not always possible. Finally, as in any analysis based on samples, the results are descriptive and indicative, rather than definitive.
180 Bill Books, vol. 8, fos. 45b, 37b–38a, 214, 215, 306; vol. 9, fos. 1, 21, 28, 49, 56, 68, 101, 141, 185. It is little wonder that Clarendon thought in 1686 that Dillon was 'in very great practice'. See further below.

181 Bill Books, vol. 8, fos. 13b, 215, and vol. 9, fo. 141.
182 Bill Books, vol. 9, fos. 49 and 68; vol. 10, fos. 37b–38a.
183 Bill Books, vol. 9, fo. 49.
184 Bill Books: vol. 9, fo. 91 (Whitfield); vol. 10, fo. 39a (Whitshed); vol. 10, fo. 28b (Langford) and vol. 10, fo. 81a (Rochfort).
185 Bill Books, vol. 8, fo. 10a.
186 Bill Books, x, fos. 37b–38a and 51b. The other plaintiffs in this case were Henry Dillon and his wife Frances, by her guardian (and mother) Frances Talbot, the countess of Tyrconnell. The countess had a reputation for avarice: see Piers Wauchope, 'Frances Talbot' in *ODNB*, accessed 23 July 2023 and Sergeant, *Little Jennings*, vol. 2, pp. 383 and 446–9.
187 Bill Books, vol. 10, fos. 39a and 91.
188 See David Dickson, *Dublin: The Making of a Capital City* (London, 2014), p. 88.
189 NLI Westport MS 40,898/6(5), 7 Nov. 1687.
190 It is highly likely that Dillon acted for Athenry on 27 Jan. 1678, Bill Books, vol. 8, fo. 17b. He may have opposed him on 31 Jan. 1681, Bill Books, vol. 8, fo. 214, and he probably represented him on 28 Dec. 1682, Bill Books, vol. 9, fo. 28.
191 Bill Books, vol. 9, fos. 1, 56 and 101. The doubt arises because the parties were virtually the same in all three cases – it is improbable that Dillon switched clients.
192 Bill Books, vol. 10, fo. 42a.
193 Bill Books, vol. 10, fo. 81a. Trant was a Jacobite knight, and an MP in the 1689 parliament. See S.M., 'The Trant family', *Kerry Archaeological Magazine* 2 (Mar. 1914), pp. 237–62, at p. 241.
194 Bill Books, vol. 10, fo. 83a.
195 NLI Westport MS 40,895/1(11), 18 Dec. 1677. In 1683 the 7th viscount gave Dillon the delicate task to effect the jointure of the dowager countess, which she claimed against the current viscount and the estate of the late viscount. The late viscount was the 6th, and his dowager subsequently married Sir William Talbot: NLI Westport MS 40,896/3(21), 26 Feb. 1683, MSS 40,898/3(8–9), 22 Apr. and 2 May 1687.
196 NLI Westport MSS 40,889/22(1–3), 10/11 Jan. 1687. NLI Westport MSS 40,889/23(1–3), 19/20 Apr. 1688. See also NLI Westport MS 40,898/2(8–9).
197 NLI Westport MS 40,898/4(19), Jan.–Mar. 1687; the verso of this document has a list of Browne's debts on 13 Apr. 1688 that amount to the staggering total of £43,000. See also NLI Westport MS 40,898/4(16) which covered the period 9 Nov. 1686–Mar. 1688, and MSS 40,898/4(20A–B), 19 July 1689.
198 *CSPD 1685–1689*, vol. 1, p. 147.
199 Talbot, *Lion' Den*, 667–71. Talbot pre-deceased Tyrconnell.
200 See Lenihan, *Last Cavalier,* p. 118, for a table of appointments by Tyrconnell in favour of members of his family and their associates.
201 Bodleian, Carte MS 167, fo. 4; NLI Pakenham-Mahon Additional Papers, MS 9476. This refers to James's income from lands granted to him under the Acts

of Settlement and Explanation, and any other land belonging to him before his accession. The text of the Commission is at *CSPD 1685*, vol. 1, pp. 89–90.

202 Lenihan, *Last Cavalier*, p. 64. McNeill, 'Rawlinson MS', p. 114. Examples of Talbot acting on behalf of the duke (and later king) can be found in *CSPD 1677–1678*, p. 187, *CSPD 1678*, p. 57, *CSPD October1, 1683–April 30, 1684*, p. 346, and *CSPD 1685–1689*, vol. 1, p. 324.

203 Bodleian, Carte MS 217, fo. 232. 15 Dec. 1686, *CSPD 1685–1689*, vol. 2, p. 321, and vol. 3, p. 241.

204 If his signature on proclamations can be used as an indicator of activity – three in 1687, one in 1688 and two in 1689: *Proclamations,* vol. 2, pp. lxi, 28, 29, 45, 54, 85 and 117. On 5 Aug. 1689 a proclamation authorising a collection for wounded soldiers was issued under his name alone.

205 Bagwell, *Ireland under the Stuarts*, vol. 3, p. 167. Sheridan's side of the story is vividly told in HMC *Stuart Papers*, vol. 6, at pp. 12 and ff. See also Sergeant, *Little Jennings*, pp. 365–9.

206 J. G Simms, *Jacobite Ireland* (Dublin, 2000) p. 82. *The Journal of the Proceedings of the Parliament in Ireland, with the Establishment of their Forces There* (London, 1689), p. 8.

207 Bergin and Lyall, *James II's Irish Parliament*, p. 10.

208 D'Avaux to Louis, 10 July 1689, in James Hogan (ed.), *Négociations de M. le comte d'Avaux en Irlande, 1689–90* (Dublin, 1934), p. 249.

209 D'Avaux to Colbert de Croissy, 30 Aug. 1689, *Négociations*, p. 438

210 Nagle's appointment 'depended on his administrative rather than his military capabilities': Hazel Maynard, 'Richard Nagle' in *DIB*, vol. 6 p. 851.

211 Lenihan, *Last Cavalier*, p. 181. D'Avaux to Louis, 22 Dec. 1689, *Négociations*, p. 617.

212 Bodleian, Talbot MS. e.1. Printed in HMC *8th Report*, app., pt. 1, s. 2, 497b–499a.

213 Arnold states that Talbot was one of the five landowners restored to over 30,000 acres in Co. Wicklow. Sir William (sic) Talbot: Arnold, *Restoration Land Settlement*, p. 145. It is possible Arnold's reference is to clause CCXXV of the Act of Settlement, *Statutes II*, p. 347. This had no effect and Sir Robert was one of the 54 nominees to be restored to their personal seats with 2,000 acres adjoining under the Act of Explanation – Section CXLVIII. *Statutes III*, p. 89. This proved to be equally futile. The land at Talbotstown belonged to Sir Hans (or Francis) Hamilton in 1670: TCD, Down Survey of Ireland.

214 Lenihan tells us that Richard secured a lease on Carton sometime after the passing of the Act of Explanation and 'eventually' installed his nephew William there: Lenihan, *Last Cavalier*, p. 69. The authority for this statement is not clear. Sergeant indicates that Richard did not acquire Carton until after being appointed Lieutenant-General of the army in 1686: Sergeant, *Little Jennings*, vol. 1, p. 323. In Talbot, *Lion's Den*, p. 182, it is suggested that Richard may have bought it from William; alternatively, the latter may have given it to Richard in exchange for being named as the remainder to the earldom. Richard Talbot and his wife Frances used Carton as their country residence:

Nolan, *Jacobite Duchess*, pp. 79 ff. In their marriage settlement, William left a life-interest in Carton to his wife Anne; it is not clear what interest he had himself: Fitzgerald, 'Carton', p. 7. When the 'capital or mansion-house of Cartown' was sold in 1703, the forfeiting proprietors were described as 'Richard late earl of Tyrconnell and Sir William Talbot or one of them, attainted': *15th Annual Report*, p. 380.

215 Talbot, *Lion's Den*, p. 126. Simms, *Williamite Confiscation*, p. 181. These numbers do not tally with those shown in the *Book of Postings and Sale of the Forfeited and Other Estates and Interests In Ireland* in the Royal Irish Academy which show the Trustees selling 557 acres in Meath, p. 14.

216 *CSPD Jan. 1686–May 1687*, p. 8 records his appointment as King's Counsel. He would have been elected Recorder by Dublin Corporation. In his capacity as Recorder, he may have come to the attention of James II when he formally welcomed the king to Dublin in March 1689: Anon., *Ireland's Lamentation* (Dublin, 1689), p. 27.

217 *The State Letters of Henry Earl of Clarendon,* vol. 2, p. 136. Curiously, this appears to have been the only occasion when Browne was considered for a judicial role.

218 NLI Westport MS 40,898/4(2), 8 Oct. 1685, *recte* 1687.

219 There are more books in the 1687 list than in 1675 that have defied identification, but even they seem to have a religious hue.

220 *The State Letters of Henry Earl of Clarendon,* vol. 2, p. 136.

221 NLI Westport MS 40,898/3(14).

222 One Mr. Ross was to be disciplined by the bishop of Kilmore: King, *State of the Protestants,* pp. 204–5.

223 A. R. Hart, *A History of the King's Serjeants at Law in Ireland* (Dublin, 2000), p. 66.

224 Hart, *King's Serjeants*, pp. 71–2. Hart did not evaluate the prime serjeant's role.

225 Blaney became the 6th Lord Blaney, baron of Monaghan in 1689.

226 Simms, *Jacobite Ireland*, p. 74.

227 Catholics who bought land after the Restoration. King thought Dillon a 'furious papist': *State of the Protestants*, p. 152.

228 J. G. Simms, 'The Jacobite Parliament of 1689' in D. W. Hayton and Gerard O'Brien (eds), *War and Politics in Ireland 1649–1730* (London, 1986), p. 67. It is not clear where this estate was.

229 Simms, 'The Jacobite Parliament', p. 9. Hazel Maynard, 'The Irish Legal profession and the Catholic revival, 1660–89' in Kelly et al., *People, Politics and Power*, p. 42.

230 This was the second Act of James II's parliament in 1689: Bergin and Lyall, *James II's Irish Parliament*, p. 9. See also D'Alton, *King James's Irish Army*, p. 29.

231 NLI Westport MS 40,899/4(9). See also D'Alton, *King James's Irish Army*, pp. 178 and 250.

232 Technically, he was a captain in Abercorn's regiment. See Michael McNally, *Battle of the Boyne 1690* (Oxford, 2005), p. 48.

233 NLI Westport MSS 40,899/2(12–13). One bill for Oct. 1688 to Dec. 1689 amounted to £13 6s; the most expensive item was a morocco saddle £7. A second bill was for £6 16s 8d.
234 NLI Westport MS 40,899/2(10). MS 40,899/4(9), 6 Mar. 1690 for £84 6s related to fitting out 53 carbine barrels and 53 cases of pistols.
235 For the Boyne, see Pádraig Lenihan, *1690 Battle of the Boyne* (Stroud, 2003), pp. 214–15.
236 All three practised on the Connacht circuit.
237 Kinsella, *Catholic Survival*, pp. 128–9.
238 For a detailed discussion see Kinsella, *Catholic Survival*, pp. 59–60.
239 Including Sarsfield, Galmoy, Patrick Plunkett and others: see Gilbert, *Jacobite Narrative*, p. 188. Unlike his nephew Dillon, John Browne remained in Ireland.
240 Lodge and Archdall, *Peerage,* vol. 4, p. 175.
241 *15th Annual Report,* p. 360.
242 16 Aug. 1677. *15th Annual Report*, p. 244.
243 24 Aug. 1678. *15th Annual Report,* p. 261.
244 Kinsella, *Catholic Survival*, pp. 204–5. Kinsella cites no source for this. Johnson was appointed 3rd baron of the Exchequer in 1703: Ball, *Judges in Ireland*, vol. 2, p. 67.
245 NLI, Westport MS 40,902/4(9), 14 Aug. 1700. ffotrell had obtained a judgment in 1697 in respect of the debts, which stretched back to 1684.
246 NLI Westport MS 40,902/6(23), 10 Aug. 1700. At this time, Browne was under enormous pressure in relation to his own affairs, of which Dillon's debts were only one part, and much of the complications are detailed in correspondence with his agent Luke Hussey in the Westport papers: NLI Westport MSS 40,903/4(1–22), MSS 40,903/5(1–22), MSS 40,903/6(1–23), July–Dec. 1701, Aug. and Nov. 1702.
247 NLI, Westport MSS 40,903/2(12–14), 9 Feb. and 7 Mar. 1702
248 NLI, Westport MSS 40,904/1(1A, B) and (2A, B), 5 May 1703. These documents are draft and may never have been executed, but they are consistent with the general scheme of the settlement of Browne's debts.
249 *15th Annual Report*, p. 360.
250 283 acres in Co. Dublin were sold a few days earlier for £1,672. *15th Annual Report*, p. 360. Kinsella suggests that Higgins may have acted collusively with the Browne family in 1708 by buying-in forfeited land, and subsequently letting it to Peter Browne, John Browne's heir: Kinsella, *Catholic Survival*, p. 207.
251 NLI Westport MS 40,904/1(5), 10 July 1703.
252 NLI Westport MS 40904/3/(15), 16 Oct. 1703.
253 NLI Westport MS 40,905/1(9), 13 Mar. 1707.

Conclusion: the Catholic threat neutralised

In 1612 Sir John Davies argued that although military force might subdue Ireland, it was essential that English common law should apply throughout the country in order to complete the conquest. The Proclamation of 11 March 1605 ordered that all people of the kingdom of Ireland were to be direct subjects of the king, and not of local lords. Furthermore, disaffected subjects were required to bring their complaints to the Crown Courts. Davies intended that the universal extension of English common law would have the most profound consequences. It would replace Brehon law and become the only legal system on the island. The common law would educate and reform the Irish so that they would grow civil and become English. But what were to be the consequences for Ireland's Catholics? This book addresses a gap in the historiography of the late seventeenth century by establishing how Irish Catholics engaged with and experienced the common law during the Restoration. It explores the writings of the Catholic intelligentsia, in particular the clergy and Gaelic poets, and illustrates how Catholics could exploit the law, whether in court or as a lawyers.

Catholics eagerly anticipated Charles II's restoration and did not advocate a change in constitutional status or the legal system, which was restored in 1660. The Interregnum had left few marks on the legal regime and a suite of new judges was appointed to the superior courts. When the judges ruled against the legal efficacy of the Gracious Declaration, the king was forced to call a parliament, which sat from 1662 to 1666 and enacted the Restoration land settlement. For the remainder of his reign Charles II ruled Ireland by fiat, something he was unable to achieve in England. No parliament sat for most of the Restoration; in its absence the law was administered and enforced by proclamations. New laws, justified by a narrative of contempt, elaborated rules and sanctions against Catholics. Thus the legislation for keeping the anniversary of the outbreak of the rebellion was an enactment of Catholic guilt for the atrocities of 1641. The Acts of Settlement and Explanation consolidated the extirpation of Catholic estates and were justified by alleged Catholic treachery. There were some potentially critical events. The emphatic closure of the Court of Claims after seven months of operation laid the foundations for generations of resentment, but did not provoke an immediate backlash. The banishment of bishops and religious orders in 1673 and again in 1678 caused hardship and resentment, but no rebellion. When the judicial apparatus of the state executed primate Oliver Plunkett in 1681, the reaction to his death was muted by fears of further outrages. The legal system underwent few significant changes until 1685 when James II's policy of catholicisation revolutionised the confessional allegiance of key judicial figures. But this had no lasting effect and the repeal of the Acts of Settlement and Explanation and Declaratory Act of 1689 did not survive the Patriot Parliament. Despite all that had happened during the century, the common law was well entrenched in Catholic Ireland.

It may seem paradoxical that Catholics would accept a legal system which in many respects was inimical to their interests. In reality there was no choice. Native Irish law was progressively undermined by the common law in sixteenth-century Irish society. Land was the principal form of wealth, and a fundamental change in the conceptualisation of the legal nature of that wealth, and how it was managed and transmitted, had taken place. As part of the process of conquest, the ultimate control of land was surrendered to the sovereign and in exchange common law titles and ownership of land were granted to the Gaelic chiefs. Sir John Davies merely articulated that the Elizabethan wars delivered the coup de grace to the Brehon system. Thus, Catholic participation in the common law during the Restoration was not a paradox, but a pragmatic acceptance of the power of the state and its apparatus, expressed in legal language, and always supported by threats of state violence though legal penalty or military action. When the opportunity arose in 1685 Catholic Ireland embraced the legal system to reverse the onslaught on land ownership under Cromwell and the legislation of the Restoration land settlement: 'It was now high time to put an end to the unspeakable sufferings of the Roman Catholic natives of this realm ... by repealing the said acts'.[1] Over 80 years a legal revolution had taken place.

While the Cromwellian land settlement was the preoccupation of the nobility and gentry, all degrees of the Catholic population were affected in their daily lives by proclamations limiting or prohibiting religious practice. The nobility and gentry had been weakened and the hierarchy had become the principal advocates for the Catholic population. Of the archbishops, Peter Talbot of Dublin was the most politically active, and least concerned with pastoral matters. James Lynch of Tuam spent barely five years in Ireland until the accession of James II. It was left to Oliver Plunkett of Armagh and John Brenan of Cashel to assume pastoral responsibility to mitigate the enforcement of the law and they chose to engage with the administration by diplomacy rather than confrontation. Their strategy was incapable of dealing with vicissitudes of English politics and failed in Plunkett's ignominious execution at Tyburn.

From the vantage of exile, John Lynch and Nicholas French engaged in a more confrontational polemic. Lynch's analysis was essentially constitutional, based on the contractual relationship between the sovereign and his subjects. He challenged the legitimacy of the English and Irish parliaments that had deprived Irish Catholics of their lands and religious rights. It was only by sidestepping parliament and through the exercise of the king's prerogative that Catholic rights could be restored. French chose to focus on the motives of the authors of the land settlement, and forensically examined the rights of those who purported to claim Catholic estates as their own. He invoked the supremacy of natural law over the legislation of the Irish parliaments. Lynch and French took different perspectives on royal authority. Notwithstanding that the contractual relationship between sovereign and subject had been ruptured, Lynch remained steadfast in his loyalty to the Stuarts. French believed that anointed kings derived their authority from God, and Charles II had to exercise the royal virtue of mercy in favour of his Catholic subjects. French did not trace the consequences if the king should fail to do so, but it is not difficult to see how his advocacy of the natural law principle of armed self-defence in the face of attacks on religion could cause alarm in royal circles during the 1670s. Bishops Edmund O'Reilly and John O'Molony did not leave an extensive literary record, but were closer in their political thinking to French than Lynch. O'Reilly was more concerned with religious freedom and, like French, had no doubt as to the superiority of divine authority over man-made law. For O'Reilly, the right to freely practise the Catholic religion prevailed over the state's interests. O'Molony was more interested in the restoration of Catholic power and the reversal of the land settlement. Both were fearless in the face of the law and were separately suspected of treason. Similarly, both showed an independence of thought that led them to contemplate radical alternatives to the Stuarts. Despite the passion and power of their critique the land settlement remained intact and the practice of the Catholic religion heavily circumscribed.

One of the greatest deficits in the historiography of this period is how Gaelic Ireland, the greater part of the population, engaged with and experienced the common law. Conventional records written in Irish are almost non-existent and the literary record is not extensive. But there is a rich resource in the poetry of Dáibhí Ó Bruadair and his contemporaries. The pre-Restoration poets were staunchly hostile to the imposition of the common law, its courts and legal processes. Ó Bruadair's poetry was more nuanced. It mirrored the rise and fall of Catholic hopes throughout his long life and showed a high level of awareness of the legal system. He disparaged the

Cromwellian regime that impoverished him, and together with Séafraidh Ó Donnchadha he recorded the shaming reversal of the Gaelic social order under upstart Cromwellian settlers. The financial decline of his patrons paralleled his own personal humiliation. The poems prompted by the trials of Sir John Fitzgerald illustrate his understanding of the dangers posed by the law, but also a naive belief in its redeeming possibilities. He delighted in the skills of Judge Keating but, following Fitzgerald's acquittal, Ó Bruadair endured another period of decline. His old pessimism was rekindled by the Popish Plot, only to be upturned by the new social and legal order brought about under James II. Both he and Diarmaid mac Sheáin Bhuí Mac Cárthaigh celebrated Tyrconnell's catholicisation of the army, the bench and public administration. But his 'Shipwreck' followed James II's defeat and in his despair he sought to establish culpability. He identified the lack of respect shown by the Irish lower classes and soldiery for the social order and the rule of law as major contributors to Ireland's ruin. In his last years he lashed out at the lawless Irish underclass, the *caitcheann*, who were no better than the English enemy.

It is in the pre-Restoration Gaelic literati that one finds the most violent objection and least accommodation to the common law system. The recitation of legal terminology in the poems reads like a raining down of curses, as if the system might be stymied by turning it on itself. The response was emotional, born out of a sense of oppression and frustration with a system that could not be changed – Dunlop's 'impotent rage'.[2] It could be argued that Ó Bruadair was such an exceptional figure that his views may not be representative. But at various times his thought was echoed by Ó Donnchadha and Mac Cárthaigh. Almost all the poetry he wrote in the decade 1682–92 is political in character. His experience over the entire period, his wide-ranging perspective and his close observation of litigation made him an acute critic of the legal landscape. The evidence is not plentiful, but it can certainly be argued that Ó Bruadair's attitude to the law, unconcerned about legal theory, highly critical when circumstances were adverse and celebratory when otherwise, was reflective of the Gaelic population as a whole in the later seventeenth century. Ó Bruadair's perception of the legal system was as complex as the events that motivated his poetry.

But the law was not always to Catholic detriment, and some chose to participate in the legal system, rather than condemn it. The 1663 Court of Claims offered an opportunity for Catholics to recover family estates. Some of the wealthiest Catholic families recovered their pre-Cromwellian estates in full. The divisions between Gaelic and Old English Catholics were evident in the court. There are few Os and Macs among the names of the litigants. Ironically, commissioners McRainsford, O'Beverly and McChurchill were in no position to render assistance to Gaelic Ireland in recovering estates.

None of the 10 largest landowners who recovered their estates were of Gaelic origin. The reasons are complex. Insofar as he chose to exercise his influence, Ormond favoured Old English claimants. The sequence in which claims were heard by the commissioners favoured landowners from the Pale. Gaelic owners were less likely to have the resources or networks to procure the assistance of agents who orchestrated successful claims and settled any difficulties with possible counter-claimants. The most effective of these agents, Richard Talbot, had few clients from Gaelic Ireland. Regardless of ethnic difference, Catholic Ireland was united in that the greatest fault of the court was its brevity; once the Protestant interest realised that the court could lead to significant Catholic gains, its duration was limited, and thousands of Catholic claimants were not heard. For them, the Court of Claims was the last opportunity to reclaim their estates by virtue of their innocence and loyalty to the Stuarts. The court could have vindicated them, but political control of the legal system ensured it failed them.

Unlike the broad mass of Catholics, only the lawyers, and particularly the barristers, had a sense of the mastery of the law. They were the most agile in adapting to legal change and in many cases they could influence the application of the law. More than any other group, they had the skills to exploit its possibilities. But even expertise was not always sufficient, and many Catholics relied on a network of family connections and other forms of patronage to make use of the law for their own advantage. Sir John Walshe's service as Ormond's seneschal is a remarkable example of a successful collaboration between a Catholic lawyer and his Protestant patron, and his death before the Jacobite era ensured his modest gains were preserved. Although Sir William Talbot and Gerald Dillon initially met with great success, the ultimate failure of their careers reflected the vulnerability of the Catholic elite in late seventeenth-century Ireland.

After 1691, Catholics were once again excluded from law-making and whatever moderation might have been exercised by royal restraint was severely circumscribed. An ascendant Protestant parliament in Dublin abrogated the protection of the treaties of Galway and Limerick, and legislated to eliminate Catholic economic and political power. Such was the Protestant abhorrence of the Catholic *revanche* five years earlier, the Protestant parliament of 1695 ordered the destruction of the official records of the 1689 parliament. Catholics could no longer rely on the protection of the law, and the opportunity to exercise the legal profession was removed. The legal system was not independent or fair-minded, the benign expression of Davies's intent to civilise the Irish. Instead it was actively and openly used against Catholic interests: a principal tool of the Protestant state to control and oppress. In these circumstances, Catholic alienation from the legal system that had oppressed and beggared them would not be surprising. Catholics had no means of changing the Irish legal system and did not trust its administration. But loyalty to the Stuart dynasty continued, and the legal system that three generations of Stuarts had imposed remained firmly established. To that extent, Davies had succeeded. The common law had thoroughly permeated the social and cultural thought of Catholic Ireland. Legal discourse was framed only in common law concepts and the Brehon system became the preserve of antiquarians. But Davies's theoretical framework could not accommodate the Catholic majority in seventeenth-century Ireland. The conflicts of 1641–53 and 1689–91 could only be contained by military force and belied his aspiration that 'the execution of the law doth make the Irish grow civil'. These conflicts were the foundation for the exclusion of Catholics from making law and a sequence of ever more repressive legislation, which served to unite Ireland's Catholics into an aggrieved, impoverished and marginalised community with a keen sense of past wrongs.

Notes

1 John Bergin and Andrew Lyall, *The Acts of James II's Irish parliament of 1689* (Dublin, 2016), p. 22.
2 Robert Dunlop, 'Ireland from the Plantation of Ulster to the Cromwellian Settlement' in *The Cambridge Modern History* (Cambridge, 1906), iv, p. 513.

Select bibliography

Manuscripts

Trinity College Dublin

TCD MSS 1995–2008/3a (Lyons collection of the correspondence of William King)

National Library of Ireland

NLI MS 31 *Book of Orders of the Commissioners of the Second Court of Claims, 1666*
NLI MS 9476, appointing William Talbot as Chief Agent and Commissioner in the management of James II's Irish estates
NLI Westport Estate Papers, Collection List No. 78, compiled by Brigid Clesham and Wesley Geddis, Assistant Keepers, 2002–05

National Archives

Chancery Bill Books, vols 8–9

Bodleian Library

Carte MS 31, 68, 167, 214, 267 and others
Talbot MS e.1

Printed material

Record publications

Calendar of the State Papers, Domestic, 1671, 1673, 1679–80
Calendar of the State Papers relating to Ireland, 1647–60, 1660–62, 1663–65, 1666–69, 1669–70

Public Records Office of Ireland, Reports of the Commissioners
15th Report, 1825
Public Records Office of Ireland, Reports of the Deputy Keeper
5th Report, 1873, App. III
6th Report, 1874, App. V
17th Report, 1885, App. II
19th Report, 1887, App. V, Abstract of Decrees of the Court of Claims for the Trial of Innocents

Records of Parliament

Commons Journal Ireland (1796 ed.), vol. 1
The Statutes at Large Passed in the Parliaments Held in Ireland (3 vols, Dublin, 1786)
The Statutes at Large of England and Great-Britain (London, 1811)
Bergin, John, and Lyall, Andrew (eds), *The Acts of James II's Irish Parliament, 1689* (Dublin, 2016)
Firth, C. H., and Rait, R. S. (eds), *Acts and Ordinances of the Interregnum 1642–1660* (Abingdon, 1978)

Publications of the Irish Manuscripts Commission

Hogan, James (ed.), *Négociations de M. le comte d'Avaux en Irlande, 1689–90* (Dublin, 1934)
Kelly, James, with Lyons, Mary Ann, *The Proclamations of Ireland 1660–1820* (5 vols, Dublin, 2014)
McNeill, Charles, 'Report on the Rawlinson MS', *Analecta Hibernia* 1 (1930), pp. 12–117
Simington, Robert C., *Books of Survey and Distribution, County of Mayo* (4 vols, Dublin, 1956)
Simington, R. C. *The Transplantation to Connacht* (Dublin, 1970)
Tallon, Geraldine (ed.), *Court of Claims, Submissions and Evidence, 1663* (Dublin, 2006)

Publications of the Historical Manuscripts Commission

Historical Manuscripts Commission 8th Report
Historical Manuscripts Commission, 9th Report
Ormonde MS
Ormonde MS, NS
Stuart Papers, vol. 6

Other documentary material

Airy, Osmund (ed.), *Essex Papers* (London, 1890)
Keane, Edward, Phair, Beryl P., and Sadleir, Thomas U., *King's Inns Admission Papers, 1607–1867* (Dublin, 1982)
Macpherson, James, *Original Papers; Containing the Secret History of Great Britain, from the Restoration, to the Accession of the House of Hannover* (Dublin, 1775)
Maryland Historical Society, *The Calvert Papers* (Baltimore, 1889)
Register of Admissions to the Honourable Society of the Middle Temple, vol. 1. *Fifteenth Century to 1781* (London, 1949)
Routledge, F. J. (ed.), *Calendar of the Clarendon State Papers* (5 vols, Oxford, 1970)
Russell, C. W., and Prendergast, J. P., *The Carte Manuscripts in the Bodleian Library, Oxford* (London, 1871)
Steele, Robert (ed.), *A Bibliography of Royal Proclamations of the Tudor and Stuart Sovereigns 1485–1714* (2 vols, Oxford, 1910) vol. 2, *Scotland and Ireland*
The Register of Admissions to Gray's Inn, 1521–1889 (London, 1889)
The State Letters of Henry Earl of Clarendon (Oxford and Dublin, 1765)

Contemporary or near-contemporary works

Bond, Maurice F., *The Diaries and Papers of Sir Edward Dering* (London, 1976)
Cunningham, Bernadette (ed.), 'Clanricard letters', *Journal of the Galway Archaeological and Historical Society* 48 (1996), pp. 162–208
Davies, Sir John, *A Discoverie of the True Causes Why Ireland was Never Entirely Subdued, [and] Brought under Obedience of the Crown of England Until the Beginning of His Majesty's Happy Reign (1612)*, ed. James P. Myers (Washington, DC, 1988)
Dinneen, Patrick S., and O'Donoghue, Tadhg (eds), *Dánta Aodhagáin Uí Rathaille* (London, 1911)
French, Nicholas, *The Historical Works of the Right Rev. Nicholas French D.D.* (2 vols, Dublin, 1846)
Giblin, Cathaldus, 'Catalogue of material of Irish interest in the collection "*Nunziatura di Fiandra*", Vatican Archives: Part 1', *Collectanea Hibernica* 1 (1958), pp. 7–136, and 'Part 2' *Collectanea Hibernica* 3 (1960), pp. 7–136.
Gilbert, John T. (ed.), *A Contemporary History of Affairs in Ireland, from 1641 to 1652* (Dublin, 1879–80)
Gilbert, John T., *History of the Irish Confederation and the War in Ireland 1641–9* (7 vols, Dublin, 1882–91)
Gilbert, John T. (ed.), *A Jacobite Narrative of the War in Ireland*, 1688–1691 (Shannon, 1971)
Hogan, James, *Letters and Papers Relating to the Irish Rebellion, between 1642–46* (Dublin, 1936)
Kelly, P. H. (ed. and intro), 'Sir William Domville, "A disquisition touching that great question whether an act of parliament made in England shall bind the kingdom

and people of Ireland without their allowance and acceptance of such an act in the kingdom of Ireland"', *Analecta Hibernica* 40 (2007), 17–72

Kelly, Patrick Hyde (ed.), *William Molyneux: The Case of Ireland's Being Bound by Acts of Parliament in England, Stated Dublin, 1698* (Dublin, 2018)

King, William, *The State of the Protestants of Ireland under the late King James's Government* (Dublin, 1730)

Lowe, John (ed.), *Letter-Book of the Earl of Clanricarde 1643–47* (Dublin 1983)

Lynch, John, *Cambrensis Eversus*, ed. and tr. Matthew Kelly (3 vols, Dublin, 1851–2)

Mac Domhnaill, Fr (ed.), *Dánta is Amhreain Sheáin Uí Ghadhra* (Dublin, 1955)

Mac Erlean, John C. (ed.), *Duanaire Dháibhidh Uí Bhruadair: The Poems of David Ó Bruadair*, Irish Texts Society 11, 13, 18 (3 vols, London, 1910–17)

Millett, Benignus, 'Archbishop Edmund O'Reilly's report on the state of the church in Ireland, 1662', *Collectanea Hibernica* 2 (1959), pp. 105–14

Moran, Patrick Francis (ed.), *Spicilegium Ossoriense* (3 vols, Dublin, 1874, 1878, 1884)

More-O'Ferrall, E. G. (ed.), 'The dispossessed landowners of Ireland, 1664', *Irish Genealogist,* 4 (1972), pp. 429 ff.

Moynes, Vera (ed.), *Irish Jesuit Annual Letters 1604–1674* (Dublin, 2019)

Ó Donnchadha, Tadhg (ed.), *Amhráin Dhiarmada mac Seáin Bhuidhe Mac Cárrthaigh* (Dublin, 1916)

O'Donoghue, Geoffrey, *The Poems of Geoffrey O'Donoghue, Dánta Shéafraidh Uí Dhonnchadha an Ghleanna*, ed. and tr. John Minahane (Cork, 2008)

Ó Duinnín, Pádraig (ed.), *Dánta Shéafraidh Uí Dhonnchadha an Gleanna* (Dublin 1902)

O'Rahilly, Cecile (ed.), *Five Seventeenth-Century Political Poems* (Dublin, 1977)

Plunkett, Oliver, *The Letters of St. Oliver Plunkett*, ed. Hanly, John (Dublin, 1979)

Power, Patrick (ed.), *A Bishop in Penal Times, being the Letters and Reports of John Brenan, Bishop of Waterford (1671–93) and Archbishop of Cashel (1677–93)* (Cork, 1932)

Williams, N. J. A. (ed.), *Pairlement Chloinne Tomáis* (Dublin 1981)

Secondary sources

Armstrong, Robert, 'Geoffrey Browne' in *DIB*, vol. 1, p. 906

Armstrong, Robert, 'Edward Butler' in *DIB*, vol. 2, pp 112–13

Arnold, L. J., 'The Irish court of Claims', *IHS* 96 (1985), pp 417–30

Arnold, L. J., *The Restoration Land Settlement in County Dublin, 1660–1688* (Dublin, 1993)

Bagwell, Richard, *Ireland under the Stuarts* (3 vols, London, 1916)

Baker, John, *Collected Papers on English Legal History* (3 vols, Cambridge, 2013)

Ball, F. Elrington, *Judges in Ireland 1221–1921* (2 vols, London, 1926)

Barnard, T. C., 'Lawyers and the law in later seventeenth-century Ireland', *IHS* 111 (May 1993), pp. 256–82

Barnard, Toby, 'Introduction: The Dukes of Ormonde' in Toby Barnard and Jane Fenlon (eds), *The Dukes of Ormonde, 1610–1745* (Woodbridge, 2000), pp. 1–53

Bergin, John, 'Richard Power' in *DIB*, vol. 8, pp. 265–6

Bergin, John, Magennis, Eoin, Ní Mhunghaile, Lesa, and Walsh, Patrick (eds), *New Perspectives on the Penal Laws: Eighteenth-Century Ireland / Iris an dá chultúr*, special issue 1 (Dublin, 2011)

Bottigheimer, Karl S., 'The Restoration land settlement in Ireland: A structural view' *IHS* 18 (1972), pp. 1–21

Boyle, Patrick, 'John O'Molony Bishop of Killaloe (1672–89) and of Limerick (1689–1702)', *Irish Ecclesiastical Record* 4th ser. 32 (1912), pp. 574–89

Breathnach, Catherine, 'Archbishop John Brenan (1625–1693), his life and work', *Tipperary Historical Journal* (1993), pp. 148–59

Burke, William P., *History of Clonmel* (Waterford, 1907)

Burke, William P., *Irish Priests in Penal Times* (Waterford, 1914)

Caball, Marc, *Poets and Politics: Continuity and Reaction in Irish Poetry, 1558–1625* (Cork, 1998)

Carte, Thomas, *An History of the Life of James Duke of Ormonde, from his Birth in 1610, to his Death in 1688* (3 vols, London, 1735–36)

Clarendon, Earl of, *The Life of the Earl of Clarendon* (London, 1827)

Clarke, Aidan, 'Peter Talbot', *DIB*, vol. 9, pp. 245–7

Coppinger, Walter A., *History of the Copingers or Coppingers* (London, 1884)

Creighton, Anne, 'Sir Robert Talbot', *DIB*, vol. 9, pp. 256–7

Cronin, John, 'John O'Molony', *DIB*, vol. 7, pp. 704–5

Cunningham, Bernadette, *The World of Geoffrey Keating* (Dublin, 2000)

Cunningham, Bernadette, 'Representations of king, parliament and the Irish people in Geoffrey Keating's *Foras feasa ar Éirinn* and John Lynch's *Cambrensis eversus* (1662)' in Jane H. Ohlmeyer (ed.), *Political Thought in Seventeenth-Century Ireland: Kingdom or Colony* (Cambridge, 2000), pp. 131–54

Cunningham, Bernadette, and Gillespie, Raymond, 'Lost worlds: History and religion in the poetry of Dáibhí Ó Bruadair' in Pádraigín Riggs (ed.), *Dáibhí Ó Bruadair: His Historical and Literary Context* (London, 2001), pp. 18–45

Cunningham, John, *Conquest and Land in Ireland: The Transplantation to Connacht, 1649–1680* (Woodbridge, 2011)

Curran, C. P., 'The trial of the primate' in *Blessed Oliver Plunkett Historical Studies* (Dublin, 1937)

Curtayne, Alice, *The Trial of Oliver Plunkett* (Dublin, 1975)

D'Alton, John, *King James's Irish Army List (1689)* (Kansas City, 1997)

Darcy, Eamon, 'The social memory of Oliver Cromwell in Ireland' in Martyn Bennet, Ray Gillespie and R. Scott Spurlock (eds), *Cromwell and Ireland: New Perspectives* (Liverpool, 2021)

Dennehy, Coleman (ed.), *Restoration Ireland: Always Settling and Never Settled* (Farnham, 2008)

Dennehy, Coleman (ed.), *Law and Revolution in Seventeenth-Century Ireland* (Dublin, 2020)

Dickson, David, *New Foundations Ireland 1660–1800* (Dublin, 2000)

Dickson, David, *Dublin: The Making of a Capital City* (London, 2014)
Downey, Declan M., 'Accommodations with the Protestant state and church: A comparative study of respective Dutch and Irish Catholic experiences' in John Bergin, Eoin Magennis, Lesa Ní Mhunghaile and Patrick Walsh (eds), *New Perspectives on the Penal Laws: Eighteenth-Century Ireland / Idir an dá chultúr*, special issue no. 1 (Dublin, 2011)
Dunlop, Robert, *Ireland under the Commonwealth* (2 vols, Manchester, 1913)
Fitzgerald, Lord Walter, 'Carton', *Journal of the Archaeological Society of County Kildare* 4 (1905), pp. 3–34
Gibney, John, 'Arthur Capel' in *DIB*, vol. 2, pp. 317–19
Gibney, John, *Ireland and the Popish Plot* (Basingstoke, 2009)
Gillespie, Raymond, 'The social thought of Richard Bellings' in Micheál Ó Siochrú (ed.), *Kingdoms in Crisis, Ireland in the 1640s* (Dublin, 2001), pp. 212–28
Gillespie, Raymond, *Seventeenth Century Ireland* (Dublin, 2006)
Harris, Tim, *Restoration: Charles II and his Kingdoms, 1660–1685* (London, 2005)
Harris, Tim, *Revolution: The Great Crisis of the British Monarchy, 1685–1720* (London, 2006)
Hart, A. R., *A History of the King's Serjeants at Law in Ireland, Honour rather than Advantage?* (Dublin, 2000)
Hogan, James, 'Two Bishops of Killaloe and Irish freedom: John O'Molony II (1617–1702)', *Studies: An Irish Quarterly Review* 34 and 35 (1920), pp. 213–31 and 421–37
Johnston, Neil, 'Politics, parliament and the Restoration land settlement in Ireland, 1660–1665' (Ph.D. thesis, University College Dublin, 2012)
Johnston, Neil, 'Charles II's legal officers and the Irish restoration land settlement' in Coleman Dennehy (ed.), *Law and Revolution in Seventeenth-Century Ireland* (Dublin, 2020), pp. 324–53
Kenny, Colum, 'The exclusion of Catholics from the legal profession in Ireland, 1537–1829', *IHS* 100 (Nov. 1987), pp. 337–57
Kiberd, Declan, *Irish Classics* (Cambridge, MA, 2000)
Kinsella, Eoin, *Catholic Survival in Protestant Ireland, 1660–1711* (Woodbridge, 2018)
Lenihan, Pádraig, *The Last Cavalier* (Dublin, 2014)
Lodge, John, and Archdall, Mervyn, *The Peerage of Ireland* (Dublin, 1789)
Mac Mathúna, Liam, 'Growth of Irish (L1)/English (L2) literary code-mixing', in Hildegard L. C. Tristram (ed.), *The Celtic Languages in Contact: Papers from the Workshop within the Framework of the XIII International Congress of Celtic Studies, Bonn, 26–27 July 2007* (Potsdam, 2007)
Maynard, Hazel, 'Irish membership of the English Inns of Court, 1660–1699: Lawyers, litigation and the legal profession' (Ph.D. thesis, University College Dublin, 2006)
Maynard, Hazel, 'The Irish legal profession and the Catholic revival, 1660–89' in James Kelly, John McCafferty and Charles Ivar McGrath (eds), *People, Politics and Power* (Dublin, 2009), pp. 28–50
Maynard, Hazel, 'Richard Nagle' in *DIB*, vol. 6, pp. 849–52
McGrath, Bríd, 'A biographical dictionary of the membership of the Irish House of Commons 1640–1641', (2 vols, Ph.D. thesis, Trinity College, Dublin, 1998)

McHugh, Jason, 'Catholic clerical responses to the Restoration: The case of Nicholas French' in Coleman A. Dennehy (ed.), *Restoration Ireland* (Aldershot, 2008), pp. 99–121

Mooney, Canice, 'Accusations against Oliver Plunkett', *Seanchas Ard Mhacha* 2 (1956–57), pp. 119–40

Moran, P. F., *The Life of Oliver Plunkett, Archbishop of Armagh: [A Compendium of the Author's Memoirs of him* (Dublin, 1861)

Morley, Vincent, 'Peter Walsh' in *DIB*, vol. 9, pp. 756–60

Morley, Vincent, *The Popular Mind in Eighteenth-Century Ireland* (Cork, 2017)

Murray, Raymond, 'Edmond O'Reilly' in *DIB*, vol. 7, pp. 848–50

Murray, Raymond, 'St. Oliver Plunkett' in *DIB*, vol. 8, pp. 191–3

Nolan, Frances, *The Jacobite Duchess, Frances Jennings, Duchess of Tyrconnell, c.1649–1731* (Woodbridge, 2021)

Ó Buachalla, Breandán, *Aisling ghéar: Na Stíobhartaigh agus an t-aos léinn 1603–1788* (Baile Átha Cliath, 1996)

Ó Buachalla, Breandán, *Dánta Aodhagáin Ui Rathaille: Reassessments* (London, 2004),

Ó Ciardha, Eamonn, *Ireland and the Jacobite Cause, 1685–1766: A Fatal Attachment* (Dublin, 2002)

Ó Ciardha, Éamonn, 'John Brenan' in *DIB*, vol. 1, pp. 799–800

Ó Ciardha, Éamonn, 'Garret (Gerard, Gerald) Dillon' in *DIB*, vol. 3, p. 288

Ó Fiaich, Tomás, 'Edmund O'Reilly, Archbishop of Armagh, 1657–1669' in The Franciscan Fathers (eds), *Father Luke Wadding* (Dublin, 1957), pp. 171–227

Ó Fiaich, Tomás, 'The fall and return of John Mac Moyer', *Seanchas Ardmhacha* 3 (1958), pp. 51–86

Ó Fiaich, Tomás, *Oliver Plunkett, Ireland's New Saint* (Dublin, 1975)

Ohlmeyer, Jane, *Civil War and Restoration in the Three Stuart Kingdoms: The Career of Randal MacDonnell, Marquis of Antrim, 1609–1683* (Cambridge, 1993)

O Riordan, Michelle, '"Political" poems in the mid-seventeenth-century crisis' in Jane H. Ohlmeyer (ed.), *Ireland from Independence to Occupation, 1641–1660* (Cambridge, 1995), pp. 112–27

O'Rourke, Liam, 'Catholicism and the Church of Ireland under the viceroyalty of Arthur Capel, first earl of Essex, 1672–77' (M Litt. thesis, National University of Ireland, Maynooth, 2010)

Ó Siochrú, Micheál, *Confederate Ireland 1642–1649* (Dublin, 1999)

Ó Siochrú, Micheál, 'Sir Richard Barnewall' in *DIB*, vol. 1, pp. 287–8

Ó Siochrú, Micheál, 'Sir Nicholas Plunkett' in *DIB*, vol. 8, pp. 187–90

Ó Siochrú, Micheál, 'Sir John Walsh' in *DIB*, vol. 9, pp. 739–40

O'Sullivan, Harold, *John Bellew: A Seventeenth-Century Man of Many Parts, 1605–1679* (Dublin, 2000)

Pawlisch, Hans S., *Sir John Davies and the Conquest of Ireland* (Cambridge, 1985)

Perceval-Maxwell, Michael, 'Elizabeth Butler' in *DIB*, vol. 2, pp. 119–20

Perceval-Maxwell, Michael, 'James Butler' in *DIB*, vol. 2, pp. 132–45

Perceval-Maxwell, Michael, 'The Irish Restoration land settlement and its historians' in Coleman Dennehy (ed.), *Restoration Ireland: Always Settling and Never Settled* (Aldershot, 2008), pp. 19–34

Rankin, Deana, *Between Spencer and Swift: English Writing in Seventeenth-Century Ireland* (Cambridge, 2005)
Sergeant, Phillip, *Little Jennings and Fighting Dick Talbot* (2 vols, London, 1913)
Simms, J. G., *The Williamite Confiscation in Ireland 1690–1703* (London, 1956)
Simms, J. G., 'The Restoration, 1660–85' in T. W. Moody, F. X. Martin and F. J. Byrne (eds), *A New History of Ireland*, vol. 3. *Early Modern Ireland 1534–1691* (Oxford, 1986), pp. 420–53
Simms, J. G., 'The War of the Two Kings, 1685–91' in T. W. Moody, F. X. Martin and F. J. Byrne (eds), *A New History of Ireland*, vol. 3. *Early Modern Ireland 1534–1691* (Oxford, 1986), pp. 478–508
Simms J. G., 'The Jacobite Parliament of 1689' in D. W. Hayton and Gerard O'Brien (eds), *War and Politics in Ireland 1649–1730* (London, 1986)
Simms, J. G., *Jacobite Ireland* (Dublin, 2000)
Simms, J. G., 'Introduction' in Geraldine Tallon (ed.), *Court of Claims, Submissions and Evidence 1663* (Dublin, 2006)
Talbot, S. E., *Into the Lion's Den: A Biographical History of the Talbots of Malahide* (London, 2012)
Walton, Julian, 'Richard Power' in *ODNB*
Wauchope, Piers, 'Frances Talbot' in *ODNB*

Online resources

Archives of Maryland, V.5, http://aomol.msa.maryland.gov/000001/000005
Carte Manuscripts, Bodleian Library, http://www.bodley.ox.ac.uk/dept/scwmss/projects/carte/carte.html
Down Survey, TCD, http://downsurvey.tcd.ie
Dictionary of Irish Biography, http://dib.cambridge.org/home.do
Oxford Dictionary of National Biography, http://www.oxforddnb.com

Index

EU authorised representative for GPSR:
Easy Access System Europe, Mustamäe tee 50,
10621 Tallinn, Estonia
gpsr.requests@easproject.com

www.ingramcontent.com/pod-product-compliance
Ingram Content Group UK Ltd.
Pitfield, Milton Keynes, MK11 3LW, UK
UKHW021840100926
8556IPUK00004B/453
* 9 7 8 1 5 2 6 1 7 6 3 5 6 *